The Sales and Marketing Excellence Challenge

ALSO BY JIM DICKIE

THE INFORMATION TECHNOLOGY CHALLENGE

$\maltese$

THE CHIEF SALES OFFICER'S GUIDE TO

CUSTOMER RELATIONSHIP MANAGEMENT

$\maltese$

INSIGHTS INTO HIGH TECH

SALES AND MARKETING

ALSO BY BARRY TRAILER

SALES MASTERY, A NOVEL

The Sales and Marketing Excellence Challenge:

CHANGING HOW THE GAME IS PLAYED

JIM DICKIE   BARRY TRAILER

Sales Mastery Press
Mill Valley, California

Copyright © 2003 Sales Mastery, Inc.

All Rights Reserved.

TERMS & CONDITIONS

Library of Congress Cataloging-in-Publication Data

Dickie, R. James (Ralph James), 1953 –

Trailer, Barry (Barry Joseph), 1949 –

The sales & marketing excellence challenge: changing how the game is played./ Jim Dickie, Barry Trailer – 1st ed.

ISBN 0-9724750-6-0

1. Leadership   2. Sales strategy   3. Marketing strategy
4. Technology innovations – Management.   I. Title

Cover Photo: ©2003 John Turner / Stone / Getty Images

"If I have seen further, it is by standing upon the shoulders of giants."

Isaac Newton

This book is dedicated to Ed Adams, Bob Boylan, and other giants who went before us and helped us along the way. We hope that reading how your peers are dealing with the sales and marketing challenges we all face today will help you see further in your own endeavors.

Acknowledgements

We wish to thank all the far-sighted industry executives who so unselfishly contributed their time and insights to the creation of this publication, and helped review and refine its many versions.

In addition, we owe a debt of gratitude to many colleagues, mentors, and advisors, without whom this book would not be possible. To list them all would be impossible, but a few deserve special mention: Our academic advisors – Dr. David Reid, Director of the Savage & Associates Center for Advanced Sales and Marketing at the University of Toledo and Dr. Bill Weeks, Executive Director of The Center for Professional Selling at Baylor University; our editing team – Sue Renner, Trisha Liu, Kim Cameron, Kelly Kusina, Marc Hodges, Tim Robinson, Dr. Diane Hodges, Arleen Virga and Dorothy Foglia; and finally the support and understanding of our wives, Wendy Dickie and Peg Videtta.

Table of Contents

Chief Commercial Officer, General Electric Corporation

Over the past decade, the role of sales has clearly been shifting to solution selling versus transactional selling, but this move has been much slower than many of us imagined. I think the reason behind this is that many companies are fundamentally weak in a few key areas.

President, Check Point Systems

The thing that has become more pronounced today is the market's continual question, 'Are you adding value?' From the customer through the partners through the whole relationship, they are asking, 'Is it of value? Is it something I really, really need?' If they can't answer 'yes,' they are not going to go forward.

Co-Founder & President, Savage & Associates

We look for people with a good work ethic who possess a great attitude. There has to be a certain amount of intellect and talent, but beyond that, they must possess great habits. We all have habits, but are they good ones? Honing good habits to improve ourselves, and getting rid of bad habits that we all have at different stages in our lives, is what helps us focus and really achieve.

Senior Executive Vice President, Worldwide Field Operations, StorageTek, Retired

Over a four-year period we took sales at StorageTek from $700 million to $2.2 billion, and we did this all through productivity gains—we did not add any additional sales people during that time. In retrospect, the main foundation of our success was that we concentrated on three things— Metrics, Process, and Tools.

President & CEO, Miller Heiman

In today's market we are deathly afraid of losing deals; we try to do whatever it takes to avoid losing. An interesting question I have been exploring with companies is, 'What is actually the worst thing that can happen when you lose a deal?' When you really consider the problem, you realize that only one bad thing can happen when you lose—which is that it takes you a long time to lose.

> *As publisher of Selling Power, I have the opportunity to talk to many CEOs and vice presidents of sales in many different industries. During these discussions, I get their thoughts on the state of the union, if you will, for selling and marketing. Two key challenges seem to be emerging that we are going to have to address if sales forces are going to meet their business goals.*

> *Sales quotas can only be met if sales people are in the field, talking to customers, meeting them face-to-face. In an age of tight budgets and self-enablement, however, many sales people spend more time performing administrative tasks than they do selling. Hiring in-house administrative staff is no longer an option. Neither is increasing the size of the sales team. If projections are to be met, if sales people (and their managers) are to keep their jobs, if companies are to stay in business, another solution must be found.*

> *The Tennant Company has been in business for 132 years. We've twice been listed as one of Fortune's Best 100 Companies to Work For and are on the leading edge of the quality movement. All of this gives us a certain perspective; we attract and hire people with a certain mindset and value set. We used this foundation to build bench strength and pull away from competitors with short-term focus and challenges.*

> *This year, while marketing spending by Global 1000 companies continues to climb and exceed $1 trillion, marketing productivity and program effectiveness are declining. The issue is not necessarily the amount being spent, but rather how and where dollars are allocated. This is being solved by an interesting combination of process and technology.*

> *Buyers are grasping the amount of leverage they have, but business execs and sellers are fighting it. The principal reason for the lack of sellers' understanding is that businesses have very poor listening skills. In business, we have been very lax about putting in systems and methods that enable us to capture as much customer input as possible.*

> *In our industry we have come to realize that it is not nearly as important that our Customers understand our strategies as it is for us to understand theirs. Our Customers will be the ones that define what 'competitive advantage' really means, whether overtly or not, and will somehow indicate that to us. To succeed, we had better be ready to listen and respond.*

> *Think of yourself as a snow skier starting off the new season. If you have skied double black diamonds the year before, you normally don't start on double diamonds for your first run down the hill. You start on an easier slope. The reason isn't necessarily that you've lost your ability to handle the challenge—the issue is your confidence about your ability to handle the challenge. So it is with sales.*

> *Sales and marketing people spend a great deal of time attempting to create a relationship-based service model that will give them a competitive advantage in the eyes of their customers. We all would like to do that. But unless we have identified a customer who is interested in a relationship with us, and have a very clear organizational focus on what the customer is trying to accomplish with our products, we are unlikely to achieve our goal.*

> *Because small companies, by definition, have a limited number of people, we have to make the most of human, financial and technical resources. This means I have to grow as a leader and increasingly release authority to others so they and the company can grow. Having a clear plan, participating in education/entrepreneurial programs, and having a trusted advisory board have been key for me.*

> *Today, it is all about making sales; that is the compelling, urgent need. To do that we need to create value-add relationships with our customers, and we have to better leverage technology.*

Editor & Publisher, *CustomerThink*

> *As I've often said, 'You ought to be smarter at the front end.' A lot of business is actually about learning by doing. When you have the data and the systems to translate that data into real information, but you don't use it to determine how to build better relationships, that's a shame. Neglecting to do this costs us money and customers and I think this happens a lot more often than we'd like to see.*

President, SportsMind, Inc.

> *Responding to the pressures of the marketplace, many companies are investing in technology, sales skills, product training, etc. to increase the effectiveness of their sales teams. Those are all valuable, but to have a balanced approach to performance improvement we should also be looking at what we can do for team members at a more personal level.*

Managing Partner, Insight Technology Group

> *In the course of benchmarking more than 2,900 sales and marketing effectiveness initiatives over the past ten years, six trends emerged that all companies are going to have to successfully deal with if they are going to survive, let alone remain competitive.*

President, Sales Mastery, Inc.

> *What kept coming up in doing the interviews for this book is how much these folks 'think' about their business. They don't just show up every day and go through the motions; they're figuring out, or trying to figure out, what's really going on, what are the trends, and what they need to do to advantageously position themselves. They also demonstrated a surprising openness to sharing what they're doing, without fearing that they're somehow giving something up, in hopes that their peers might gain insights from their experiences in the trenches.*

Introduction

In 1912, football was already well established at the collegiate level, but it was a different game than it is today. Football during that era resembled rugby, in that the entire game was focused on the run. You lined up 11 players on each side of the line, the offensive center hiked the ball to the quarterback, who in turn normally handed or lateraled it to a swift halfback, who then carried the ball until tackled.

A powerhouse team of that era was the U.S. Military Academy at West Point. Army had mastered the game and had strong seasons in 1911 and 1912. Their domination of the sport might have continued unabated had it not been for a twist of fate.

Then, as now, football schedules were determined well in advance. Army had its opponents lined up for the 1913 campaign when Yale decided to cancel its November 1st game with the cadets. The Army team manager, Harold Loomis, contacted all the major East Coast teams, but was unable to schedule a game for that date with another local opponent. He then expanded his search to include football teams in the Midwest, and finally secured a commitment from a then-relatively-unknown Catholic college in South Bend, Indiana—Notre Dame.

During the summer of 1913, two of Notre Dame's players, quarterback Gus Dorias and offensive end Knute Rockne, worked together as lifeguards at the Cedar Point resort in Sandusky, Ohio. In their spare time, they practiced to stay in shape for the fall season. In thinking about the game with such a dominant power in football, these two players realized that even if their team executed all the basics—blocking, tackling, running, etc.—flawlessly, it was unlikely that those maneuvers alone would be enough for Notre Dame to be able to win the game.

To pull off a major victory, they needed to innovate. Out of their desire to overcome tremendous odds came a major advance in how the game was to be played—the perfection of the forward pass, which had been legalized in 1906 but hadn't drawn much attention because of tough rules against its use.

When football practice started back in South Bend in the fall, Gus and Knute introduced their concept to the coach and the rest of the team. The rulebook clearly spelled out that the objective of the game was to advance the ball; "how" was left up to you, and the passing rules had been liberalized. With this understanding in mind, the team quietly practiced and perfected their new style of play.

The Sales and Marketing Excellence Challenge

On November 1st, Notre Dame went over to West Point for the appointed match, and introduced Army and the rest of the football world to a brand new way to play the game. The first forward pass shocked the cadets, but the referees quickly noted that nothing in the rulebook prevented Notre Dame from throwing the ball if they chose to do so.

Well, Notre Dame chose to do so often and connected 14 times that day. Army put up a valiant fight, but its game was thrown off by the confusion caused by the unheard-of execution of this new play. Notre Dame prevailed with a 35-13 win and changed the course of the sport forever.

As a sales or marketing professional, you may be wondering what does this story have to do with me? Fast-forward almost a century from 1913 to today. If there ever was a time when running a sales and marketing organization was easy, NOW is not it! Dealing daily with a wide range of issues – such as continuing economic uncertainty, increasing global competition, collapsing product life cycles, expanding product complexity, increasing customer expectations, decreasing customer loyalty, never-ending profitability pressure from Wall Street, etc. – results in a flood of "Maalox Moments" for all senior management team members, especially sales and marketing executives.

When looking at the challenges we need to overcome to continue to be successful, many of us must feel like Notre Dame's coaches and players did when they first found out they were going up against Army.

Businesses across all industries are recognizing that in order to deal with the pressures of the marketplace today, they need some innovative plays. They need to make fundamental changes in the way they market to, sell to, and service customers. At a strategic level, management teams are analyzing a variety of issues, such as:

- Do I continue the dependency on my direct sales force, or should I expand my sales through channels?

- How do I optimize my marketing mix to attract the right types of potential clients?

- Is the e-business model totally hype, or does it still need to play a role in our customer acquisition and service plans?

- Should I move from a product specialist sales strategy to a universal rep concept?

- Do I continue my current sales strategy, or should I look to adopt a formal sales methodology and target my sales teams toward a more consultative sell?

- Should I jump on the technology bandwagon and look to Customer Relationship Management (CRM) solutions to solve all my problems, or, in light of the high project failure rates, should I shy away from additional CRM tools?

- Do I target the majority of my resources at acquiring additional market share, or should I focus on maintaining the customer base I already have?

- Is now the time to control costs, or should I be looking to expand my sales and marketing investments?

And while thinking about these types of critical issues is keeping executives awake at night, a never-ending stream of tactical issues challenge them each and every day, including:

- How do I find and hire great sales and marketing talent?

- How do I get new team members up to full productivity faster?

- Once I have great reps, how do I minimize turnover in sales?

- How do I foster better teamwork between marketing, sales, and support?

- How do I maximize the success of new product introductions?

- How do we do a better job of cross-selling and up-selling?

- How can I get more visibility into the forecast?

- How do I ensure our compensation plans are motivating the right behavior?

- How can we reduce our no-decision rate?

- How can we shorten our sell cycle?

- Why are we discounting so much?

The days of treating sales and marketing as an art are rapidly fading. We have no choice but to evolve what we do into more of a science. To be successful going forward, we must better understand our customers, live process instead of talking about it, optimize our sell cycle to more closely support our customer's buy cycle, maximize the success of our channels, integrate our workflow across the enterprise, and provide real customer value to re-instill loyalty. And, we need to do all this quickly if we are going to meet our revenue and profitability goals.

When we shared the forward pass story with one executive, he remarked, "That's the challenge. I need to be able to look at how we currently play the game, decide which strategies and tactics are still working, which ones are not, and then come up with innovative new plays to replace the failing ones." The mission is clear, but *how to accomplish it is not*. Many of the sales and marketing executives we have talked to this past year report that they are struggling with the task of determining exactly where and how they should evolve their operations.

In dealing with the challenges they face, sales and marketing leaders are at a significant disadvantage compared to other functional areas. When CEOs need insights into how to optimize global business plans, they can turn to any number of strategic consulting firms. When CIOs are looking to develop their long- and short-term technology road maps, they can turn to any number of research houses for assistance. CFOs have long depended on input from their accounting and legal services firms for counseling on optimizing their back office operations. But who today provides the same type of coaching and support for sales and marketing executives?

Lacking access to these types of formal resources, those of us who have run sales and marketing teams have developed our own informal network of friends, confidants, and advisors who we go to for help and guidance. We always have treated this as an extremely valuable resource.

What would it be worth to any of us to double or even triple the reach of that network? That is the objective we have set for the creation of this book: *The Sales & Marketing Excellence Challenge: Changing How the Game Is Played.*

Over the past ten years, as part of our benchmarking activities, we have surveyed more than 2,900 companies to assess how they are leveraging people, process, and technology to optimize the way they market to, sell to, and service their customers. During the course of this work, we have had the opportunity to interface with numerous business executives on this key business topic. In addition, we also have had the opportunity to meet with the various consulting firms, training firms, Customer Relationship Management (CRM) technology vendors, and industry watchers to whom these senior managers turn for help.

During the first half of 2002, we tapped into this network and sought the opinions of several hundred individuals regarding how to best meet the sales and marketing challenges we all face. We then did in-depth interviews during the second half of the year with a number of these individuals around specific topics they previously discussed. This was a tremendous learning experience, and provided us with a wealth of insights.

In determining the most effective method for presenting the knowledge we have collected, we reflected on the observations of Peter Drucker, who noted that communication is effective when it has "both information and meaning…To have meaning there must be communion."

With that in mind, we decided to avoid the approach most business books take, in which the authors aggregate research and distill and filter it to a particular message. Instead, we felt the format of this book should let you learn directly from the individuals who graciously shared their insights and impressions with us – to commune with your peers.

We wish we could tell you that we found the perfect answer for how to deal with all the business challenges that confront us today. Unfortunately, since no two companies are exactly alike, we did not find the universal truth for sales and marketing excellence. But we did collect a wealth of great ideas and concepts.

What you are about to read is a collection of some of those perspectives.

For each of these opinion pieces, we have provided a brief bio on the person we interviewed, which includes the position they held at the time we interviewed them, along with a one- or two-sentence synopsis of the topic they discussed with us. What follows are their thoughts and insights on how to optimize sales, marketing and support.

As soon as we started this project, it became clear to us that when you are dealing with a topic as broad and complex as sales and marketing excellence, no single book will meet everyone's needs. To try to overcome that limitation, we came up with an innovative approach for providing you with information specially tailored to your organization's needs.

For the book itself, we selected a subset of interviews that we felt covered a broad range of issues and ideas that would be of general interest to many sales and marketing executives. Some of these interviews deal with strategies, some talk about tactics, some focus on services you can leverage, and some explore very "bleeding edge" concepts. There are perspectives from Fortune 500 firms, as well as mid-sized and smaller companies. While not every perspective piece may apply to your organization, our hope is that you will walk away from reading this book with at least a dozen ideas to explore.

But your exposure to the top experts we interviewed doesn't end there. To provide you with further insights into strategies and tactics you can use in dealing with the specific challenges your organization is facing, we are offering to send you up to ten additional perspectives over the next year free of charge.

The Sales and Marketing Excellence Challenge

To receive these additional interviews, all you need to do is visit our website, www.CSOInsights.com, and fill out a brief profile to help us better understand the topics that specifically interest you. As we continue our research efforts and develop additional perspectives that fit your areas of interest, we will e-mail them to you with our compliments. Through this continuing exchange of insights, we hope to make this book an ongoing educational process instead of a one-time learning event.

This is timely material. The concepts presented here will have value in five years when you pull this down again from your bookshelf, but they will never be more useful than they are now. As we said, these interviews were conducted in the second half of 2002, a time when we are all struggling with very unique challenges.

All indications are that the business environment described (and endured) here is the one you'll be facing through 2003. So hopefully, the insights you are about to read will be of assistance in helping you weather that storm.

We believe these issues have broad applicability, but even so, we encourage you to only use this information as the basis for brainstorming how to deal with the operational challenges your organization faces. Everyone can benefit from understanding what strategies and tactics others are using, but in the end we must implement solutions that fit our specific business needs and not those of other firms.

If you have any questions about the information contained in this book, would like to discuss your specific challenges, or if you would care to share some of your experiences and lessons learned, please feel free to call or e-mail us.

We wish you good luck in successfully changing how the game is played for your organization.

Jim Dickie	Barry Trailer
jimdickie@aol.com	barrytrailer@aol.com
(303) 530 6930	(415) 383 3484

J. Jeffrey Schaper

Jeff Schaper is in the newly created role of Chief Commercial Officer (CCO) and has responsibility for leading major sales and marketing initiatives across all businesses within the $126 billion GE Corporation. Previous to being named CCO, Jeff was Vice President of Sales for GE Industrial Systems, a $5.6 billion global business headquartered in Plainville, Connecticut. Jeff joined GE in 1973 as a sales representative in GE's plastics business, where he held numerous sales and marketing roles. In 1987, he joined GE Medical Systems, where he held various commercial positions, including three years based in Paris, France, managing a 2,000-person, $350 million technical service P&L throughout Europe, Africa, the former Soviet Union, and the Middle East. Jeff graduated in 1969 from Allegheny College with a BA and worked for Sinclair-Koppers in manufacturing and sales until he joined GE in 1973.

Jim Dickie (JD)

> **Over the past decade, the role of sales has clearly been shifting to solution selling versus transactional selling, but this move has been much slower than many of us imagined. I think the reason behind this is that many companies are fundamentally weak in a few key areas.**

The basis of solution selling is providing what the customer wants, instead of concentrating on the products we want to sell. This is easily said, but achieving this goal requires a major mindset change on the part of companies, because for decades we have delivered products to the sales force, instead of solutions.

If all you are doing in today's market is selling products, then you are very vulnerable to e-auctions or new methods of bidding that are continuing to surface in the marketplace. Companies need to differentiate themselves by offering value over and above the products they sell. Frankly, if we cannot achieve that objective, the effectiveness of a sales force significantly decreases, and the odds that a customer will leverage an alternative buying strategy becomes much more likely.

Optimizing Market Development

If the need to change is evident, why have so few organizations successfully made the transition to solution selling? From looking at the businesses I have run into, the first weakness I see is in the area of market development.

Market development is separate from product management. In the majority of cases, companies already have a solid understanding of product management. This function has been, and will continue to be strong. But the market development function—the concept of identifying market segments, anticipating the movement in those segments, effectively directing deployment and alignment of resources to target those segments—is where the weakness lies. And it becomes evident every time there is an economic downturn.

I am mainly talking about sales outside of the retail environment. Some retail firms excel at market development already. But very few commercial or industrial companies have strong competencies here. One of the underlying causes of this trend is that during the past two years, as we have been impacted by the economy, the focus on market development has been waning. And yet I would argue that this is one of the more critical success factors impacting business performance going forward.

History makes it clear that all customers are not created equal. At any given point in time, some market segments are growing, some are stagnant, and some are in a tailspin. To succeed consistently over time, it is critical that market development be able to identify growth segments, identify targeted value messages for those segments, and then redirect the organization accordingly.

Blending Tactical And Strategic

If we can turn market development from a weakness into a strength, then the next challenge we need to deal with is generating a mindset shift inside of our companies. A major issue we face today is that the short-term always wins. It doesn't matter what industry you are talking about; making the sale now takes precedence over a longer-term sell.

Solution selling tends to be longer-term. It requires you to understand the individual needs of each client. It requires you to differentiate your offerings in the minds of the customer, that you help them translate how your product solves their business problems. That type of selling takes time. But in a tough economy, when you are under the pressure to sell today, it is all too easy to get pulled back into short-term thinking.

Another issue we have to contend with is that many sales organizations have separated sales people into hunters and farmers. Hunters are the ones that go out and kill something, but frankly they get bored with dragging it back, dressing it, cooking it, all those kinds of activities required to complete the job. This type of selling mindset does not lend itself well to solution selling, as the quick kill becomes all-important.

To overcome these issues, you need to differentiate your organizational structure. Business needs may dictate that part of your selling activity be focused on the here and now. If that is the case, then dedicate some of your resources towards that task.

But then we also need to set up a separate group to do relationship building. These people should be measured and compensated differently, and they should be focused on the total package, even when the market pressures are to sell today.

Unless we make that organization differentiation clear, then ultimately everyone, relationship sellers included, will shift back into that 'I have to make it today' mentality, and we will always continue to sell at the transaction level.

Focusing On The Ultimate Customer

If we can organize our companies correctly, then the next challenge in doing an effective job of solution selling is to start to view things from the customer's perspective. Customers typically want more than just a product. If all they need to do is complete a transaction, they can go on the web and put it out for bid.

Our goal, therefore, becomes to understand what a customer really wants and needs, and in order to accomplish that we have to change our focus from the product out, to the customer back. By that I mean seeing things from the perspective of the customer looking back into the organization.

This often tends to be a struggle. We talk a lot about concepts like customer centricity, but at the end of the day we often get confused about what that really means. One of the biggest mistakes I see companies making is focusing on the 'internal customer.' Personally, I hate that concept, and I fight with people all the time about that phrase. Yet it's used every day by many, many functions—marketing, HR, manufacturing, technology, etc.—all focusing on satisfying the 'internal customer.'

You can be in technology, and you can satisfy the needs of your 'internal customer,' which may be manufacturing. But at the end of the day, does what you have done ultimately serve the needs of the real customer, the 'external customer?'

For example, technology may have done a great job of supporting manufacturing in their quest to produce vanilla ice cream, and manufacturing's productivity may be great because they are making vanilla. But what value is all of that if the external customer base wants strawberry, chocolate, and raspberry? We can easily lose sight of the needs of the marketplace if we focus only on our internal customer.

The biggest struggle most companies have, whether they realize it or not, is how to rally an entire organization, an entire company around the ultimate external customer, the one that is really paying the bills. How do you really have a customer-centric company if you have phrases like 'internal customer?'

This challenge gets even more complicated when you weave the impact of the supply chain into the equation. A typical supply chain might involve a manufacturer, a distributor, a contractor, and then, ultimately, a customer.

Your distributor wants to be treated like a customer, but they aren't your customer. They are part of the supply chain to satisfy the ultimate external customer. We need to develop that type of customer focus, and make sure we live and breathe that concept every day; and we need to blow up phrases that divert us from that focus.

Changing Our Measurement And Reward Practices

If we are going to overcome that hurdle, and really start to look at things from the external customer's point of view, we may well have to fundamentally redesign our internal measurement and reward practices. Let me share the reason why this is true.

A while back we did a survey of a cross-section of people within GE. The research project dealt with a number of topics, but it included six or seven questions that revolved around the customer. In all cases, our people rated customers very high in terms of their priority and their focus.

We then followed up on this study with a focus group involving 250 people regarding what was at the heart of their day-to-day activities, and during those sessions the customer almost never came up.

I never hear anyone say, "I don't care about the customer." Intellectually, we all care. However, that being said, we can easily lose that customer focus. The reason this occurs is that much of what we are evaluated on is internally-focused metrics versus customer-focused, and it is human nature to give priority to the tasks by which we are measured.

We need to develop new measurements that keep the customer visible.

We need to make all employees aware of their performance relative to the customer. We will still need compensation plans that reward growth, but we need to balance those with quantifiable programs that reward customer-oriented performance.

This is not just a sales or marketing issue. You need to expose virtually everybody in the company to the customer, whether they are in finance, manufacturing, maintenance, technology, it doesn't matter. Everyone should hear what customers are saying. You need to develop active feedback mechanisms from the customer.

The customer may not always be right, but they are always the customer, and we should never lose sight of that fact. Ultimately, if you are not sensitive to customers on a daily basis, you are going to lose them. If that occurs, you are not going to attain the growth or the profitability you are counting on. And, if you don't attain growth and profitability, there is no reason to exist.

Turning Solution Selling Into A Reality

Clearly, dealing with these issues is going to involve a lot of work. So what are some practical steps you can take towards transitioning a company into a solution selling organization? Let me share some of the things we at GE are doing.

Currently, we are reviewing all of our businesses, all of our divisions, with the goal of surfacing best practices (and not so good practices) that may already exist to facilitate these changes.

In addition to internal answers, we are not shy about borrowing or taking good ideas from other companies. We have definitely gotten over the 'not-invented here' syndrome that had existed up to the early to mid-1980s. We are spending a great deal of time going to different forums or working with suppliers and customers to collect other best practices.

▶ Advisory Boards

One of the practices that we have seen a number of our divisions generate a lot of value out of is creating customer advisory boards. These types of groups can really help open your eyes to what the marketplace thinks of you, instead of what you think.

I remember taking part in my first advisory board a number of years ago. During our initial meeting we asked our clients what they thought of us, and they rated us a B+ on presentation and an F on execution. That was one of the more humbling experiences I've ever had. But it was critical for us to hear their feedback, and we took it to heart.

The advisory board became an integral part of setting our priorities. All the top managers, including the CEO of that business, were involved in these meetings. After each session we took the feedback we received from the customers and used that to develop action items. At the next meeting, we would review what had been accomplished and again ask our customers to rate how we were doing.

I remember one specific instance where, frankly, we thought we were doing a superior job in the area of customer service. Our internal numbers showed we were achieving a 90% rating in terms of our ability to serve. To bask in our own glory, we asked the advisory board what they thought of our performance.

Well, after they checked with their people, they came back and informed us that we were way off the mark. Their internal ratings put us at around the 40% to 45% range. I remember them telling us that they used to hold GE up as the gold standard in terms of execution, but we weren't operating at even the brick standard in the eyes of their people.

Without that feedback, which was 'customer back' instead of 'business out,' we would never have known we needed to change. So the value of customer advisory boards is priceless.

▶ Market Segmentation

Another aspect of business that deserves significant attention is market segmentation. If you are going to sell solutions, you need to start by really understanding what the specific needs are for individual market segments. To do this effectively, you need people with specialized knowledge.

For example, if you go to an automotive company and don't know the automotive industry, you will have difficulty talking their language. You might be able to go in and talk about plastics, or metals, or composites, but at the end of the day, you need to relate those elements to issues that are important to the automotive segment. How do those items affect fuel economy, cost reduction, or safety enhancement? These are the over-arching drivers of what that industry cares about, and those are the things our marketing and sales processes need to address.

We also need to do a better job of understanding the cyclical nature of market segments. Take the telecom segment, for example. It kind of came out of nowhere and returned from whence it came, in a relatively short period of time.

For three years or so the market represented a huge opportunity for suppliers and buyers. If you didn't anticipate it coming, you were six to nine months behind having access to those opportunities; and if you didn't anticipate its decline, you experienced six to nine months of significant losses. Dealing with the issue of 'lead-lag' is where effective market segmentation can be invaluable.

If you have people that excel at market segmentation, they can help you make more intelligent choices across the enterprise. Their input can help you determine where to make investments in development, manufacturing, and service by helping to define where the biggest opportunities lie. They can help you deploy your best and brightest people to focus on the opportunities that represent the biggest growth potential. We can miss a lot by not investing properly in this type of expertise.

Unfortunately, market segmentation is an area that is all too often exposed to the winds of the marketplace. In good times we make investments, and in bad times it is often one of the first areas cut. This does not need to be a huge group, but it needs to be afforded some degree of protection so that the job is always being done adequately.

▶ Optimizing 'Touch Time'

Another of my key objectives at present is to determine ways to increase sales value-added time; an important element of this is customer 'touch time.' Increasing touch time, particularly when focused on finding new accounts, adds capacity while driving increased volume.

Value-add time is a core factor in solution selling. If value-add time increases, volume should increase. Most sales companies have touch time in the neighborhood of about 30%. We want to take this to 50%, or even 70%.

Frankly, what we are finding is that our sales people's days are consumed doing any number of non-value-add administrative tasks. Here you have a sales professional, whose compensation and benefits package could be $80,000, $100,000, $150,000, or more, chasing down the status of a delivery, checking on the status of a pending shipment, or spending time responding to simple technical questions. It is crazy.

You want your sales people out creating demand for your channel. You want your sales people out finding and developing new accounts. You want your sales people out developing stronger relationships with your existing customers and anticipating their future needs.

You need sales focused on activities that generate business rather than doing the 'Mickey Mouse' administrative tasks that currently wipe out the majority of their day. This is a huge issue for us, and we need to capitalize on digitization and other improvement techniques to create streamlined and repeatable processes for handling those tasks.

Optimizing the Sales Process

In addition to our administrative processes, we are also taking a long look at our sales process. Our objective is to develop a strategy that would allow a 30-day sales person to be as competent in providing information to the customer as a 30-year sales person. If you have to have 30 years of experience to be truly competent, then by definition you have a flawed process.

In a company like GE you have many businesses that say, "You don't seem to understand. We're unique." However, looking at the selling process, if you take it to the 10,000-foot level, we all are trying to guide the prospect through a solution selling process. We go through interest development (prospecting), qualification, education, proposal generation (selling), closing, post-sales support, and then we all have some type of reporting requirements. So there are some synergies we can leverage.

Here too, we are looking for best practices. Across GE some of our businesses are very strong on the hunting and prospecting side, some are very strong on the post-sales side, still others are strong in their closing, etc. We want to understand each of those strengths so that we can leverage what one business is doing, and increase the effectiveness of another part of the company whenever possible.

Boundary-Less Solution Selling

In my new role as Chief Commercial Officer (CCO), a position that never existed before at GE, my value will ultimately be measured on the specific things we've done to facilitate growth. As you can see, there are a wide variety of issues we are going to have to confront. However, these are challenges that all companies need to deal with if in the end they are going to be able to deliver what a customer really wants to buy.

Ultimately, we would like to create a boundary-less selling environment at GE. By that I mean that we are organized to optimize our ability to have multiple divisions and businesses working together to deliver solutions that focus on the needs of a single account. In that regard, we are changing to more of an industry focus rather than just a geographic focus. When we achieve that objective, we will have made major strides in the transition from transactional to solution selling.

JERRY UNGERMAN

When I first met Jerry Ungerman in 1986, he was Vice President of Sales for National Advanced Systems (NAS). They sold what were called plug-compatible mainframes and competed with IBM and Amdahl. He was then, and remains today, one of the most honest, upright, and smart individuals it has been my privilege to work with. NAS was acquired in a joint Hitachi-EDS venture becoming Hitachi Data Systems. During Jerry's last years at HDS, he was Executive Vice President of Worldwide Operations. Today, he is President of Check Point Systems. I consider Jerry to be a consummate sales professional and will be surprised if you don't get at least a couple insights and good ideas from the interview that follows.

Barry Trailer (BT)

> **The thing that has become more pronounced today is the market's continual question, "Are you adding value?" From the customer through the partners through the whole relationship, they are asking, "Is it of value? Is it something I really, really need?" If they can't answer 'yes,' they are not going to go forward.**

A Solutions-Oriented Perspective

It's interesting to have conversations with friends who say, "I could never be a sales guy," or, "I could never be in sales." To them, sales is about getting people to do unnatural things. Whether their perception is the old cliché about a used car salesman or someone else, they equate selling with trying to get somebody to do something they wouldn't otherwise do—and probably isn't good for them.

I think people who are really good at selling are really good at listening and understanding. They take time to understand customers' needs, problems, and issues, and try to solve them. The best sales people are those who sell something that somebody needs. And if they don't need it, they don't sell it.

I say to those same friends, "Wait a second. You 'sell' your wife, you 'sell' your kids, you 'sell' your friends or co-workers on an idea or concept. In other words, you get them to do something. That is what selling is all about. Now, hopefully, you are getting them to do something that is good for them, like going on vacation, doing their homework, cleaning up their rooms. You are convincing them, selling them." Some can do it through intimidation. Some can do it through motivating and leading. But I think it's really about being able to provide to somebody something that he or she needs.

I think sales excellence is providing a solution to a problem. The basic problem we at Check Point help corporations solve is connecting and protecting their people on their networks and while using the Internet. We look at a lot of IT (information technology) spending surveys of CIOs, and know that security technology spending has been at the top for the last few years. It's been number one or two. We sell both firewalls for security as well as VPNs (virtual private networks) to provide connections to the Internet that have security elements embedded. This year, in three or four recent studies, security and VPN are again on the top two priorities.

So, we've been fairly lucky that this is a segment that has an awful lot of awareness and is a high priority issue in today's enterprise marketplace. Currently, we have 60% to 70% market share on a worldwide basis in the enterprise market. Now, everybody has his or her own definition of an enterprise. Obviously they're the largest corporations in the world. We define the enterprise level as companies with 500 employees on up and with multiple sites; and we have over a hundred thousand customers today. This leads to a perception that the market is saturated. Yet in reality, there are over 20 million businesses connected to the Internet today, which means there is a huge market opportunity for our firewall and VPN solutions.

Real Business Challenges: Knowledge Transfer & Education

We've brought to market a lot of new technology and we're moving into a lot of new segments, so we're challenged in new, different ways. How do we take our brand, which is the de facto standard in the enterprise market and with the largest companies in the world, and build awareness in the small/medium business market? How do we get into the small office/home office market segment? And moving into the consumer market place—what do we need to do to get the consumer to say, "I need Check Point?"

We have an added challenge because we have a 100% indirect sales model. Our product is sold by a broad range of partners, including distributors, value-added solution providers, systems integrators, consulting companies, the major telecommunications companies, and a wide variety of managed service providers. This complexity represents one of our biggest challenges today: the effective transfer of knowledge.

Currently, we have the largest group of R&D engineers in the world focused on building security solutions. Additionally, we have double that number of people in support, sales, and systems engineering who need to be fully up to speed, as well as thousands of channel personnel. Taking that core group and extending it to our thousands of partners that sell our technology and our solutions around the world leads us to ask ourselves, "How do we get the information to this wide audience, and from them to the customer?"

We just announced the fifth major version of our software, Check Point NG, which has over a thousand new features. Given that, how do we go out and educate people? How do we communicate the full capability, the robustness, the functionality, and the features in that security technology so they can go out and talk to somebody and ask about his or her needs and requirements? It's a very complex problem to address and solve.

We've developed a series of communication mechanisms, most of which try to take advantage of technology. We still do direct mail and seminars. We're probably running a seminar in some part of the world every single day of the week. We do big regional seminars and tradeshows. We also conduct a webcast the first Thursday of each month so partners can plan it into their schedule.

To ensure a consistent level of quality, expertise, and current best practices, we have a certification process. To achieve a certain level of partnership status, each partner has a specific number of certified engineers they must have on staff. To maintain that partnership level, they need to stay continually qualified and up to speed on the latest versions, etc. It is a daunting challenge—for us and for our partners—but it is necessary and valued by our customers.

To assist, we archive many of our lessons, especially the webcasts. On our Partner Pages, we keep a wide range of information (e.g., white papers, technical notices, archived webcasts, upcoming events, sales tools, etc.) that help our partners be educated and stay educated. We do a lot of web-based training, so partners can pick times best suited to them.

If they want to do a self-paced class, people can sign up for a web-based training course. We use a lot of different vehicles because it is so important to have knowledgeable people—the more knowledgeable they are, the better job they can do for their customers and therefore for themselves.

A Solutions-Focused Organization

We just re-oriented the whole company because, since the beginning, it has had a product orientation—people knew they needed a firewall, and we sold firewalls. It's getting more complex today so we've gone to a solutions orientation. This is going to be a long-term change for us, and we are just starting the shift.

Rather than walking in and talking about our products, we'll ask customers questions about their environment, their network, their issues with security, what they are trying to accomplish. Are they trying to increase their productivity by tying two sites together or trying to connect remote employees? Or are they building out more points of presence to the Internet that need to be secure? Whatever the case, we respond with a solution as opposed to a product. In fact, we have to go about five levels down in a discussion with a prospect before we start to get to specific product information, whereas, historically, our products would have been the first thing we talked about.

Today, we probably have 60 or 70 various products and solutions. They are all in the security arena based on firewall and VPN technologies, but there is a lot of different functionality and capability that's been productized. So you can't just walk in and talk—which product are you going to talk about? You need to start asking about problems and the customer's issues, or the vision of what they are trying to achieve. You need to listen and then respond with the appropriate solutions.

Indirect Versus Direct Sales Models

Since I have mentioned our 100% indirect sales model, it may be of interest how this began and has played out. From day one, Check Point started out with an indirect business model. The company was founded by three individuals in Israel, which has a very small home market. They knew they had a global solution and wanted to export right away. Once you decide to go global, where are you going to get the expertise, capability, and leverage to sell in all the different markets around the world?

I find many companies start up in the United States and say, "Okay, we are a U.S.-based company, and until we get successful in the U.S. market, we're not going to Europe." European companies start up in Europe with the same attitude.

Check Point started in Israel and went to the rest of the world right away. As a result, our revenue stream is very balanced between the United States, Europe, and Asia—successfully accomplished through the power of resellers.

I talk to a lot of people about their sales model(s). Some say, "Yeah, we'll probably get to an indirect model, but we are going to start out with our own direct sales force because we have to educate the customers, or we have to show corporate support, or because it is a technical sale, etc."

If you have to educate the customer about your product or your technology, rather than going out on a one-on-one basis, why not educate ten resellers at the same time? Instead of hiring a sales person to call on an individual end user, have him organize a seminar with ten resellers and educate them. If they each have five sales people attend the seminar, you now have 50 people the next week going out and replicating that story.

A lot of companies say, "Yeah, but we've got to give the reseller margin to do that." If you take a look, you may find they offset enough cost from a sales standpoint that it's worth giving them the margin. Some companies try to do both by selling direct to some accounts and indirect to others. I don't think that approach works, since the world is dynamic and the line in the sand moves.

The market will pay a fair price for the product and, along with the margin on services, that's where partners make most of their money. There's no value associated with not letting the channel sell. We have a direct touch organization: about half of our people recruit, develop, and train channel partners; the other half makes sales calls on users.

We call it a 'direct touch' model because we don't fulfill business directly, but we do work with customers as necessary. This usually occurs with a channel partner when a customer wants to talk to the manufacturer. But every commitment we get is processed through a channel partner. A partner will process the PO, and receives his margin on the order for product plus from the margin on the other products and services he wraps into the solution. With this approach, we have a business model we are proud of and believe we generate results that compare favorably to others.

Even with big accounts that want to have a direct relationship with our company for whatever reason, we explain our direct touch model and the value of the channel as an added resource and security expert. If necessary, we'll introduce the customer to three partners capable of closing and servicing the business, and let them decide. As you know, it gets down to personal relationships eventually.

Check Point is the product, the vendor, and the technology behind what customers are ultimately buying; and we are always there to be involved as necessary. We ensure our customers get all the information and support they need to complement the service and support they receive from the partner they have chosen to work with locally.

One thing that is different with partners, since they are independent businesses, is that you don't have as much visibility into when a transaction will close. That's the theory. However, even when I ran a direct sales organization, I had a lot of sales people that didn't really have a good handle on the forecast and didn't provide much visibility into the pipeline. The only issue here is that you are a little further removed from the decision maker and the timing of the decision. However, we do hundreds of orders every day, which smoothes the uncertainty of any individual order.

Historically, our price point has been between $3,000 and $20,000. We've now brought out some products that go as low as $300. We're newly entering the consumer market as well as home offices and small offices, and that's probably going to change the dynamics a little bit. Today, through our partners, we handle a large volume of purchase orders each day.

Say I've got 300 sales people. There is no sales person that goes out there on a one-on-one basis and signs one or two contracts every day. Instead, we have all our partners selling, so it's a highly leveraged model. It's also a run-rate model. You can almost look at what you've done for the last 30 days to predict what you're going to do for the next 30 days, although there are seasonality issues that impact results as well as monthly differences within a quarter.

Smoothing Out The Revenue Flow

Often in a direct model, revenues are back-end loaded. By contrast, our revenues are split pretty evenly. Our quarterly revenue breakdown by month is about 30%-30%-40%. I know some companies say they'll do 50% to 60% of their quarter's number in the last two weeks of the quarter. There are a lot of issues associated with this phenomenon, including discounting and resource allocation. Even though they have direct organizations, what visibility does that give them? They're on pins and needles waiting for the last two weeks.

We don't incent end-of-quarter behavior. We're not quarter-motivated to the extent that we will promote unnatural behaviors even though we are a public company. We've been fortunate, though this economy has been a challenge to us like it's been to everybody else. It's been tough from both the macroeconomic environment as well as the IT spending slowdown. But we find that the inability to forecast by not having a total direct sales force is offset by the run-rate nature of the business and having so many partners globally.

We have thousands of partners selling every day. They are not all waiting for the last day of the month. They all have different fiscal years, they all have different motivations, and they're not caught up like a direct organization with quarter-end issues and the actions or incentives associated with the fiscal period as may happen in a company that is direct.

I'll tell you an interesting story. The end-of-quarter fire drill was one of my big frustrations when I managed a direct organization. Even though it was in the mainframe business and was one company, there were three different owners over time. It went from being called Itel, to National Advanced Systems, to Hitachi Data Systems.

What was interesting was the influence of quarter-end and year-end on sales activity. Starting with Itel, the fiscal year coincided with the calendar year. December was our biggest month out of the twelve by far. No other month was even close. If you looked at the graph over the twelve months, you'd see little spikes at the end of each quarter, but December was huge.

Then National Semiconductor bought us and renamed us National Advanced Systems (NAS). NAS closed their business in May. Guess which became the biggest month of the year? It wasn't December; it was May. Next, Hitachi bought the business with a March year-end. Guess which month became the biggest month of the year then? March. Were there external elements associated with this behavior? Same product, same customers, same management, same sales people. Three different fiscal year ends. The 12th month of each one was always the biggest month.

We don't face that situation with thousands of partners around the world that are all on their own systems with their own compensation, with their own motivations, with their own pressure of when they're trying to do something. It levels out. Usually the third month is the biggest of the three months in the quarter, but not by a wide margin. To a certain extent it may be inherent in the market; customers know about March, June, September, and December. So whether or not they are trying to spend money before the end of the quarter, we see the 30%-30%-40% pattern repeat, but the variations are not like we experienced with a direct organization selling big-ticket items.

Effective Partnering

As you would expect with literally thousands of partners, we have the 80-20 rule: 20% of the partners write 80% of the business. Some management theory says each year you cut the bottom $X\%$; however, rather than eliminating the bottom percentile, we focus on providing more tools and information in a highly leveraged fashion to make them successful. We're more interested in their commitment because out of this group could come the next big partner.

We look at several factors when we discuss partner commitment: revenue, the number of Check Point certified security engineers, and year-over-year growth. We look at the number of training sessions they attend, the seminars they run, and their marketing activities. We are interested in all these elements, because *we are really looking for a relationship, not just revenue*.

Today the discussion is increasingly about solutions, but there is still a large technical element. The CIO says, "You need to connect Boston, Chicago, New York, London, and Frankfurt. I want to be able to quickly and easily connect to all my remote employees who are traveling. I've got to cut the communications costs, but I want to do it in a secure fashion." So we relate to their business issues. What are our solutions to deal with that? You can't lose sight of the fact that the problem and solution are technical in nature. This is why we are so focused on partnering with quality companies who are security experts.

Six years ago, we helped create the OPSEC Alliance—the Open Platform for Security. Our company's philosophy is based on partnering and to be open in everything we do. We've opened up our software and have over 20 APIs (application program interfaces) today that other people write to. OPSEC now has over 300 companies that are building security products. They take their technology, whether it's content filtering, URL filtering, intrusion detection, anti-virus, authentication—all are what we call complementary technologies— and write to our APIs. Then their product goes through a certification process so they can say it is 'Certified by Check Point.'

Working with technology partners who are focused on bringing to market best of breed security products is a tremendous benefit that we bring to our customers and channel partners. This was not only done on the software side but also on the hardware side. Today we run on open servers—whether it's Linux, UNIX, or NT—as well as purpose-built security appliances. We've built this very big family, or Check Point ecosystem. I spoke earlier about our open approach with our indirect channel partners. This same openness with technology companies has helped our leverage model. We believe in the power of partnering. Partnering, using an indirect sales model, and having an open business philosophy have paid huge dividends for us.

Maximizing Value For The Customer

As I said earlier, the thing that has become more pronounced today is the market's continual question, "Are you adding value?" You have to be focused on what value you are bringing. Is it something that is needed? Dot-coms—were they all needed? Apparently not. So, what I challenge all of our people to really think through is the value proposition of what we are doing, what we are bringing to market, is it something the customers need? This value question is our orientation.

People ask about competition. My response is always, "We're aware of them; we know we are not going to have 100% of the market." But we don't even think about them. We focus on the customer. We are always focused on the customer—their needs and requirements. If you listen to them, and respond to what they are saying, you're much better off than following a competitor who may be going down the wrong path.

Now, we know customers can't always tell you exactly what they need a year from now or two years from now. We're lucky in that we can respond to needs in a matter of months. The founder of our company is one of the great Internet visionaries. In 1993, he saw what was coming in 2000, and sees where it is going to go in the future. Clearly, it helps to have somebody with that level of insight and intelligence to help drive the direction. But it's also because he has always been focused on the customer and he happens to be one himself. We all use the Internet. Because we use our own product and see how other people are using it, we understand first-hand the problems we are trying to solve.

Selling is about listening and problem solving. Our view is always about value and whether we are bringing value as our customers define it.

ROBERT SAVAGE

Robert Savage leads Savage & Associates, a financial services firm based in Toledo, Ohio, which was founded by him and his late older brother, John F. Savage. Since 1993, Savage & Associates has been recognized nine, and soon to be ten, years in a row as a Top 100 firm by the General Agency Manager's Association (GAMA) International, an organization made up of all the life insurance-based financial services firms in the United States, including firms such as Equitable and Northwestern. This is especially notable since Toledo is one of the smallest markets in America. GAMA International also selects one person for their Management Hall of Fame each year. Bob Savage was inducted in 1999. The Savage brothers received the local Entrepreneur of the Year Award presented by Ernst & Young, Merrill Lynch, and INC Magazine. Bob's other sales awards include being a four-time member of the $10,000,000 Forum and a 26-year recipient of the National Sales Achievement Award. He also serves on numerous community and corporate boards. I caught up with Bob for this interview as he returned from speaking engagements in Singapore, Toronto, and Australia.

BT

> **We look for people with a good work ethic who possess a great attitude. There has to be a certain amount of intellect and talent, but beyond that, they must possess great habits. We all have habits, but are they good ones? Honing good habits to improve ourselves, and getting rid of bad habits that we all have at different stages in our lives, is what helps us focus and really achieve.**

Company Culture

Our company is a bit unusual in several ways. First, we bring in young college graduates, usually about five a year, and we teach them the financial services business. Second, every member of our management team has personal clientele in addition to management duties, which is a very unusual structure.

We teach our people to look at themselves as individual entrepreneurs. They can't give great advice to business people if they don't see themselves in that category. We promote teamwork by having everyone's office be a similar size, whether you are a 24-year-old rookie just graduating from the bullpen or our executive vice president. We have 50 offices and each one is distinctive. That is rare in large service companies. We encourage individual office decoration because we believe that it is very important that each office reflect its occupant so that the clients think of their chief financial advisor as a distinct individual.

In our kind of sales, it is important to get inside peoples' heads and know exactly where they want to go in life. We do that by asking penetrating questions about exactly where they are today, both financially and personally. Once that is determined we ask more questions to determine their personal dreams, goals and objectives—where they see themselves in 10, 15, or 20 years.

Our job is then to take all that information and develop a financial superhighway that gets clients from where they are, no matter where that is, to where they want to be. We help them figure out how to get organized, overcome financial hardships, and have a successful financial path through life. We do that with businesses as well as individuals.

Using our approach, a new mentee should become productive at the end of the fourth year at the latest, and at the end of the third year in most cases. Every once in a while somebody will become productive in two years. So our game plan is aimed at a three-year ramp where a person is mentored every day.

Our biggest investment is the enormous time we take and the patience we demonstrate in bringing in our new people. We look at 23 candidates, mostly college juniors and seniors, for every person we invite to join our firm. We spend an enormous amount of time in selection. The last thing we want is for somebody to come in and have a bad experience. In an industry where bad experiences are common, selection is key. And, if you can find the Larry Birds, Michael Jordans, and the Tiger Woods', you will win the ballgame.

A quick aside about athletes: we have had two great athletes come to work here. Athletes are very common in our industry, but neither one of ours made it. There is certainly an argument that the really great ones have so much natural talent when it comes to playing sports that they never had to work at it. But when they had to do the blocking and tackling in our industry, they didn't relate. I completely ascribe to the theory that somebody who gets knocked down a lot learns to get up. That's the reality of what it takes. It's not just great talent.

Ongoing recruiting is key to our business, so we develop relationships with many universities and colleges. We ask the professors to let our younger people into their classrooms to talk about our business. Our goal is to entice the students who are impressed by the career opportunity demonstrated by our young associates to come by our office and visit. We talk about the greatness of the industry and how we feel we can put them in a position to have a great walk through life. We are looking for those who can walk through the woods and never see the shadows. That is what it takes to be effective in our kind of business.

We know exactly what we're looking for: people with a history of success; people with leadership abilities, who other people follow; who are assertive, honest, have a great work ethic, and a sense of humor. We want people who are articulate and poised, who possess great communication skills and who you'd like to spend time with. That is what we are looking for in our business.

When I was in school in the late '50s, the education system thought there was only one form of intelligence. The formal education system recognized that one form, and people who were good at it got Ph.D.s. Having served on two university boards for a total of 19 years, and working a lot with the university community, we know today that there are many different forms of intellect. We are hunting for people who are operative, who are first-rate communicators, and that people have chosen to follow during their college years.

Given our business needs, we'd rather have the person that was vice president of the student senate, was president of his fraternity or her sorority, or the one who put together the yearbook. We need people who help clients organize their money. They need to be leaders, not just theorists who pontificate wonderful philosophies.

I don't talk to candidates until the management team has interviewed them and everyone agrees that the selections make sense. When I talk with the candidates, I'm really not looking for talent. I assume they have the talent or they would not have made it this far. I'm looking for character flaws, personality flaws, or lack of compatibility with the kind of open space that we coordinate.

We have a true open door policy. When you walk out of here at night, every individual office door is open. It's a trusting relationship that is very unusual in business, but that's the way we built our space and we don't want somebody who doesn't fit in.

What we really offer our associates is independence. If they have intellect, a good work ethic and decent people skills, they'll make a great living wherever they go. We can give them something very few corporations offer: control of their own time. They can arrange their hours so they never have to miss a kid's ballgame or play. They can take five-week vacations in national parks every year if they want. They can decide when they work and when they don't. The reality is, by year's end, they will be putting in a lot more hours than people who work in typical corporate structures, but the beauty is they can do it their way. There's a lot to be said for that kind of freedom.

Investing In The Profession Of Sales And Marketing

I was a trustee at the University of Toledo for 11 years. Five years ago, the president of the university came to me and said that they wanted to develop an Advanced Sales and Marketing Center in the College of Business. They wanted me to become involved, but I told them I would not do so while I was a trustee.

Six months after I retired as a trustee, the president of the university approached me again, and after consulting with our management team we agreed to sponsor what has become the Savage & Associates Center for Advanced Sales and Marketing, in the College of Business at the University of Toledo.

In many ways our business structure is similar to a law firm—a service business that does not attempt to accumulate cash reserves. For that reason we were not in a position to write a large corporate check. Because of their great love for the University of Toledo we were able to get 26 of our associates and a couple of our friends in the community to write checks. Collectively, we gave $600,000 to the university to establish the Center for Advanced Sales and Marketing that bears our name. I continue to be its strong advocate as we bring this Center to life.

Many professors think that people in sales skin somebody or take advantage of them—unfortunately, that is part of our image in academia. But I smile at this because, having had a long career in sales, the sales people that I've known are the most creative and most helpful people in business. In fact, a major common denominator amongst CEOs of small- and medium-sized businesses is their background in sales and communication. I think it's important that we move sales into an academic environment. We will all benefit when the future sales people are well prepared by a college of business to go out and intelligently represent companies.

I'm very convinced that if we could crank out 1,000 sales majors a year who really understand the communication process that is needed in business, every one of those people would get three job offers. Every business has a never-ending need to attract and retain people who can articulate the value proposition of their employer.

Here's our vision for the Center for Advanced Sales and Marketing. Toledo is a town of 600,000 people. The environment in a town like this allows the members of the business community to know each other fairly well. Thirty of us from different industries are involved in the Sales Center. In developing the classes, at least once or twice a week the professors will call in a successful business person that fits well into that particular part of their curriculum. The business person arrives, talks with the class, shares his or her wisdom, which has been developed from hands-on experience, and then answers student questions.

At the end of the courses, the students have all these wonderful, rich experiences from real life. When you combine that experience with the professor's ability to give them structured learning and insight from an academic viewpoint, the students end up with the best of both worlds. This has not been done much in the past. Now, though, a lot of places are beginning to look at it and are trying to get centers started. We believe we can build this into a real model, at least in the Midwest and perhaps beyond.

Sales Excellence

Sales excellence depends on what you're trying to market or sell. In our kind of business, the sales person must totally understand the products which are solutions to people's long-term financial planning. They must communicate both on the human-value side and on the product side. We view our people as specialists who help their clients prepare for the future and protect themselves from life's financial pitfalls.

Some people in our business are concerned about the threat of the Internet. I think the Internet will work for a few analytic souls, who are data-driven decision makers—but only a very few. The Internet gives you an enormous amount of data and information, but most people are not hunting for more data and information. They are already inundated and overwhelmed by having too much data and information. What they're hunting for is knowledge and wisdom. Our job is to take all that data and information and provide clients with the parts that apply to their personal or business lives. We help them get organized in a way that makes their lives better. I tell people all the time, "We're in the wisdom business. None of us wants to know how the telephone works. We just want to know the right phone number to call."

Making Our Business Better

My view is that each associate should do whatever it takes to make Savage & Associates a far better business. It seems strange to many people that our business with 130 associates does not have any individual job descriptions. That is because we have a view of what each associate should do to make Savage & Associates a far better and more effective business.

We have a sign that says it all. It is posted in our training area, as it has been for more than 25 years. It says four things:

Do what's right and avoid what's wrong.

We all know right from wrong; nobody has to tell us that.

Treat other people the way you want to be treated.

The next time you're in an argument and you're about ready to knock somebody over with this great line you just thought of, imagine yourself on the other side of the table. Would you like that line to be delivered to you? If not, then be quiet.

Always do the very best you can.

That's all anybody can expect. We all have been given gifts and talents. If we are doing the best we can—that's great.

Keep in touch with God.

We have Jews and Moslems and 27 kinds of Christians here and we've never had anybody cause any trouble with the understanding of this point. We've also never had anybody object to it.

We hire two or three high school juniors every year. They work here for one year answering the phones and greeting people. Probably 80% of our appointments are here in the office. Our doors open at 7:30 a.m. and close at 6:30 p.m., so for 11 hours a day these young kids keep the doors open.

I am not involved in their selection. They just know that 'Mr. Savage' is the president. The first time I bump into them, I look them right in the eye and ask, "Do you know what your number one job is?" They look at me and it is clear they don't have any idea. I tell them, "Your number one job is to smile and to add to our business environment. We have the best business environment in Toledo and your job is to make it better."

Later, I'll come around the corner and they'll see me and have this kind of 'overdone' smile—as only teenagers can do—which is very out of place, but over the next few weeks, as things get more relaxed, the smile is very natural and very pleasant. I tell these young people that everybody has some personal problems and concerns and they should leave them outside in the parking lot when they enter our office. When they appear to be in a great mood it truly enhances our office and business environment.

I believe we get what we ask for, so it's very important for those of us in leadership positions to be very clear about our expectations.

Mentoring

All of our associates are generalists at the beginning. Once they move through the process, and by the time they've been here seven or eight years, about half the people have become specialists. It's very interesting. When you get associates as young as we do, by the time they're 30 years of age, they are seasoned veterans and have a 30- or 35- or 40-year career ahead of them if they choose.

I think the greatest psychological reward from being a member of our management team is seeing new people join us, develop confidence toward whatever their specialty becomes, and then truly become expert in that phase of the financial business. These days, it is important that you become a real expert in one thing, because our business is too complex for our people to remain generalists. As their knowledge grows, other associates will bring them into cases that need their expertise. Today that is how we generate a great deal of our business, especially in estate planning, pensions, financial planning, and business insurance.

Our average marketing person, not including the clerical or staff people, joins us at age 21. Out of our 69 representatives, 54 of them joined us at age 21 and have been here an average of 17 years. In a business that nationally is noted for having enormous turnover, that is an incredible record.

I think our turnover is low because we have great role models and mentors. We mentor very, very well and it's a huge part of our operations. In the first week somebody joins us, he or she is assigned a mentor who's not in management. The mentor is somebody who is successful, can tell the mentee where everything is, and can answer any kind of question he or she has. The mentor becomes the big brother or big sister who can help guide them by sharing their years of experience about our operation so they have a smooth introduction to our organization. The mentors and mentees work extremely closely together and in many cases become lifelong friends.

Our program includes a great deal of formal classroom education, which is taught by our management team. They teach the new people everything they will need to know about each aspect of our business. This includes basic financial planning, estate planning, pensions, and group insurance. We cover the intricacies of different kinds of life insurance, the tremendous variety of investments, when they're appropriate and when they're not.

In addition to teaching, the mentor's job is to coach the new person about the reality of working with clients and their expectations. If new associates did not grow up in a business household, then they may never have been around business and may not know what to expect. The mentors usually take the mentees along on client calls so that the mentees can watch them in action. It gives them an opportunity to see successful people giving appropriate advice and doing successful things.

Sometimes we get personalities that don't work well together. We change the mentor very quickly when that happens, and continue to monitor the situation.

In our business, many people are called managers, which I think is an antiquated term. I believe we're all in the coaching business, and should think of ourselves every day as coaches. Nobody has ever heard of a world manager, political manager, or a religious manager. The reality is, each day we all follow world leaders, political leaders, and religious leaders. We are coaches and leaders and should think of ourselves in those terms to be effective.

Perfect Practice Makes Perfect Performance

If you talk to anybody in the life insurance-based financial services industry, they'll say you have ten suspects, three prospects, and one sale. Twenty-five years ago, we said that was the dumbest thing in the world.

We expect that if you meet one person, you'll have one sale. You may not—and probably won't—have it now, but if you truly understand financial planning and it is clear you are concerned about your customers and their financial future, you should eventually do some business.

If you are relatively bright, know your products and their proper solutions, and know how to communicate effectively, almost everyone with whom you spend the proper amount of time should do business with you. It may take five years, but the idea of not spending in-depth time with people to help them understand what you offer is ridiculous. Our job is to create a high-quality environment with all the people with whom we communicate so that they recommend us to their friends who are in relatively similar circumstances.

Training people correctly is our business. If our organization can't teach people the intricacies of the financial services business and how to communicate, then we have no business at all.

Learning The Insight To Communicate Well

So far, we have not employed any particular technology on the sales side. We have a full-time technical director whose job is to make all our technology work on an ongoing basis. But at this point, we're using technology to back up a lot of processes, including our financial planning reports, but we do not use technology directly in sales. It is a tool that is very important and saves us an enormous amount of preparatory time, but we only show the client the end result. That does not mean that some day we won't; we are walking our way along the technology curve, and we certainly see the enormous potential of technology.

Leading By Example And Enthusiasm

I read a great deal, actually every night, and apply what I learn whenever I can. I'm one of those people who gets up early every morning and stays energized hoping to be a proper role model and a positive force. One of the things I have done for 25 years, and continue to do, is give eight hours every week trying to make Toledo, Ohio, a better place.

I think that is very important that all of us try to positively affect the towns and neighborhoods where we reside. A community's greatest resource is the talent of its leadership and we all have a huge obligation to make things better. Every time we meet anyone, we can either lift them up a little, or knock them down a little. I think it is important that we all become uplifting human beings. People gravitate to others who smile, are pleasant, upbeat, and have positive things to say. No one likes to be around complainers. The reality is, in a historical sense, most of us have very little to complain about.

I think our organization's actions have been value-based because of the example set by our parents and friends early in our lives, a long time ago. I am reminded of the story that is told of President Franklin D. Roosevelt who, in the early '40s, flew over the Pacific to meet the Commanding General Douglas MacArthur. The President was trying to entice the General to come back to America at a time when he was hoping to win a third term. When his approach was not motivating the General to fly back to the mainland, it is said that the President told him he should come back to see all the many changes that had taken place over the years the General had been out of America. The General is quoted as saying, "The things I believe in never change." I am not sure of the accuracy of the quote, but it is a compelling story.

The things that have made Savage & Associates one of the great financial services organizations over the last 43 years are fundamental: quality people who are well educated and are trying to truly help people understand and better prepare for life's probable economic events and pitfalls.

JOHN WILLIAMS

John Williams' accomplishments in achieving world-class sales productivity have been profiled in Newsweek, CRM Magazine, featured on CNN, reviewed in-depth in George Columbo's Sales Force Automation (McGraw Hill), and more. John is a 35-year veteran in the high tech marketplace, and is probably best known for the work he did while serving as Senior Executive Vice President for worldwide sales, marketing, and support for StorageTek. Prior to that, John was the Vice President of sales for Grid Systems, managing the company through its startup phase to ultimate acquisition by Tandy Corporation, and he also worked for Memorex. John has recently retired but still lectures on how to optimize sales force performance. When I interviewed him I asked him to review his experiences at StorageTek, since the issues he successfully dealt with there are the same challenges many sales organizations are facing today.

JD

> **Over a four-year period we took sales at StorageTek from $700 million to $2.2 billion, and we did this all through productivity gains—we did not add any additional sales people during that time. In retrospect, I think the main foundation of our success was that we concentrated on three things—Metrics, Process, and Tools.**

We live in an era where increasing shareholder value is of critical importance in every boardroom across the nation, around the world. Each corporate officer is being turned to and asked to come up with new innovations to optimize the performance of his or her piece of the business to help contribute to that goal.

I'm a firm believer that today the biggest return on anything you can do in a company is to make your sales people more productive. It is not optimizing back office processes more. It is not fine tuning finance more. It is not about improving the quality of manufacturing more. The biggest contribution you can generate to the bottom line comes from increasing the efficiency and effectiveness of the sales force. I say this from experience.

Our Own Sales Excellence Challenge

When I took over all the front-office functions for StorageTek worldwide, we were just coming out of bankruptcy. The focus of all of us on the executive management team was to rebuild our credibility with our customers, our investors, and Wall Street. Based on the current economic climate I would venture to guess that many other companies are facing those same issues today.

At StorageTek, each of us on the executive team made a personal commitment to ensure that our operations directly contributed to the success of the company going forward. For my part, I had a two-year window before our next generation technology would come to market. During that time I had to revamp the sales force and get them ready for a new age of business. We were looking at massive changes: new products, new ways of selling, and new tools.

Well, we survived that period of massive upheaval. I am personally very proud of the fact that over the next four years we tripled sales revenues, increased customer satisfaction, and actually reduced our cost of sales, not just in terms of sales as a percentage of revenues, but in fixed dollar costs as well. Perhaps some background on what we went through would be useful.

Getting The Lay Of The Land

When I took over the position of Senior Executive Vice President of Worldwide Field Operations, I was actually coming back to StorageTek. I had worked as a sales executive for the company in the 1980s, before leaving to start a PC hardware company.

While I had some previous knowledge regarding how things worked, and in fact had kept in touch with people in the company over the years, upon my return it occurred to me that it would be a mistake to let any of that influence my decision process on where to take things from here. I decided that I needed to do my own due diligence analysis of the company, as it existed today. I needed to get a current perspective on how operations were currently managed. So I personally visited every major sales office, analyzed how we did business, and I was shocked at what I found.

▶ Process Morass

First, the company's processes were very antiquated and overly complex. The sales process was full of inefficiencies. It took on average 50 calls to close an order. I am talking 50 'real' calls: face-to-face meetings with a customer, over an average sell cycle of nine months. We computed the expense and determined that each of these calls was costing us about $1,200.

Once we got an order, things didn't get any better. To fully understand the quote-to-cash cycle, we produced a workflow chart that documented everything that needed to be done to produce an order. I am not joking— the final document ended up being eight feet long, even after using miniature print. We calculated that it was costing us $700 to process the paperwork using these procedures. I actually put that chart up in my office, hanging from the ceiling, and I would look at it and shake my head.

▶ Relationship Versus Solution Selling

The second thing I found was that I had good, solid sales people. The majority of the members of the sales force had been around the industry a long time. During that time they had developed very solid relationships with their customers. But an issue was that they relied very heavily on those relationships to close business.

The new products coming down the pipe were going to be more innovative and more complex than anything we had to sell before. Taking these new solutions to market was going to entail a much higher degree of strategic selling than any of the current team members had ever experienced, but it was clear we had to make that transition to be successful.

▶ Dart Board Forecasting

We had no Customer Relationship Management (CRM) tools in sales. Consequently, forecasting at best was black magic, with no consistent logic to the black magic. Worldwide, I had over 1,000 direct account executives doing business over 1,000 different ways. People were not even using the same rules in this guessing game.

Because of this, we were creating problems for other parts of the business. Finance never knew exactly when sales were going to close. Manufacturing never knew exactly what those orders would include. Services never knew exactly who would be needed where and when to get the units operational.

Even with all of this, the company was still fairly stable; we were making money. But I looked at our sales force and knew they were going to get killed in the future because they were not in a position to handle what was coming at them. There was a tsunami headed their way, and they didn't see it.

Based on the numbers we were going to have to put up on the board, it was obvious that we were going to have to turbo-charge sales; we needed a massive increase in productivity and effectiveness.

Charting The New Course

As the top executive in sales, I made it clear that I was personally committed to champion the project. I explained to everyone the difference between 'committed' and 'contributing' by using the old ham-and-egg breakfast analogy. Regarding the breakfast, the chicken contributed, the pig was committed. This time I was willing to be the pig.

In optimizing sales in the past, I had looked at new ways to leverage people, process, and technology. It had already been made abundantly clear to me that I would not be getting any additional headcount for a long time to come, so process and technology became the two major items that we focused on.

▶ Create the Vision of What 'Better' Looks Like

My first task was to create the vision for how we needed to sell going forward. The vision document reviewed the metrics of how we were presently performing; detailed the holes in the way we did business; laid out the new sales process; pointed out where efficiency, effectiveness, and communications improvements needed to be made to implement that process; and finally, defined the technology tools the team would need to support their work efforts.

Before rejoining StorageTek, I spent ten years running the sales operations for a laptop computer company, so I understood technology from both a software application and hardware standpoint. I put together the vision of how I wanted us to operate. My ultimate goal was to provide each of our sales people with a personal administrator and a personal engineer to support them; they would just happen to be in the form of a laptop computer.

I presented this vision to the board to get their approval. The initial plan called for spending $3.5 million—nearly $18,000 per sales user—for hardware, software, application customization, training, and support to equip the sales people in North America. Based on the success we achieved in the States, we would then roll the systems out worldwide.

As I said before, we were in a period of very austere budgeting at that time, not unlike today for many companies, so getting money for this project meant taking it away from other people's budget. Because of this, I had to develop a detailed project plan showing how we could generate an ROI for the project within 12 months.

I had to personally commit to achieve that number. I made sure I had a firm commitment for the funds before I said anything to the sales force. In addition, I had to sell other departments on why they should support me in this endeavor, so I gave a lot of thought into what was in it for them if my plans were put into action. Ultimately, I gained complete support for this initiative.

▶ Take a Phased Approach

The code name for the project was Apollo, since just like the moon-landing program, we were phasing our reengineering efforts in over time to minimize risk. Our first goal was to win the sales force's support for the initiative. To do that we needed to pick a few things, two or three, that could really make a difference to them, and do those extremely well.

We were not going for a Rolls Royce right out of the chute; we were going for a steady, reliable Jeep. Something we could get out quickly, something that could go wherever the sales force went, something that added real value.

The initial rollout included a proposal generation system, a presentation system, and an opportunity manager that functioned as the sales peoples' right-hand desk drawer, holding all of their customer files, which allowed them to be more effective when working remotely. We also had a number of capabilities to support improving communications between the members of the sales force.

▶ Get a Support Crew

To increase our chances for success, and to speed up the creation of the system, we enlisted outside help to make this project happen. When we started the initiative, Apple had what I considered to be the best laptops available. They not only provided the hardware, but they also gave us five of the best software engineers I ever met, and they wrote the software applications we needed to support this program and had them beta ready in about three months.

On the process side, we brought in what was then Andersen Consulting (now Accenture). One of their key partners, Phil Tamminga, was invaluable in helping us analyze our current operations and then define the new ways to do business. I am a big believer in getting some outside eyes involved in a project like this, because you need the involvement of some people who have no vested interest in the status quo, who are ready to look for innovation.

▶ Push the Team

We had a very aggressive project time line. I had heard about two- and three-year implementations for CRM projects like this, and that was unacceptable. We needed problems solved now. Beta testing lasted two months. This was then followed by a one-month pilot where we trained a set of users across the States and had them kick the tires. A month later, we brought all the sales people together and did three full days of training to make sure they felt totally comfortable with the new processes and the tools.

▶ Get User Buy-in

Notice I said sales people; the sales managers were not invited to the rollout. In fact, they had to stay back in the offices and cover the local accounts while the account execs came to HQ for the launch. We did this to make a statement that the tools, processes, and technology that the sales people were being given were truly meant to increase their productivity, their efficiency, and their effectiveness. I had already seen too many of these projects fail when the sales teams perceived that what they were being given were things that had sales management's best interest at heart, and not necessarily theirs.

After training, during that first quarter of usage, we set aside a $50,000 budget to reward success when using these tools. If someone gave us a story about how the systems helped him or her win a deal, they might get $1,000. Give us a great idea for how to improve the applications or processes and you'd get a $500 night on the town. We spent every cent of that money, and it was absolutely worth the investment.

▶ Continuously Gather Metrics

Within two weeks of the launch we had a 55% adoption rate. By that, I mean sales people were using the tools on a daily basis. After six months we were up near 90%. All along the way we gathered new metrics on our performance so we could see if we really were improving or not.

After six months of active usage, I was able to go back to the board and show in hard dollars, to the CFO's satisfaction, that we had achieved the full ROI that we had set for the project. By focusing on new ways to do things, and giving sales people the information and tools they needed to do their jobs, we collapsed the sell cycle down from 50 calls to 35. We reduced the sell cycle length from nine months down to seven. We reduced the cost of a sales call by 60%. We dramatically increased our service revenues. Prior to starting the project, I would have been happy if we had achieved any of these numbers, and here we did them all in six months.

▶ Repeat All Over Again

From that point on, I never had any problem getting money from the board. They saw the real returns their investments were generating. Over the next several years we rolled out a new release of the system every six months. Each phase of the project had the same objective; find three or four new problems still impacting the effectiveness of sales teams, design solutions for those challenges, train the people how to use the new tools and processes, and start all over again.

Over time we added tools to help the sales force do financial analysis, design the lay out of the floor space of a computer room, do detailed expense analysis, and we streamlined the sales order entry system. Yet with all of that, when I retired we still had plenty of areas for improvement. The vision kept expanding over time, based on new business needs, new technology, new competitors, sales force reorganization, and so on. So anyone starting down this road should be aware that this is a multi-year endeavor. You will continually be finding new ways to innovate.

Lessons Learned

If I were going to give any advice to my peers, based on what we learned, first I would say that executive sponsorship is critical to the success of the project. As the sponsor, you have several roles. First, you need to set the vision—no one else can do that for you. If you do not have a corporate officer willing to take on this responsibility, then don't even start.

Second, you need to gather metrics before you do anything else. These are not always easy to get, they can be very time consuming to collect, but I don't know how you can build your vision for improvement without them.

Third, be ready to break some legs. I don't want to make it sound like everything went smoothly every day. It didn't. We did have some sales people and even some sales managers who pushed back against the changes we were making. If you find terrorists who are trying to sabotage the project—kill them. You cannot afford to keep these people around.

Fourth, make sure you know what the purpose of the pilot really is. Too many people think the goal of the pilot is to ensure the software and hardware works. Well, that is what alpha testing is for. The intent of the pilot is to prove that you can generate true business value using the tools. If you don't see a clear ROI during the pilot, stop the project and redesign the systems and processes until you do. Never give the users something that has no value.

Finally, fund the project appropriately. i know in the current business climate, we are all worried about spending money today, but this is an investment, not an expense. Figure out what it will cost to do the project the right way; calculate what you need to spend on training, consulting, tools, etc.

Next determine what your current levels of inefficiency and ineffectiveness are costing you. How many deals are you losing because you are slow to respond to opportunities? How much margin are you giving away because your sales people cannot sell the true value of your offerings? How much revenue are you losing because it takes a year or more to get new sales people productive? If you know these costs then you can figure out the payback, and if the numbers look right, then commit to invest the funds.

Back when we started down this road we were way ahead of the pack. The way we leveraged technology and process was a real competitive advantage for us. Now these systems are a matter of competitive survival. My message to other sales executives is prepare now for the tsunami coming to your industry. To delay today is to court disaster.

SAM REESE

As President and CEO of Miller Heiman, the leading provider of sales development services, Sam Reese is constantly exposed to the real challenges and opportunities facing sales leaders. Sam joined Miller Heiman in 1999 as both an alumni and advocate of their sales process. Prior to that, he was the Corporate Vice President of Sales and Marketing for Corporate Express, the world's largest corporate supplier of office products and services. Sam provides the leadership, experience, and a sales practitioner's insight which helps Miller Heiman provide relevant solutions important to today's sales leaders. He's held senior sales leader positions with Xerox Corporation, British Telecom, and Kinko's, where he served as steward for the Commercial Sales organization, doubling the productivity of its sales force in less than one year, while increasing average account billing five-fold. Sam received his Bachelors degree from the University of Colorado. His company's website is www.millerheiman.com.

JD

> **In today's market we are deathly afraid of losing deals; we try to do whatever it takes to avoid losing. An interesting question I have been exploring with companies is, 'What is actually the worst thing that can happen when you lose a deal?' When you really consider the problem, you realize that only one bad thing can happen when you lose—which is that it takes you a long time to lose.**

This concept is very eye opening for many sales executives and their teams. When you evaluate your losses, and you realize how long you take to lose, and how many resources you waste in the process of losing, you start to appreciate the magnitude of the problem. We have got to organize how we sell so if we are going to lose, we lose really fast. It's great if you win fast, and it's okay if you win slow, but you cannot afford to continue to lose slow.

In talking with sales executives recently, a recurring trend I have been seeing is that over the past two years, there has been a lot of confidence lost in our sales organizations. People once felt as if they had these finely tuned machines that could withstand any type of economic pressure. However, as soon as it really got ugly out there, many sales executives began to realize that part of their sales force actually consisted of high-priced order takers. While these types of reps are good at servicing accounts, they are not great at winning new business.

Because service account reps are not great at understanding what it takes to win deals, they spend a lot of time and company resources losing bad deals. So, how do you avoid losing slow? The firms that are making headway in addressing this issue are doing a few things fundamentally differently from their peers.

Understanding Your Value Proposition

My company is currently being engaged by a number of organizations to help identify the source of their sales performance problems. When we talk with these companies, a common pain point keeps recurring: support resources are being consumed faster than ever before. The common lament I hear across sales teams is, "We need more resources to close deals."

Imagine the dilemma this is causing. Companies are incurring the same level of expense or more, providing support services that get gobbled up as fast as they are made available, while at the same time the sales people are often selling less than they did a year ago.

And what happens if the resources aren't made available to sales? Well then, in order to help close business, the sales force comes back and says, "We need better prices." The end result of either situation is lower margins.

In our experience, relying on excessive resources in order to close deals is a symptom of a more fundamental problem: you are going after the *wrong* deals. The sales organizations that are figuring this out understand that the world is not their oyster. You can't just look at a marketplace and say, "We have such a great product, and anybody can use what we offer."

What sales teams need to do, using a Miller Heiman term, is to understand clearly their value proposition. To do this, you need to know what problems you solve, who has those problems, why your solution is better than any number of alternatives, and what is the associated ROI for making that issue go away. When sales people take the time to think through this process, they develop a much more pointed, focused sales approach.

How many times have we all sized up an opportunity, realized it did not represent an ideal target, yet still went ahead and chased the deal because the dollars seemed attractive? We dedicated loads of resources—sales support people, pricing analysts, engineers, whatever it took—going after business where the odds of winning were extremely low. We cannot afford to do that anymore.

We need to introduce a new rigor around how we sell. We need to focus on the ideal customer. We need to install a sales process that puts a guardrail around resources. We need to make it clear that sales reps are not going to get help selling to a prospect unless they have done their homework and can show that the opportunity represents a high-win, solid margin opportunity.

Customers of ours, like Kinko's, are achieving sales performance success by implementing this type of discipline. Today at Kinko's, sales people can't get any help with their major accounts on pricing, sales support, proposal creation, etc. unless they do a full account plan that has been signed off by key members of the executive team. The reps have to convince the rest of the company that the opportunity is the type of business that the firm wants, and can win.

Adopting this mindset does not guarantee that you will always win fast, but it will significantly reduce the number of times that you lose slow.

Proactive Versus Reactive Selling

There are a number of industries that have problems today as a result of their wild successes in the '90s. Business was so good, for so long, that many sales professionals have become seriously dulled in their proactive, new business development skills.

When we look at sales forces today we find numerous sales people who do not engage in a sales process until the customer says, "We have a need." At that point, the sales person begins determining how to fill that need as it has been defined to him or her.

The problem with starting the sales cycle at this stage is that you are coming into the process late in the game. The buy cycle started long before the sales person engaged with the customer, so he missed out on a number of critical events. He wasn't involved as the customer was forming their concept of what needed to be fixed, accomplished, or avoided. The rep waited until the customer got to the end of that thought process.

When you enter the decision cycle at the tail end, a number of things can happen, most of which are bad. First, strategic discussions have already taken place and the evaluation process most likely has been delegated to a group of lower-level individuals. Given their own self-defined view of the problem, these folks will consider a multitude of vendors looking for the best fit at the best price.

When you are not able to provide any value on the front end of the process, you have assumed the role of an order taker. Sell cycles drag out because the sales person is not in control of the process, and in fact he or she never was. Since a high number of alternatives are often being considered in this type of sale, if you win at all you will win long, but far more likely you will lose long.

The sales person in this example has become too complacent. He or she has become dependent on marketing to identify opportunities that are already in a decision mode, and then just focused on closing.

When you constantly come late into the sell cycle, even if you are closing deals, you are only getting good at doing a fraction of the job of selling, and that is not a sustainable model for business. We have to wake up the sales force and get them to be much more proactive versus reactive.

The proactive mindset is one where the sales force doesn't wait for marketing to give them leads. Instead, the sales organization determines which accounts to target and systematically goes after those prospects. By systematically, I mean that they adhere to a very structured, step-by-step approach for moving a customer through a sales process.

Creating A Proactive Sales Force

▶ Separating the Players from the Pretenders

The type of person that is successful in this type of sales environment is not an order taker; he or she is a true sales professional. If you are going to adopt this type of proactive sales model for your sales force, the first question you need to ask is, "Do I have the right people?"

There are a number of ways to determine whether you have the right players or not, but an easy model that we use is based on the premise that a successful sales person needs to be evaluated on three key metrics: skills, activity, and revenue.

During an economic downturn, you have a perfect opportunity to expose the pretenders in your sales force and bring them back up to speed or replace them. In an up market, pretenders can appear successful—they're bringing in revenue and hitting their sales plan like everyone else. Conversely, when times are tougher their revenues decline, and if you take a broader look you quickly see that the two other critical sales success factors, activity and skills, are not evident. When a great market no longer blinds you, those flaws surface quite clearly.

Keep in mind that identifying pretenders doesn't mean immediately getting rid of them. Many pretenders are actually players who just got off track. We need to refresh their skills and hold them accountable for activity. If poor performers can show they are making progress, we need to support them in continuing that shift. However, if they don't improve their skills or they do not increase their selling activity levels, then we need to let them go. This is the time to build muscle by either improving the people we have or bringing in new talent.

▶ Focus on Activity

If we are sure that we have the right players, then we need to be vigilant about monitoring their activity. There are a lot of activities you could measure, but the model I like best is the one that John Chambers was famous for using at Cisco. The key metric Chambers touted was that the health of an organization can be represented by the amount of physical time sales people spend in face-to-face business meetings with customers.

Notice the key words here. This is not about talking to a customer over the phone. This is not about doing a customer service check up call. This is all about the right type of activity, which boils down to having regular, meaningful discussions with clients and prospects about their business challenges.

When you focus on that key metric, as we have been doing for a number of clients this year, you find a huge disconnect between perception and reality. Management almost always believes there are a lot more sales calls being made than are actually happening.

So, reality has to change to match expectations. We need to focus on getting the sales people on track to increase the amount of true selling they do, and that all starts with face time with clients. If we have meaningful business conversations, we will uncover problems. If we uncover problems, we can surface opportunities to get much more involved in a customer's decision cycle. If we are actively involved from the start, we will honestly know if we have the best solution for their problem or not, and we will then know early on if we should walk from the deal or aggressively fight for the business.

▶ Strategic Selling Skills Versus Tactical Product Knowledge

What we are talking about here is strategic selling. You cannot pick up a sales magazine or book without finding that we should be selling solutions versus products. Everyone knows that. But it is surprising how many sales people do not know how to do that.

For years, they have been able to be successful by relying on their detailed product knowledge; today that is not enough. As a potential customer, you can often get all the product details you want off of a web site. What customers want from a sales person today are insights about how to apply the product or offering to their specific challenges.

Clearly, during the sell cycle we need to answer all the questions of the evaluation team regarding the features, functions, and specifications of our product. But in order to close the deal, we need to sell not just to the recommenders, but to the economic buyers as well—the CXOs of the company.

This creates a significant challenge for many sales forces. Sales people will meet with their manager, and the manager will say, "Go out there and have a strategic discussion with the CFO at ABC Company." The sales rep will dutifully agree, walk out of the sales manager's office, and then realize that he has no earthly idea of what it means to have a meaningful discussion with a CFO.

That one issue has become the focus for much of our consulting work this year. Companies cannot just teach their sales people the high level steps in the sales process; they have to help them develop the skills to implement specific tactics. That means getting down to the details, such as how to structure the conversation, what questions to ask, what responses/ objections to anticipate, etc.

We have been doing a lot of work crafting that type of communications flow, and have found that when you give sales people the 'how' for each step in the sales process, they respond very positively. If we are going to enable sales people to function at the strategic level versus the product level in selling, we are going to have to make this type of investment.

Management's Focus On Execution

▶ Executive Management's Role

Another thing we are finding, and I was guilty of this too, is that as business leaders, we let the revenue successes we achieved in the past cause us to take our eye off of what was truly happening in the marketplace. It became easy for us to sit on top of our business plan, view things from a purely strategic perspective, and then just expect people to implement the strategy.

While in the good times that seemed to work, the negative side effect was that we lost touch with what our company was doing, and more importantly what our customers were doing. Today, senior executives have to get involved with execution. How ever a deal turns out, win or lose, if you don't know why, you won't know how to maximize the positives and fix the negatives.

As a CEO, I have taken it upon myself this year to become involved in a lot of the details. I have to. Although I was coached against that by a lot of people, my direct involvement is what is giving our business traction. That's significantly different from what we learned in our management classes. We were told to delegate and let smart people figure it out.

I still want smart people to figure it out, but I'll do it at the same time. I need us all working as one team. I do not want 100 smart people doing 100 different things. I want 100 smart people doing one thing, the best thing; and I want to constantly analyze and improve that thing.

▶ Sales Management's Role

Key changes also need to be made at the sales management level if we are going to be successful going forward. One of the first things we need to focus on is holding sales managers more accountable for their team's performance.

I find it interesting that, when talking to sales managers, the conversation will sometimes shift towards how poorly their people are performing or how weak the team is. I generally listen for a while and finally ask a tough question: "Who hired these people?" Usually, I find it is the person saying how bad they are. Well, how can that be? When first hired the person was great, yet now he or she is horrible.

Remember the three key metrics for successful sales people: skills, activity and revenue. This is the same model by which sales managers need to be measured. If a sales manager tells you that one of his reps is weak, he needs to also relay the specific steps he is going to take in order to help the rep overcome that problem.

For sales managers, this is a sobering change. For a long time they have been able to deflect the light off of themselves by blaming the performance of others. Well, sales rep turnover is too big a cost to a company in terms of lost revenue opportunity, and we cannot let this issue continue unchallenged.

Another change we are going to have to make with many sales managers is to get rid of their 'us versus them' mentality. The old time attitude that 'nothing starts until there is a sale, and everybody else is overhead' will divide a company. We cannot afford to have adversarial relationships between sales and the rest of the corporation today, because sales needs to rely more than ever on other parts of the company in order to meet customer expectations and needs.

Sales management should be an advocate for their sales team. They need to know what their people need to be successful, and build relationships with the other functional parts of the enterprise to support that. It is a proactive course of action. A sales manager cannot just sit back and wait for things to come from marketing, engineering, or finance, and then criticize the work because it doesn't reflect what is going on in the field. Sales managers need to make sure the rest of the organization knows exactly what they need before it comes time to deliver.

CRM And Sales Process

I think the last part of the sales success equation is developing much more effective ways of evaluating our activities so we can find the trends, good or bad, and focus on what to optimize and what to replace. Many companies I talk to thought that Customer Relationship Management (CRM) systems were going to be the savior here, and I'm troubled by how few sales teams are really getting what they want out of CRM.

The Achilles heel for CRM is that if you have a flawed sales process, all CRM is going to do is help you do ineffective and inefficient things faster than you have ever done them before. You need to take the time to optimize your processes before you implement a CRM system. Some CRM vendors don't like to hear that because they think that is going to delay their sale by months, or more. But I think companies need to demand that their sales process providers and CRM vendors work more closely together for the customer's good.

Sales teams need much clearer visibility on how they are performing. The only real option is to integrate your sales process directly into your CRM applications so you can constantly collect metrics on who is doing what, what skills are they leveraging to do that activity, and what impact that activity has on success rates.

Finding Your Starting Point

Sales excellence is a significant undertaking, but it is what will decide who dominates in a marketplace. Sales excellence is not an elephant that needs to be eaten in one big bite. The key is in finding the right starting point, the area that will have the biggest impact on your current business, and dealing with that challenge first.

The Sales and Marketing Excellence Challenge

For some of our customers, it has meant working hard to better define their value proposition. For others, it could be upgrading the skill set of the sales team, or improving the performance of managers. There is no universal answer, but there is one universal goal. If we are going to lose, let's lose fast so we have more time to work with the right prospects.

BENSON P. SHAPIRO

I was introduced to Ben Shapiro by a friend who had attended an executive program at Harvard. Ben is a well-known authority on marketing strategy and sales management with particular interests in pricing, product line planning, and marketing organization. He is also the Malcolm P. McNair Professor of Marketing Emeritus at the Harvard Business School, where he taught a wide variety of MBA courses, including Industrial Marketing, Sales Management, Creative Marketing Strategy, and Integrated Product Line Management from 1970 to 1997. He continues to teach there in several executive programs, including the CEO Program, Young Presidents' Program, and Business Marketing Strategy. Professor Shapiro is the author, co-author, or editor of 14 books and 19 Harvard Business Review articles. Since 1997, Professor Shapiro has concentrated his professional time on consulting, speeches, boards of directors, and writing.

BT

> **As I look at the marketplace today (September 2002), there are two broad areas I'd like to address. The first is in response to the clamor in the business press about corporate abuses. Many feel the need for greater governance and ethics, which may directly relate to everybody on the frontline dealing with customers—especially major account management. The second is the lack of strategic thinking in pricing and its impact on sales.**

Do The Right Thing

There's been a lot of talk about empowerment and about getting people who are on the frontline to do what's right for the customer. This is particularly true when you're dealing with major accounts. An account manager who is responsible for a single account that represents significant business is treated as a high-level executive and is told, "Use your good judgment."

At the same time, the company has a strategy, a set of policies or guidelines, and lots of other people who are using their good judgment. The tension comes when, for example, a national account manager says, "Of course we can make that custom item. We'd be delighted to, particularly given that you're going to give us $5 million in sales on it." That account manager then goes back to the plant manager, who says, "Hell, no; I can't schedule that in for the next two months. The setup will take three days and I don't have the capacity."

This can create enormous tension between what is right for a single customer, large or small, and what complies with your set policies, procedures, and strategies.

I express this as a governance issue because, if you look at what caused the problem at Arthur Andersen, a lot of it involved conflict between responding to a revenue opportunity and doing what made longer-term sense. Arthur Andersen had a group of people in Houston who wanted Enron as a customer. Those people were responsible for generating certain amounts of revenue and Enron was an enormously successful account for them.

Meanwhile, the Andersen central accounting group was responsible for accounting procedures and correctly performing accounting protocols. The Houston group sent their work through this audit protocol group and it was turned down. What ensued was a big fight between doing what was fundamentally right in the long run, which was to say 'no' to Enron, or making short-term revenue and profits, which the Houston people wanted.

This issue in governance—the tension between centralization, strategies, procedures, and local empowerment—becomes most important when we're dealing with individual sales people.

A less controversial and more common example of this same dynamic would be a vice president of sales saying to his or her organization, "We are not going to lose one point of market share this year, but I don't want to see any Mickey Mouse deals."

This could be interpreted as, "No price cutting." For example, at the end of the quarter, companies that have very high fixed costs, such as high tech and software companies where incremental revenue turns into profits very quickly, will sell as much in the last two weeks as they sell in the other eleven weeks of the quarter. That means there's price-cutting. It may not be illegal, but it is often inappropriate and dumb. If you take that one step further, you encourage your sales force to literally bribe the buyers.

In addition to giving your people mixed messages, which is a governance issue, you also train your buyers to wait until the end of quarter. I traveled with a key account saleswoman for Xerox in 1990. What one of her customers did to her on June 29th, the last business day of the half-year, was brutal. The buyer said, "I'm buying three of those big copiers. I can either buy them today or I can buy them on Monday. How are you doing on your quota for the quarter?" He knew he had nothing to lose.

Xerox wasn't going to turn down the order if it was placed on Monday, but the customer could squeeze out as much as he wanted. It seems to me that this is a very big issue that never gets talked about.

When Everything Changes

I think it became clear during the summer of 2001 that the game had changed. If you were a vice president of sales in 1999 or 1998, you had the wind at your back. Everybody was worried about not losing orders, and about keeping their growth tracking with everyone else, particularly in the same industry. The relevant question was: are we investing fast enough so that somebody doesn't get in front of us?

The trouble was that, in some industries, people lost sight of what were the important metrics. For example, in telecommunications and Internet services you had some companies—WorldCom is a great example—that were reporting profits when they should have been reporting losses. So, not only did you have the generalized euphoria of the market but the specific euphoria of an industry, which naturally led to overcapacity.

If you look at high fixed cost industries, you'll see that this has been going on for an enormously long period of time. In the railroad industry there was something called the Panic of '73 (note: 1873). That's when the railroads had all over-invested. Between Albany and New York City, for example, three parallel railroad lines might have been built. Each line competed a little on service, but mostly on price because they already had invested their fixed cost. Essentially, whatever was run over those lines would give some incremental revenue.

The overcapacity problem with telecom and Internet services is analogous because they had built parallel systems and were battling for *any* revenue. The overburden was compounded by both the natural bias toward growth, and the fact that these emerging industries were high fixed cost industries with lots of 'network externalities,' or 'network effects.' That is, the more customers I have, the more variable is the product. This is true of eBay; the more people who are selling and buying on eBay, the more attractive eBay is to the new seller or buyer.

Faulty Signals

In addition to this problem, we now know the situation was exacerbated by greed and what clearly look to be illegal activities. In a normal and honest arena, other competitors would have been seeing a yellow or red light in terms of investing in more capacity. Instead, everyone was seeing a green light.

In a normal market, it's as though you have an intersection of five streets. Some of the lights are red, some are turning yellow, and one is green. With the misreporting and cooked numbers, the net effect was that all the lights were green. Everybody was investing and you got a collision as they all came together in the same space. The shenanigans played made it worse.

Now, let's return to the vice president of sales who says you have no choice but to make quota. As that person, I can't go to the board and tell them we're growing less than 30% a year when the whole industry is growing 30% a year. I have investors who are piling on saying, "GBF—get big fast." And, I've got to use up all the regular capacity plus all the additional overcapacity invested in due to the shenanigans. In this pressured situation, 'good judgment' can fly right out the window.

As a result of past events and current questioning, I think that we're going to be rumbling around in this lukewarm environment for a while. The trick will be to make very, very efficient and effective use of your sales and marketing resources to generate revenue and build a long-term position. Those are very tough things to do simultaneously, particularly if you're a public company under quarter-to-quarter pressure to realize profits—with the added scrutiny of today's environment.

All of this conflict has to be sorted out. I think that we're in for a couple of very challenging years and I don't think that, at least in the next decade or two, we'll see another period like the recent big bubble. It got bigger than normal, yet its correction is proving less painful than I expected, mostly because home building has held up so strongly along with other consumer durables, such as automobiles. But if there are problems in those areas, then I think we're going to see even more long-term problems.

A contributing factor is the very low interest rates. They are so low partially because inflation is so low and partially because productivity is so high based on all those investments made during the late 1990s. In some ways that means employment, particularly of professionals, may be quite limited for the next couple of years.

There's an interesting circularity that comes back to the issue of governance. People throughout the organization are asked to make very good decisions, but those decisions are very hard to make objectively if their very jobs are in jeopardy. This is why you've got to have a central set of strategic precepts and shared values that guide people. We've seen that these precepts will be challenged when you're dealing with very large chunks of revenue.

Big Deals, Big Dilemmas

That's another difference that we hadn't seen before. Through the 1990s and going back to the 1980s, we had an enormous amount of consolidation. A simple example, if you're old enough to remember it, is the independent neighborhood toy store. Today, three retailers—Wal-Mart, Kmart, and Toys R Us—do about 85% of the retail toy business in the U.S. If you built and sold locomotives years ago, you had lots of independent large customers, possibly up to 40 in number. Now there are two or three. We have seen this consolidation in industry after industry.

This has put enormous pressure on prices, and it means that the orders have become huge and come in big chunks. You either get Wal-Mart or you don't. And it's not going to impact a single territory (e.g., Boston, New Jersey, Cincinnati). Either you have Wal-Mart or you don't. I think this has added to productivity in some ways, but it's also put enormous pressure on companies to lower prices even as total deal size has gotten much larger.

What You Should Know

I am amazed that very few major account managers, especially those who are responsible for a million to well over a billion dollars in revenue, have been thought of in terms of their ability to negotiate. Very few companies have provided enough training in negotiation or looked hard enough at pricing.

There's no question that companies are paying more attention than before, but the complexity and the stakes have gone up faster than companies' ability to analyze them. It's interesting to me that over the last couple of years, there has been a big surge of interest around the issue of pricing. If I were running a good-sized sales force, I would spend a lot of time making sure that my key account and global account sales managers understood an enormous amount about negotiating and pricing, and that they were supported by the best kind of analytics.

Most companies aren't very skilled at pricing. They figure out what they think are their costs, add on some margin, or charge what they think the market will bear until the competition shows up. But there is damn little going on in actually understanding what value they contribute to an end user, their customer. They don't understand the customer's perception and quantification of value.

When you set a price, it's absolutely critical to understand the value that customers experience. One of the jobs of the sales person is to make sure that the perception is as high as the reality. The second thing that you've got to keep in mind is your own cost structure; yet very few companies understand their costs well.

Further, most companies don't know who their most profitable customers are. We've got so many different pieces of data, whether you look at it from an operations perspective, a marketing perspective, or an accounting perspective. People have to be able to figure out the profitability at the order level—at the customer level.

I was teaching a cost accounting case on account profitability to a group of senior executives at Harvard. Here are a hundred people in one of our big amphitheater classrooms. I was halfway up the aisle and turned around to walk back to the board. As I did, I was responding to someone's statement about strategic accounts. I asked, "What is a strategic account?" Someone from the back of the room yelled out, "It's an account where you lose money!"

I turned around and nobody would admit to saying it. It is interesting that sales people can inevitably find a good reason to sell to somebody. And what you often hear is, "Hey, this is a great piece of business." What you don't hear is, "It's commissionable. How could it be anything but great?"

In most organizations, the sales people get commissions whether an account is profitable or not. Many sales managers get so enamored with accounts of high testimonial value or size that they neglect the profitability issue.

Strange Bedfellows: Finance & Marketing?

Back to the governance issue, finance and marketing are coming much closer together. In today's world, the sales and marketing vice presidents better go to lunch with the CFO because the strength of your balance sheet may determine how aggressively you can operate in the market today.

As an example, General Motors just signed (Fall 2002) a deal with their Canadian unions that keeps General Motors pumping. Now, the UAW in Canada is taking a look at whether they should go after Chrysler or Ford, who are in much weaker positions. They have less cash and their market share is going down, whereas it looks like General Motors' market share may have stabilized or even gone up a tiny bit. What you see here is the circular relationship between marketing strength and financial strength.

Marketing strength enables you to price well and get paid more for something than it cost you to produce. If you're really strong, you understand the perceived value, cost, and long-term situation, so you are constantly upping your price, making money, and building financial strength. If the CFO has been doing this right, you're not giving the money away through stock buy-backs or other activities. There's a strong balance sheet to go along with the strong income statement.

I would argue that a strong income statement is, to a good extent, the responsibility of the sales and marketing vice presidents; the CFO is in charge of the strength of the balance sheet. Ten years ago, you didn't see that kind of intimacy between sales/marketing and finance. One of the things that we must improve is managing our large accounts, not only from a sales perspective and a competitive perspective, but also from a financial perspective.

We must get better at playing a chess game over many moves. It isn't simply, "I'll do this and see what they do." It's much more: "I'll do this, the customer will respond this way, and the primary competitor will respond that way. Then I'll do another thing and, in all likelihood, those two players will do these things. And then I'll do another thing." Very few companies think that way proactively or have a strategy down at the major transaction level.

They may have a vague strategy up in the clouds, but when you're dealing with big orders that have enormous financial and competitive impact, you need a definitive structure. You've got to figure out what you will do if you get the order, what you will do if you don't get it, what your competitor will do if you get it, whether or not you have to cut your price, and so on. Most people are still running in reactive mode. They are still walking into the next boxing glove hitting them in the face rather than questioning, "If I duck now and hit him, where can I then move to protect my face?"

For companies that may be feeling on the ropes, or may in fact be there, it can be especially difficult to take the long view. A lot of the American psyche still goes back to the gunslinger mentality. We could sit around and try to figure this out, but instead we elect to just go shoot something.

This condition isn't surprising given that most sales vice presidents are sales people who learned to be reactive. Plus, they entered into selling because they were action oriented. Now we're asking sales vice presidents to act—but to think before they act.

▶ Metrics

Yet the folks who do sit back and think are generally operating more off their experience or intuition than analytics. If times have changed as much as we're talking about, then a lot of what they may be intuiting could be completely wrong.

There's no question that if I built my intuition in a different world, then it won't work here. If I'm used to hiking in the northern temperate forests and I get stuck in Death Valley, I won't know how to operate. One of the questions I like to ask is how often people do post-audits. For example, you hire a sales person and he doesn't work out. Do you sit down and ask why this person didn't work out, and what can we learn from this so that we don't repeat the same mistake?

I don't know any company that regularly post-audits pricing decisions. There are some companies that post-audit investment decisions and there are a few that post-audit new product failures. But I don't know of a single company that post-audits pricing or sales force decisions that addresses the issue, "Here was our goal in this pricing decision, and here were our expectations. Did those things happen?" If you don't have a feedback loop to do post-audits and learn, then you are bound always to be reactive.

If you are running a sales force with 100 people today, you have 100 individual experiments going on at the sales person level. If your people average three calls a day, you've got 300 natural experiments going on daily.

I once sat on the board of a large wholesale company that had 220 branches in the United States. We figured out which branches were best at pricing, analyzed what they were doing, and shared these insights with the other branches. If you look at post-audits and figure out what is successful, then you have a chance of learning. Without that, you're going to fail. Their activities were still a series of experiments, but they proved to be immensely successful because they were done with rigorous discipline and analytics.

▶ Customer Relationship Management (CRM)

The most frequent place to hear anything about process and/or metrics in conjunction with sales or marketing is Customer Relationship Management (CRM). However, CRM is stalled out right now because a) companies don't have much appetite for more software, and b) a lot of them are hugely disappointed with their forays into this area.

Tom Siebel is saying CRM is dead, and what's needed is ERM, which is basically linking CRM to enterprise resource planning (ERP): back and front office all combined so that everybody has perfect knowledge. But that idea certainly hasn't proved out to date.

It's been my experience that the smaller, simpler information system projects have been more successful. Siebel has been incredibly successful, so I hate to disagree with him, but *if big isn't working, you don't go to humongous.* Anybody who has done an SAP implementation hated it.

In fact, I've heard several CEOs say to me, "I'll go through this once in my life. I'm going to retire before it comes up again." I would argue that, if I was Siebel and recognized that 'big' has been difficult, then I'd want to put in smaller, more focused projects. I would select, for example, a simpler sales reporting system than an integrated CRM-ERP system.

I think Siebel has a problem in thinking that either they or SAP are going to win, depending on which one brings this humongous system to market. I think that for the next N years, smaller projects are going to be the watchword, and being able to put them together will be very important. We need to get the little things done and then go to the next level of getting the big things done.

Siebel may not agree because that's not their strength. In some ways, it plays to the strength of their more limited competitors. But humongous systems such as SAP that take forever to install and force you to run your business around their system architecture are often misdirected. Most people can't implement them because their business was developed instead around the customer's needs, and the secondary need was to make a profit.

When you try to drive corporate architecture with software architecture and tell the customer to organize the way you want them to organize, most customers are going to say no. Customers will find a company that's easier to do business with.

In fact, the phrase 'user friendly' does not apply only to software; it applies to companies. I don't want to do business with you if you force me to do business your way. And if I have another option, I'll take it. With Microsoft on my PC, I don't think I have an option, so if Mr. Gates makes it hard for me to use Excel, I'm out of luck. With CRM, it's different. There are lots of options and people want something with a short payback, not an enormous return on investment in 15 years.

Parting Thoughts

For many people, the confluence of sales management and selling on the one hand, and pricing on the other, is where the action is. You should think about this balance between transactions and relationships every day and ask, "What am I doing to make myself more valuable for my customer? To make my people more capable and more motivated? And, at the same time, to make more money?" Notice the order: customer, employees, company.

If you think about it that way then you can gain one hell of a lot. Marketing leadership means understanding that you don't make money unless your customer does well. And, you can't do well unless your employees feel like they're doing well—only then can you make a lot of money.

TANYA CANDIA

Tanya Candia has over 20 years of experience in the high tech software marketplace. She is currently Senior Vice President of Marketing at Sigaba, a secure enterprise-messaging firm. Prior to Sigaba, she was Vice President of Worldwide Marketing at F-Secure Corporation, a Finnish technology company which she positioned for the most successful IPO in Scandinavian history. Candia has served in executive positions at Amdahl, DEMAX Software, and Unison Software. She began her career in academia, as Chairperson of the Department of Translation and Interpretation at the University of the Americas in Puebla, Mexico. She is the author of the recently published guidebook for high-tech marketing, Hit the Market Running.

JD

> *The critical mistake many firms make on a regular basis is that they don't see how the tactical decisions they make today are mortgaging the future. There is a set of rules we create for our business plans, yet there is often another set of rules we live by when we encounter rough times in the marketplace. When we let these rule sets become wildly different, we get into trouble.*

When I look back on most of my career, I see that I was often brought into companies that had been around a few years, had cycled through a couple VPs of Marketing, and weren't going anywhere. After being at these firms for just a short period of time, I would often discover the same problem regarding the way they were operating.

Strategy Versus Tactics

Somewhere along the way, these firms lost their strategic vision and fell into the trap of reacting tactically. You can turn these types of organizations around, but it can be very, very painful. And in reality, the problem should have been avoided in the first place.

That is probably why I really enjoy working with Bob Cook, the CEO here at Sigaba. What I admire the most about Bob is his persistent strategic thinking. That is a really hard thing to do when you are pressured by revenue expectations, because sometimes your gut-level reaction is to think very tactically.

Bob does not give in to pressure; he keeps stepping back and asking, "Where do we want to be a year, two years, or five years from now? What decisions can we make today to get us there?" That attitude is reflected throughout the company, and it actually gives sales and marketing enough of a perspective to say, "This is a bad deal; walk away from it."

I don't know about any of the other people you have interviewed, but I rarely have been in a company where anybody walked away from any deal, at any time, for any reason. Unfortunately, the pervasive attitude is, "If it moves, kill it. If they've got any money, take it."

We need to get rid of, or at least minimize, that attitude. The axiom for today has to be, "The sale is just the beginning." This is true not just from a sales standpoint, but also from a marketing standpoint, a support standpoint, and an engineering standpoint as well.

The sale is absolutely just the beginning, especially in the early days of a company or a new product life cycle. You're going to sell somebody something and then you have to step up to support, maintain, and enhance that offering—and, all too often, deal with all the freebies that you gave the customer in order to close the deal.

It is critical for management to keep a mindset for where they want to be at the end of the year, or end of two years. This viewpoint means looking at deals not just in terms of, "Are we going to make our numbers this quarter?" Instead, we need to decide whether or not it is a good business investment.

That being said, I know sometimes we've got to be pragmatic. Very few companies have the luxury of being able to just sit back and say, "We're going to be purists. This is the plan and we're going to stick to it no matter what." If you are a for-profit company, you have a huge spotlight shining on you to perform. With that being the case, sometimes we may end up doing deals that aren't perfect, but the key is to keep those to a minimum.

Creating A Strategic Culture

Much of what ensures that those cases are the exception versus the rule is the type of corporate culture you establish and manage your company by. I think sales and marketing management have a big responsibility in setting the guidelines for what kind of firm you become.

▶ Know Your Value Proposition

The first thing you need to focus on is clearly defining your true value proposition: what problems your product solves, what features you currently have (and don't have). You need to get everyone in the company on the same page as to what your perfect prospect looks like, and how those needs map into your solution. Then you really need to encourage the sales force to do a very disciplined, comprehensive job of qualifying, to identify prospects that fit that model.

I hate to admit it, but at one recent company we talked the talk, but we didn't walk the walk. Everyone in the company—sales, marketing, engineering, senior management, etc.—knew exactly what the product did, but all too often we would develop selective amnesia.

A prospect would ask, "Well, can it do this?" And even though the real answer was no, we would say, "Yeah, it can do that, sure. We can enable the product to do whatever you want." Those conversations didn't happen once or twice; they happened way too many times, and they killed us.

I have learned well from sins of the past. Today at Sigaba, we are very clear with customers. We tell them upfront that we are the best security software company in the business, bar none. We have the best, and just about the only, secure document delivery product in the business.

We know the ROI we can deliver with all of our products, based on their existing features. When we sell, we know who in the prospective organization is feeling the pain, and we know how to go in and present how our product can alleviate that pain. It is a solid, well thought out business message.

When we are asked a question about a capability or function that is outside the scope of the product as it exists today—such as, "Oh, by the way, do you have a way for me to FTP large files securely?"—we give the customer the honest answer, which is, "No." Although we know our engineers could deliver that functionality, we stick to the fact that we already have well-defined products that solve current pains, and they are available today. We are always wiling to add suggestions to the list of potential future enhancements, but we focus on selling what we have, versus selling futures.

How do you create a culture in sales that supports this fundamental concept? First, you need to build a unified front among executive, sales, and marketing management. Then together, you need to clearly explain to the sales force, "Here are products on our price list. If you sell these products, you will receive a commission. Now, if you sell something that is not on the price list, not only are you NOT going to get a commission, but we will not deliver what you did sell, and you will have to explain that to your customer."

Living the culture has to start at the top and flow down throughout the rest of the company. You need to live this every day, and I know it is a hard thing to do, believe me. But if you leave a crack open in your compensation plans, the sales force will drive a semi-truck right through it in an instant.

We all have days when we have our doubts. We are afraid that maybe one of our products isn't good enough, or maybe there really isn't a market for what we do. But everything we build is based on solid market research. Early on in a company or a product life cycle, that is a critical element. The key, then, is believing in your value propositions and sticking to them, versus caving in at the sound of the first marketplace objection.

Taking the Message to Market

Marketing has to be right in the thick of it if you are going to create and maintain this type of culture. Marketing has to drive the initial research to make sure that what you've got is really what people want to buy; that a product is going to solve a real and definable problem.

Then, to prove you are right in your assumptions, marketing has to work hand-in-hand with sales to do the initial selling. You need to go out on sales calls with sales people and to do some evangelizing with them. If you are going to turn the sales force into big believers, you are going to have to prove your theories about the product and the customer's needs.

Marketing has to constantly remember that the sales reps are out there on the front lines every day being told, "No, no, no," by prospects. In that type of environment, it's easy for them to lose faith in your company and your products. Part of marketing's job has to be to make sure that they keep the faith.

With that in mind, we have to do a better job of shelling the beach and getting our message out to the world at large. We need to saturate the world, the analysts, the press, and the prospects with direct marketing campaigns, phone calls, press releases, and the like, that will continue to educate the marketplace, so sales people don't have to keep hearing, "Who is Sigaba?"

One of the key reasons we don't always do this job effectively is that too often we see marketing as a series of tactical activities; we don't see it as a strategic business process. I remember an instance at a company I had just joined, when our tradeshow organizers wanted to raffle off a HumVee at the next major tradeshow we'd be attending. When I asked why, their response was, "Well, wouldn't it be cool and generate a lot of attention?"

Well, I don't want to be cool, and I don't want to generate attention. I want to generate qualified leads at a tradeshow. Whenever we do any activities or campaigns, we need to look at what we are doing in terms of how those things support an overall marketing strategy. What are we trying to achieve? Let's look at goals first, and then let's look at ways to accomplish them. Let's not 'ready, fire, aim.'

We have to turn marketing into more of a science, and less of an art. I think that starts with setting measurable goals; we need to state what we are going to be held accountable for delivering. Once the goals are in place, you can look at each marketing activity under consideration and evaluate how it is going to help achieve those goals. When put to that type of test, you discard the HumVee raffle ideas and replace them with solid marketing plans.

Once you put your plans together and implement them, you measure the results. That's a fun challenge, isn't it? Some companies really struggle with measuring the impact that marketing has on their business.

▶ Measuring Marketing Performance

To support this endeavor, I have actually built a leads calculator. The logic behind the model is to start at the end of the sales funnel and determine what the revenue expectations are for the company, division, or a given product. You also make assumptions about the deal size, close rates, etc.

Next, you make some assumptions about the sales process itself: the specific steps for closing a deal, how long those steps take, and your expected fallout rates at each stage in the cycle. As you backtrack through the funnel, you end up at the top, and now you have a target to shoot for in terms of the number of leads that need to be created to fill that funnel in the first place. Also, based on your understanding of how long the sell cycle will take, you can also determine the rate at which those leads need to come into the funnel to keep the sales process flowing smoothly.

Now that we know what we are shooting for, we have to figure out how to get that number of leads. At this point, it's a numbers process. We can make assumptions based on past performance of what the lead return will be for any given marketing program, and we make sure that we are maximizing the value of each dollar we invest in those programs.

Navigating this process is how you get to a point where you have something to measure. I heard a comment recently that I found very revealing. A marketing executive observed that half of their marketing activities weren't working; he just didn't know which half.

Well, if you track how many leads each program generated, how many of those turned into prospects, how many prospects actually bought something, then the half of what you are doing that isn't working becomes very clear. At that point, you double-up on your winners and get rid of your losers.

▶ The Master Schedule Process

Another thing that marketing can do to help the company avoid the tactical management trap we have been discussing is to coordinate regular checkpoint meetings to ensure that all of the various parts of the organization are working together and communicating exactly where things stand, so that there are no surprises.

Years ago, I started holding master schedule meetings, and I've carried that concept to every single company I have worked with. The master schedule meeting tends to be a focal point for the executive team because during these sessions a lot of tough decisions are made. On a weekly or biweekly basis, we reiterate and re-examine our mission, our focus, our plans and schedules.

The master schedule concept is a key process because basically it takes the company mission and financial expectations, generally looking at least 18 months out, and then marries those to the current product development schedule.

The core attendees for these meetings are the heads of sales, services, customer support, marketing, development, the CFO, and usually the president or general manager if he or she is a hands-on person. Based on the fact that you can be dealing with company-making or -breaking trade-offs, you really have to have executive attendance. There are also a number of selected individuals who move in and out as needed.

The master schedule meeting becomes the regular forum for tracking whether or not we are on target. Are the products going to be released according to schedule? Are the marketing plans on track? Are the training programs happening as planned? Are there additional strategic opportunities that have surfaced since we last met that call for a goals re-evaluation? During these meetings, a lot of rough and tumble politics take place, but they happen in the open, with input from every key stakeholder.

Every part of the organization has to communicate with every other part. Anytime anyone wants to change a commitment, or introduce something that is not on the master schedule, they have to write a mini-business case and explain why, what the impact to the business will be, and how this will be managed. You also have to explain where the resources and dollars are going to come from. Are you going to add additional investments to make this happen, or are you going to swap out something that is already on the plan and put this in its place?

The benefit of managing a company's vision this way is that it effectively bulldozes all the little towers of isolation that can be erected between different functional areas of a company. It eliminates sales working their agenda, marketing working their agenda, engineers doing their own thing, etc.

The master schedule gives everybody a chance to see how a decision we make today could impact us a year and a half down the line. And that's critical to what I was saying earlier, when we were talking about ensuring that you make the right decisions for the right reasons. This process forces you to look beyond an opportunity that may look lucrative today, and discuss the hidden costs you might incur in the future by making that choice.

To the extent that you possibly can, the master schedule process allows you to continuously manage your company strategically. And, if you are going to change your strategy based on marketplace pressures, at least you'll know the things you need to work on to minimize the downside of those decisions.

Promote Your Success

On a more day-to-day level, what advice would I have for my marketing peers? Well, based on what I am seeing in the business environment today, the most cost-effective thing you can do in marketing is public relations. I think this is clearly the case for all companies, but especially true for smaller firms.

When you are a new entrant into a marketplace, you need to make your company look big, solid, and reliable as a business partner. The way you do that is by standing on the shoulders of big customers.

One of the first things I tend to focus marketing groups on is case studies. Here at Sigaba, we recently published our first case study based on the work we did for a 137-bed hospital on the Texas-Mexico border. With that case study in hand, we were able to get an article in *Network World* and two articles in healthcare magazines, one of which was a cover story.

Sales people at every company where I have worked are always clamoring for more case studies. They know the value that these reference pieces provide, the impact on a prospective sale, when they can say, "Here is what your peer at ABC company is achieving; wouldn't you like the same results?" It's not threatening and it contributes significantly to your credibility.

Case studies are time consuming, and you often have to jump through lots of hoops to get them approved, but they are invaluable. They really become the basis for so many other marketing functions. When you go to the press, for example, and say, "I've got a hot product I want to talk about," the first thing they say is, "Who is using it? Who can we talk to?" We know that is how the game is played, and based on that we plainly and simply have to do a better job of promoting our successes.

Communications Is Key

Another thing I feel strongly about is that sales and marketing ought to be joined at the hip. As I mentioned before, the very best thing marketing can do is to go out with the sales reps on sales calls. I think that is the only way marketing can truly know what the customer is really thinking and saying and feeling.

At the same time, I think sales needs to develop a better understanding of, and appreciation for, marketing. I think the only way to achieve that is through really close, frequent communication.

The field sales force, sales management, and marketing have to have an awful lot of face time. You need to set up a weekly sales conference call, monthly inside sales training, or web-based sales training to ensure everybody is up to speed on what you are doing, publish a biweekly marketing newsletter, etc. Don't expect people to pick up the phone and talk to you or come by and see you. You need to take the responsibility yourself to encourage communication, especially with sales and development.

If anything, make sure that you are over-communicating, that you are sharing how things really are, good or bad, and always try to maintain the strategic vision that got you into the market in the first place.

BERNIE GOLDBERG

After graduating from C. W. Post College, and then spending four years in the army, Bernie joined IBM Corporation, where he went on to become one of their top sales people and sales managers. In his last position with IBM in 1979, Bernie managed a pioneering facility in direct marketing and telemarketing, learning all the intricacies necessary to make these operations successful. After IBM, Bernie's entrepreneurial spirit fostered two different telemarketing companies. Today, he is a frequent speaker at direct marketing and telemarketing events and has written numerous articles on both subjects. He has served as Vice Chairman and Programming Chairman of the Business-to-Business Council of the Direct Marketing Association. Bernie is also the author of How to Manage and Execute Telephone Selling and The Lead Generation Handbook, *and publishes bi-monthly* The Business Marketing Note Pad. *His web site is www.dmpublishers.com, which contains a wealth of resources for innovative sales and marketing methods.*

JD

> **Every sales executive today knows that the economics of sales are dictating the necessity to leverage telephone selling in order to supplement and complement face-to-face selling. Yet as companies try to combine these two approaches, we are still seeing plenty of program mis-starts, and a number of outright failures. When initiatives do not succeed, the underlying cause is almost always the result of at least one of three critical elements not being adequately addressed.**

We are all aware of the problem. The cost of a face-to-face sales call today exceeds $400 and continues to escalate. That poses a problem for serving smaller accounts, as many of them cannot generate the sales volume necessary to support that type of expense. How do you then service these accounts? Many companies abandon the smaller customer because they're too expensive to support.

Direct marketing, especially telephone selling, is the ideal vehicle to manage smaller accounts, and it is clearly getting a lot of attention today. But that attention is rarely turning into successful action. Why?

I have had the opportunity to interface with hundreds of people who have tried to integrate direct sales and telesales. Speaking from decades of experience, for this to be done successfully, three critical elements must be addressed: 1) organizing correctly, 2) compensating people appropriately, and, 3) providing a common database and Customer Relationship Management (CRM) environment that the phone and field sales people can use to share information.

Typical Mistakes

Let's consider why we look to telesales to begin with. What I have witnessed is that many businesses are product-based. The company comes out with a new idea and turns it over to the field sales group to take to market. These sales people are smart and focus their selling efforts on their largest accounts, which offer the biggest potential. Because of this, the smaller accounts go largely under serviced.

Over time, the company adequately penetrates the larger accounts and then realizes that in order to continue to grow they need to go after that next tier of customers. Based on this need, they decide to start an inside sales organization.

Here is often where they make their first mistake. Initially, with whom do they staff this inside sales group? Typically, it is their under-performing field sales people. These individuals earn $90,000 to $120,000 a year, versus their best sales people who earn $150,000 to $200,000. We will come back to these economics in a minute.

The second mistake occurs when these sales people come inside. They immediately start to manage their territories like they did when they were selling outside. They have no concept of how to organize their time, how to develop calling plans, what to do if they can't reach the person on the phone, etc. Consequently, they spend 40% to 50% of their time trying to figure out whom to call, another 10% to 15% getting ready to make the call, and precious little time actually on the phone.

They get minimal help from their management, who typically have a direct sales background. Selecting a direct sales person to manage telesales groups is the third mistake companies commonly make. A direct sales manager is someone who has gained all of his or her management experience based on the end-of-month focus of direct sales teams. These managers do not understand the value or concept of giving telesales people firm directions on whom to call, how may calls to make, how to generate results, what daily production goals to achieve, and so forth.

So far we are not off to a very illustrious start, and it gets worse.

The fourth mistake occurs when creating territories for the telesales groups to service. Many times, a company will take all the small- to mid-sized accounts away from the direct sales force. The field sales people, who now see their territory being cut, resist this enormously.

Then the fifth mistake is made in focusing the telesales group on prospecting new accounts. This is the hardest part of sales. Telesales people have no previous relationship with these accounts, and now they are going to try to start developing one over the phone.

So the telesales people start calling into these accounts, and most of the time they meet rejection; however, occasionally they do close something. Here the sixth mistake surfaces because management often neglects to define upfront how people are compensated.

As soon as the first order is generated by telesales, the field sales rep screams, "I got that order!" Now sales management is faced with the challenge of arbitrating sales between these two organizations.

All of this started with a misunderstanding of how telesales should be staffed, how it should be organized to complement direct sales efforts, and how people should be compensated. Programs burdened with the challenges just outlined never work.

Structuring For Success

▶ Organization

Whenever I have helped companies build inside phone operations, the first thing we do is recruit someone to run the group. We need to start with an experienced inside sales manager, someone who has proven that he or she can build this type of organization. This requirement is non-negotiable. If we get job applications from field sales managers, we ignore them; we will not put a field sales manager in that role.

We then want to hire the right type of people to work the phones, and this is a different profile from a direct sales person. Generalizations are always dangerous, but we do tend to see certain traits in direct sales people. They have large, but very frail egos, are very money oriented, hate paperwork, are very protective of information and their territories, won't do anything that doesn't provide a personal gain, and are over achievers. These people do not want to spend eight hours a day in a very structured environment making phone calls.

Based on my experience, the profile for telesales people is very different. Great telesales people want a good, secure income, have a strong personality driven by teamwork, are willing to follow guidelines, are protective of customers, see themselves as part of a team, and are steady achievers. I find that customer service-oriented people tend to make the best telephone selling representatives.

Once we get the right manager and the right people to staff the group, we want them to focus on contacting the right prospects. To make telesales work, you need two things: a relationship and an offer. A prior relationship is key, so the best accounts to target first are your existing customers, big and small. And this should be done alongside the field sales people, not in place of them.

Instead of calling up and saying, "I am Bernie Goldberg and I am your new sales person," I want to say, "I am Bernie Goldberg, and I work with Jim, your field sales person. I am not replacing Jim; he is always available to you. However, from time to time I am going to contact you about your current needs, the service you are receiving, and any questions you might have. I will also keep you up to date on new products or services we might offer."

Now we have a cooperative environment for maximizing the value of that account. The telesales person can handle the smaller orders, and if a bigger opportunity is uncovered, the telesales person can involve the field sales person. The key here is to design the compensation program so that these two people are motivated to work together.

▶ Compensation

I always design and develop compensation plans for telesales people around the quota performance of the direct sales person being supported. For example, a telesales person might support five direct sales reps, so I want to measure his or her performance based on the success of their direct counterparts in the field. If we do that, then everyone is working together.

Here's how this works: Let's assume a field sales person has a $1,200,000 quota, and I, the telesales person, am supporting five of these people. In this example, when the field sales person makes a sale, he gets paid a commission of 5%. That means he earns $60,000 in commissions if he attains his quota goal for the year.

When we implement a telesales operation, we initially want to keep things simple. We therefore assign telesales people the same territory and accounts as the five field sales people they are supporting. Based on this scenario, the telesales person's annual quota is now the total of the other quotas, or $6,000,000.

In this case, I would hire a telesales person for $30,000 in salary. In addition, I would be willing to pay that person $1,000 a month as an incentive. The telesales person now has a monthly personal target of 1/12 of the annual number, or $500,000 a month.

To determine the commission rate for this telesales person, I would take the percentage of total quota attained for that month by the five field sales reps, and multiply by $1,000. That is how much commission or incentive the telesales rep has earned for that month. In addition, you might offer quarterly or annual bonuses, or additional incentives for implementing specific programs.

A lot of people are surprised when I suggest these types of numbers, especially if they have already started to staff the telesales center with former field sales reps. Remember when I said it is a mistake to staff the phone center with field sales people? One of the biggest reasons this is a mistake is because of the economics.

If I bring a field sales person inside, he comes in with a huge salary expectation. Even as a mediocre performer, he may currently be earning around $100,000 a year and wants to make at least that much on the phone. If you do that, you are significantly overpaying these people, and in many cases are ruining the financial model that makes telesales attractive to begin with. In today's marketplace, you can get great telesales talent much, much cheaper than that.

When you adopt the approach I have been advocating, you create an environment of cooperation, trust, and teamwork, and you do it within an economic framework that is very profitable. You set yourself up to achieve net new incremental growth. As the combination of the field and telesales rep model produces results, you can then adjust the field sales quotas in the second year to reflect that growth, because now you see where those extra revenues are going to come from.

▶ Customer Relationship Management (CRM) Environment

Now that we have created a teaming concept, we have also set the stage for a working environment that will contribute to the success of a CRM initiative. When you take an in-depth look into why CRM projects fail, you quickly discover that sales people rebel against these systems. They view using these systems as additional work, with no personal payback. What benefit do they get for spending time keeping account records up-to-date, just so their manager can see what they have been doing?

Telesales people tend to embrace CRM because, in a very structured environment, it can increase their efficiency and effectiveness in managing their time. It is a great way for them to set up regular schedules for whom to call and when, and then have access to all their past notes when making the next call.

As telesales continues to use CRM applications and update account records, field sales people begin to view the system as an advantage. Even on the road, they can easily track what their telesales person is doing. They can also use these systems to assign tasks to each other and see the status of those items.

CRM becomes a critical component for determining the success of a project. There are a number of critical success factors that come into play here. You need a system that supports both direct and telesales peoples' needs. You also need to start with a clean database and refresh it on a regular basis. You need to provide training and ongoing support. All of these investments will have significant paybacks in terms of the productivity of your people.

Putting Phone Sales Into Action

Now that we have a framework for success, let's review some of the basics of putting it into action. First, when you set up this type of environment, you should never use the term 'tele' -anything. This prefix gets everybody's blood boiling, and spawns a number of negative connotations.

I have been using the term up to now because 'tele' is how most people think of this concept. In reality, I always give the function a different name. Here is one of my favorite analogies: Just as we might call a field sales person an 'account executive,' we can also call the person on the phone an 'account manager.' This new organization is then called the Account Management department.

Second, you should plan for a significant amount of turnover, especially in the beginning. Inevitably, if I want to have four account managers, I will hire five or six, because during the first 90 days I am going to lose one or two of those people. Mis-hires are a fact of life that you should be aware of.

Next, you want to make sure that the Account Management organization is adding incremental value. How do you do that? I advocate identifying a control group of accounts and seeing how your phone center-covered accounts compare before you roll out a program en masse.

I have done this a number of times. Let's say you have 50,000 customers. I have found that while the average direct sales person can make about 400 face-to-face calls a year, the average rep on the phone can make 4,000 calls. [Refer to charts below for following analysis.]

Field Sales Productivity:

Available Sales Calls 400

Required Orders 24

Sales Calls to Close Each Order 3

Closing Ratio.. 25%

Required Sales Calls for Orders 288

Remaining Sales Calls for Customer and Prospecting 112

Sales Calls per Year per Customer....................................... 4

Number of Customers that can be Supported 28

If a field sales person is expected to close two orders per month and it takes three sales calls per order with a closing ratio of 25%, the field sales person will make 288 sales calls to generate new orders. The remainder of the sales calls will be utilized to service existing customers and prospect for new business opportunities. Assuming the sales person makes one sales call per quarter on his or her existing customers, he or she can only support less than 30 customers. This demonstrates why so many customers are never serviced properly.

On the other hand, an inside telephone sales person supporting four field sales people can handle a significant number of customers. The example below demonstrates a phone sales person making two phone calls to every prospect and only 15% converting to customers.

Telephone Sales Productivity:

Telephone Sales Calls per Year 4,000

Number of Sales people Supported 4

Number of New Orders Required 96

Phone Calls per Order 2

Closing Ratio 15%

Required Sales Calls for Orders 1,280

Remaining Sales Calls for Customer and
Prospecting 2,720

Sales Calls per Year per Customer 6

Number of Customers that can be Supported 453

In this scenario, the phone sales person can handle over 450 customers. In addition, the phone coverage will eliminate some of the field sales calls made by the field sales people partnered with the phone sales person. Productivity improves dramatically.

When you initially start a phone center, you need to create enough of a critical mass for it to work properly. I think the minimum size you want to start with is four people, plus a manager who does not make calls. This group then needs to report to the same sales management organization as the rest of the field sales team. Do not put it over in customer support. Remember, we are creating a sales 'team' here.

Assuming we give each account manager 600 accounts, we would choose a total of 2,400 accounts for the phone group to work, and then we would choose another 2,400 accounts at random to serve as the control group. Now you are in a position to measure the revenue contribution of both groups. If you do this, in a very short amount of time you will have quantitative feedback on the value a phone center can represent for your company.

You should be able to see results within one quarter, but you should plan on giving a new phone center a year to reach its full potential. And during that first year, make sure there are no changes to the field's compensation program or their territories. Leave those items as they are.

Going Forward

After the first year, what you should do going forward will become self-evident. Now that people see how the program works, you can change compensation plans. For example, you could go back to the field sales force and implement a sliding compensation model. You might pay them 1% on any customer who orders under $10,000 per year, 3% on customers in the $10,000 to $25,000 range, 5% on customers valued between $25,001 and $50,000 and 6% on orders over that.

You must make it clear to the field rep that it doesn't matter who sells the deal. They can do it, customer support could take the order, or their phone counterpart can, but the commission rates don't change. What the field people will do, if they are smart, is pass the smaller opportunities over to the account managers, which is what you wanted them to do in the first place.

You can also offer the phone people a bonus for passing the bigger opportunities over to their direct counterparts. It is now clear to each of these individuals exactly what you want them to do. Now you have an environment of cooperation, trust and partnership, all operating within an economic framework that makes sense.

I saw some numbers recently stating that the size of the average field sales person's deal is $75,000, while the average phone order is around $18,000. In today's world, it is not a question of either/or; we need both of these types of orders. Because of this reality, we have no alternative except to make a direct selling and phone selling model work.

Success boils down to three things: find the right people for the right job; establish the programs to motivate those people to do the right things; and then give them the tools and the databases necessary to do the tasks the right way. If you cover those basics, a lot of problems we have encountered in trying to integrate field and phone sales will disappear.

RALPH YOUNG

Ralph Young is Vice President of the Enterprise Sales Strategy Group (ESSG) at Microsoft Corporation. The group is responsible for worldwide enterprise sales strategy, including the development of the enterprise sales force and the models, processes, tools and training it utilizes. Ralph joined Microsoft in 1998 as the General Manager for TransPoint Sales & Marketing. TransPoint was a joint venture between Microsoft, First Data Corporation and Citibank that was responsible for developing the Internet Bill Delivery and Payment business. CheckFree Corporation acquired TransPoint in September 2000. Before this he was the Executive Vice President Sales, Marketing, & Business Planning for AccessLine Technologies, a telecommunications enhanced services start-up company. Prior to AccessLine, Ralph spent eleven years with Tandem Computers (now HP/Compaq) where he last held the position of Vice President, North American Telecommunications.

BT

Microsoft is well known as an innovative technology company that provides great productivity tools to the desktop. To compete at the enterprise level we, along with our business partners, need to understand the Customer Conversation and demonstrate keen understanding of their business issues and provide great solutions.

Recently I gave a presentation to 3000 Microsoft partners in Anaheim, California, to make sure that Microsoft and its partners are well coordinated, and that together, we are developing the kinds of solutions that our customers want. At Microsoft, we want to make sure that we're doing everything we can to align our partners with us; in return, we need to be a *predictable* partner for them, so that they can build successful businesses.

As most people know, Microsoft has grown up on the desktop with great productivity tools and technologies for desktop operating systems. My responsibility is developing the right enterprise-class sales strategy and sales model for the Enterprise Sales Strategy Group (ESSG)—a different business model than the desktop model that Microsoft has been most known for in its past.

So, the lens I look through on a daily basis is different than what might be considered traditional Microsoft. My perspective is of big companies looking for solutions and partnerships that provide the technology foundation for their businesses; my comments here will reflect that.

Focus On the Customer Conversation

When I say desktop, I mean an individual in an organization as opposed to an individual consumer. Obviously all those individuals in corporations are part of the enterprise segment, but their experience with Microsoft and their knowledge of Microsoft value is really reflected in how they interact with Microsoft products on more of a personal basis. Yes, as a consumer, but more as an information worker.

Our group is challenged with going up to the next level and taking a look at how Microsoft products and solutions add value to the enterprise as a whole. We're looking beyond empowering individuals using technology to increase productivity and efficiency, to establishing Microsoft as the enterprise-class standard for deploying mission critical applications. So our focus is on the server world more than strictly the desktop world.

We are now experiencing the need to increasingly re-focus our lens on customers and their business requirements, and on solving their specific needs. More than ever, we need to ask the age-old question, "What keeps the CEO awake at night?" And what can Microsoft do to help with that?

What this means, in my view, is transitioning from more of a transaction model to a customer intimacy model—having the *customer's conversation*.

In years past, it's been about having Microsoft's conversation: here's the next product; here are its features and capabilities; here's how it compares to the last version; and here are all the additional, cool things that this version does.

Our conversation is relevant only if we're addressing that customer's needs and pain, and understand how a particular set of innovations helps to solve their concerns or address their objectives. It is a different business model, a different conversation than we typically had in the past, and it permeates everything. The entire culture of the company changes: compensation systems, scorecards, reviews, training, and marketing all need to reflect the shift.

So now, as we engage with the customer, it's not just, "Microsoft, yep, they're the ones that can help me with desktop productivity tools: e-mail, PowerPoint presentations, and spreadsheets." It's a very different conversation. Some of those tools may be used in the solutions that help address the customer's particular need, but additionally we want the customer to view Microsoft as a meaningful business partner.

The Importance of Partnership

My goal in the next two years is to have each CEO across the enterprise segment worldwide, when faced with a purchase requisition from their staff for a technology-based solution, respond by saying, "Have you spoken with Microsoft about this?"

For our customers to experience us as a valuable business partner, who along with our partners provides great solutions to their business challenges, is a big shift. It says that we're in a very different position in regards to the IT community in the enterprise segment than we have been traditionally.

The two key investments that enable us to achieve success are in leveraging and improving our partner-centric model and in developing a sales force that is properly aligned with our customers' needs.

First, when we review the marketplace, we see that there are already partners—some on Microsoft platforms, some that we'd like to see on Microsoft platforms—who are already having the customer's conversation. On this field of play which ISVs deeply understand the retail business? Who are the systems integrators with the ability to really impact an enterprise's competitiveness in Eastern Europe?

Many of these partners are further down the path than we are. They will actually aid and accelerate our transition from an innovative technology-based company to an enterprise solutions company. The value-add our partners provide is key to Microsoft's strategy, because it enables us to analyze the market with a specific solutions orientation. You can take the IDC work and the Gartner work and all the industry technology assessment and map it specifically into industry sectors that are looking at how to drive or how to solve the requirements in a particular vertical industry.

A lot of our energy goes into our joint sales approach so that our solutions look seamless to the customer. This means joint account planning and making sure that our partners are enabled with the latest technology and are supported in a way that allows them to provide great solutions to customers.

Second, this past year we recognized that in order to build very deep customer relationships we have to resource that way, and charter the account management role that way. The goals we set must be consistent with building solid relationships with customers, with this customer focus.

The customer's account plan is based on a matrix of customer segment, geography, vertical industry and specific offerings. Therefore, in addition to building specific, relevant solutions, we need to build an appropriate set of roles within the company that support those offerings as well as the customer relationship properly. This sets up a delicate balance: on the one hand you have a deep customer relationship built over time; on the other, you need to provide specialized solution selling expertise based on that customer segment's requirements.

To this end, we have both a selling function that pushes solutions into the market and we have an account management function that pulls those solutions into specific customer cases. For example, they either have very deep horizontal expertise with regard to solutions (e.g., CRM, ERP or solutions that span multiple industries) or deep knowledge and experience in a vertical industry. You'll be seeing a lot more Microsoft field people with the capability of having business conversations with those potential customers about their challenges because they came from the industry.

I'd say our partners have warmly received this strategy, and are cautiously optimistic about how it will play out over the next couple of years. The challenge for us is to be a consistent, predictable partner for them on a market-by-market basis. As a partner in either a geography or a vertical industry, I need to know what to expect from Microsoft, and how to partner with Microsoft in a way that is advantageous to me as well as to our mutual customer.

Partner Strategy: Enabling and Engaging

Partners want to leverage Microsoft's brand and ability to engage with customers, as long as we do that in a collaborative fashion. The focus of the tools and process that we've developed has to do with sales engagement—making sure that it works in the trenches. When Microsoft takes a partner's solution to market, each player's role is clear. We've put a lot of energy into making sure that this joint engagement is beneficial to all parties involved—that it allows Microsoft to compete as a solutions provider while focusing on core competencies, and enables the partner to provide a successful, differentiated solution to the customer.

We need to avoid the 'beauty pageant' approach where we identify a number of partners that could potentially provide solutions and say, "Here's our partner list and here are the pages you need to turn to in your category.

Select from any one of fifteen." Theoretically, this approach could benefit Microsoft, since the solutions would be Microsoft-based. But what it doesn't do is recognize Microsoft as a key stakeholder in that customer's success. Rather, it lengthens the sales cycle and abdicates our responsibility for helping the customer successfully deploy Microsoft technologies and the solutions that ride on top of them. This scenario doesn't give the customer any confidence that Microsoft is *engaged* as a stakeholder and truly understands how they intend to use our products and technology.

You'll see more and more that we're engaged in the partner selection process. We want to be in position to truly understand which partner makes the most sense in each case whether it's a local partner, a global systems integrator, or an ISV who has a great track record in doing what we're trying to accomplish. This is not intended to be exclusive at all. It's based upon recognizing and truly understanding the customer's needs and requirements and providing value, more like a consultant.

Arguably we do the one-to-many relationship very efficiently and productively today. The role of the Microsoft partner in terms of totally owning an opportunity, totally driving that into a particular customer segment or marketplace will absolutely continue.

There are two big pieces to our partner strategy: *enabling and engaging*. Partner enablement is how we make sure every partner across the world is enabled to sell solutions on Microsoft platforms. The second piece of the strategy is engagement. Some corporate enterprises require that Microsoft be present as a stakeholder and need to have a close relationship. We need to be able to engage in a way that meets that need and also recognizes that the business value, from an applications standpoint, will still come from a partner.

In many cases, the partner is capable of going to market on their own. They have the right bandwidth and field coverage. What they need from Microsoft is to be enabled with all the best technologies, innovations and products that underpin their solution. We don't need to personally have every conversation. It's the combination of the two that we have a great model for engaging in the field with partners on a customer's behalf, or we greatly enable partners to be successful with customers in the marketplace on their own.

A Solutions Education

We've added a significant number of resources for educating the channel. Whatever the medium, our partners have the opportunity to understand what we're doing, where we're going, and how to take advantage of the new technology and products. We've implemented everything from one-to-many programs over the Web, to local and industry-specific seminars.

We've started a vertical industry approach in the way we manage relationships with particular ISVs. We've aligned our sales and partner organizations along industries, so that as you look specifically at retail, or healthcare, or financial services, we have very deep training efforts geared toward the different needs of each. All of this is aimed at the enablement and the readiness of partners in the field.

I think a lot of what we've done is to focus on our internal functioning so that we're in a stronger position to be able to solve customer needs. The first tenet of our enterprise sales strategy is the partnership focus. The focus on solutions, not products, is really the second tenet. Obviously there's a direct link to the partner aspect of that, but this focus on solutions also requires the understanding of each person in the company.

Now remember, we're coming from a very product-centric culture here at Microsoft. So in the past year we sent every one of our field people to a mandatory integrated solutions selling training. We made this investment when the economy challenged most training budgets, and when many companies viewed training as a discretionary expense that they didn't really have to continue. We really felt training in this area was a necessity, and stuck to our commitment.

All the product group people responsible for building the marketing materials, business value propositions, competitive analysis—all attended the same training as our sales people. We need to make sure that as they build sales tools and collateral around a particular product, it resonates with the demands of the marketplace and has a solutions orientation.

We also changed the tenure in the field and the compensation program to incent deeper customer relationships. As a company, Microsoft has one of the lowest turnover and attrition rates in the high-tech industry; yet we found that the churn rate for customer-facing roles was way higher than we'd like to see. People would begin in an account manager role, and then move to a marketing or product role in Redmond. This is a vibrant company that for many years has been on the list of the 100 Best Companies to Work For. But it wasn't viewed as a company to come and build a sales career.

So we changed the leveling process within the company. We changed the way we compensated for tenure and incented people to stay engaged with customers. Now you're able to grow a career in sales at Microsoft by staying put. These are real tangible efforts in recognizing that we needed deeper relationships with customers, and a consistent, tenured knowledge base facing the customer.

It's also a recognition that the more you understand your customer, the more credibility you have in helping them address their challenges, their competitors, and their strategy. This knowledge and credibility translates directly into the level of trust required for you to provide guidance and solutions to meet those needs. And if there's a new person on the scene every year, then there's no way to establish that depth of trust and relationship.

Our customers don't have time to keep training this year's new account manager. So, we recognized that we needed to do two things: build deeper relationships, and provide solutions expertise by virtually teaming a pool of resources with an account manager. This is a two-pronged approach we can go to market with.

In the enterprise server segment we weren't achieving the product sales results that we wanted. The company recognized at the very highest level that we fundamentally needed to change our sales model. However, there was no real understanding of what that meant except that the desktop sales model may not be the right model to get us into the enterprise segment in the way that we believed we were capable of adding value. Now, after making these changes that I just described, if you look at the growth for the enterprise server product line in the past year, we're starting to get some real traction especially in our database business, with Microsoft SQL Server, at a time when the overall market is flat and the incumbent in the market is seeing negative growth.

At the beginning of this process, what we recognized was in the enterprise segment, the product may only be 25% of the solution. You also need to effectively address what applications will ride on top of this platform. What benefit will a customer see in this approach? What services are you offering in order to make this solution real? What kind of support infrastructure will be provided for recognizing that this is a mission critical application? There are a lot of additional elements on top of what would otherwise be a great product and a great innovation that make that product real for an enterprise customer.

We can invent all the best products in the world for our enterprise customers and if we don't know their business, they'll never see the light of day.

Selling The Microsoft Way

The Microsoft Solution Selling Process (MSSP) is a process in which we have made tremendous investments and in which we have trained the entire Microsoft sales and marketing organizations. MSSP allows us to develop collateral and deploy resources based on a consistent process around the world. It allows us to forecast and sell consistently across all areas.

Now, we can focus on certain stages of the sales cycle where we seem to be encountering either more obstacles or spending more time than expected. It allows us to look more systematically at what we need to do to help a customer believe a proof of concept. Is there something that we need to do with our licensing, or with a partner that's more proactive? Is there something that we need to do for a Rapid Economic Justification (REJ)? Is there something that we can do to shorten the sales cycle and clarify the business value proposition for the customer?

As we review anecdotal information, as well as real analysis of the sales cycle, we can see where we seem to be spending a lot of time and explore how best to address improvements to the sales process. This is a more scientific way of viewing each stage of the sales cycle. The solution selling process is also more customer focused and provides guidance on how to go about recognizing a customer's pain points and priorities. So with more consistency internally and a more customer-centric approach externally, the goals of MSSP are realized by having more satisfied customers and shorter customer time to benefit.

Every step in the sales process has a percent of probability based on where you are in the sales cycle. The MSSP also includes a customer evidence element. Each step is not just a milestone of what we've done internally, but very specifically what customer evidence should be present in order for the opportunity to move to the next level of probability. So it's an internal process item and a customer process evidence item. Both are required in order to achieve the next level of probability, and unlock additional resources.

We also look at the pipeline. We've just in the last quarter provided some aging analysis that shows how long a particular opportunity resides at each stage of its cycle. Based on what we find, we consider options for modifying certain steps, shortening or possibly eliminating them entirely.

We've also focused on providing a role-based tool for the field—a tool that gives each person the information they need when they need it. For example, we've created a sales intelligence portal that gives sales people the information they need on their pipeline, including a real-time calculation of the incentives that they'd achieve. We put everything in one place: pipeline statistics, a view of each customer, their relationship and contract details, any open support issues, and any available news on that customer. The information is directly in front of our sales people, so they don't have to navigate all the backend systems to be current about their customer. The 'stickiness' of this site and the amount of cycles given back to the sales person is beating our expectations.

Our sales people are much more knowledgeable about the customer because every morning we put in front of them relevant news and data. In a very reduced amount of time, they have very specific knowledge of what's appropriate for their next call.

We want to make sure that the account manager knows exactly what customer issues are outstanding and when they were logged. We've brought this information forward via .NET, in a way that the account manager and anybody on that account team with the right access and the right privacy conditions can see it.

We want to provide via the sales portal a 360 degree view of a customer. And so as information about the customer that's applicable and appropriate is determined, it gives everybody on that virtual team the ability to benefit from that knowledge of the customer and be that much better at performing their specific function.

In the interest of better understanding our customers, we maintain some fairly specific information about our customers. At the same time, we go to great lengths to maintain the privacy of those customers so that information is shared only with the virtual team on an appropriate basis, and is used only according to the terms of that specific customer's relationship with Microsoft. So for instance, does this customer or individual want to be made aware of local events that are happening in their area? We take great care to never misuse the information, but we also make sure that anybody whose role is in providing a richer customer experience is informed.

We have completed a lot of work in this area, because if we want to change the culture of the company and put the customer at the front of our thinking, then it has to permeate through the entire company, not just on the sales side.

ALAN WARMS

Alan Warms is Founder, Chairman of the Board, and Chief Executive Officer of Participate Systems, Inc., a provider of enterprise software and online community management services for more than 100 corporations, including Wrigley, BEA, Cap Gemini Ernst & Young, and IBM. Prior to founding Participate Systems, Alan served as vice president of strategic business development for eShare Technologies, Inc. and FreeLoader, Inc. Alan is an advisory member of the Economist Intelligence Unit's Ebusiness Forum and IBM's Institute for Knowledge Management. In 2001, the World Economic Forum selected Alan as one of its 100 Technology Pioneers. He received a Masters degree in business administration from the J.L. Kellogg School of Management at Northwestern University. He earned a Bachelor of Science degree in electrical engineering from the Rensselaer Polytechnic Institute. His web site address is www.participate.com.

JD

> **There is not a single sales executive in the world who does not want to significantly improve the effectiveness of his or her sales organization. We all want that. What shocks me is that as companies chase this goal, their single biggest asset for dealing with this problem is rarely leveraged.**

When times get tough in sales, there are a lot of places we can turn to. More often than not we look to outsiders—sales training firms, benchmarking organizations, reengineering specialists, and so forth—for advice on how to improve our operations.

But the truth of the matter is, the solutions most often reside within our own sales ecosystem; within the sales, sales support, marketing, and product marketing organizations that face the customer. Improving sales performance is about servicing our customers better throughout the sales process. In an increasingly complex and information-driven selling and buying environment, the ability to get relevant, contextual answers to customer inquiries and comments, as soon as possible, is the key differentiator between leaders and laggards.

At the end of the day, who is it that already knows the most about our business, the challenges we face, and probably has already thought through a number of potential solutions for dealing with those issues? Wouldn't that be our own people inside the company, who live and breathe these problems everyday? Are we really leveraging that asset, their knowledge and insights, to its full potential? Are we allowing our sales forces to harness the entire expertise of our corporations to bring value to our customers?

Harnessing The Expertise Of The Sales Ecosystem: The Killer Application For Sales

When we are able to respond quickly, succinctly, and knowledgeably to our clients and prospects, the payback is immediate and impressive:

- Sales people significantly increase the amount of time they have available to do more selling, as they are freed from the task of chasing answers.

- Sell cycle times decrease as we remove all the 'dead time' we have injected into the process while the prospect waits for us to get back to them.

- Competitive win rates increase, as our sales people are able to tap into all the best practices that have been developed by their peers worldwide, allowing them to outperform their less experienced and less knowledgeable counterparts.

- 'No decision' rates go down, as we are able to provide detailed, comprehensive responses to clients' questions or concerns that, left unanswered, would indefinitely delay their purchase.

- Intellectual capital surrounding the actual Q&A dialogue with customers and prospects is preserved when annual reorganization, corporate downsizing, or new product directions occur.

- The productivity in many other parts of the ecosystem increases as people in finance, manufacturing, engineering, support, etc. only have to deal with an information request a single time, versus dealing with the issue time and time again.

- Finally, the voice of the marketplace is now available for everyone to see. By reviewing the questions that come in from the field, marketing can see which messages are clear and which are confusing; R&D can see where the shortcomings are in their product lines; training is able to surface the holes in their programs; senior management has an early warning for significant trends in the marketplace; and so on.

I remember a Pogo cartoon that showed Pogo and his compatriots walking in a circle around a tree. When they realize what they are doing, Pogo makes the observation, "We have met the enemy, and he is us." Well, in regards to solving a huge portion of the sales effectiveness challenge haunting our companies today, I think we can make a similar observation: "We have met the solution, and he is us."

A Historical Perspective On Harnessing Ecosystem Expertise

We used to do a much better job of working together to service customers; it was a logical extension of our everyday work environment. Recently, I had a discussion with an old IBM'er who was talking about sales in the '70s. During that period, IBM had huge regional sales offices in major cities across the country, housing literally hundreds of sales people and representing all the different product lines they sold.

Also located in these centers were sales support, sales operations, finance, training, marketing, and sometimes even product specialist personnel on loan from the various manufacturing plants—in other words, the entire sales ecosystem. You worked with these people everyday, you knew them by their first names, you would see them outside of work at your kid's baseball game, or at the grocery store.

If you had a sales issue back then, the way you handled it was to tap into the existing brain trust. Within the four walls of a single building you had a wealth of expertise about changes in the marketplace, competitive announcements, trends in buyers' needs, effective value messages, answers to questions and objections, who was a good reference today and who wasn't—you name it.

And this know-how was not just about the current market. Since many of these people were sages, having been at IBM for not years but decades, you could tap into the history and the evolution of the marketplace as well.

Accessing these insights was as simple as walking over to someone's desk, hanging around the water cooler, or offering to buy someone a cup of coffee down in the cafeteria. Almost anything you needed in order to deal with a sales challenge or a customer issue was at your fingertips.

Today's Challenges

As a sales professional, you cannot listen to a story like that and not feel a twinge of envy. What a great competitive advantage that must have been. But what happened? Where is that resource today?

The huge regional office centers are gone. The real estate costs got too expensive to provide permanent office space for sales people who spent a fair amount of their time out meeting with clients. Smaller distributed offices have also been significantly scaled back in favor of having sales people work out of their own home offices.

Another interesting trend is that the tenure in sales has dropped precipitously. Even if sales people do have offices to go to, they are now rarely populated with decade-seasoned sages. That is not to say these people do not have experience. Over the course of their career they may have spent 20 years in various sales roles, or 15 years in marketing, but rarely today do they get all their experience at a single company. So much of the history of sales of our own companies has been lost.

With these changes, the sense of community is gone. Since people come and go so quickly, and since we rarely see them face-to-face anymore, relationships on a first name basis have been dramatically reduced. And with that, the number of people we can turn to easily for help has also decreased.

The Changing Sales Challenge

Other changes are occurring that make the profession of sales more challenging than ever before. First, product cycles are collapsing. Sales people are being bombarded by a never-ending stream of new product or enhancement announcements, not just coming from their own firm, but competitors as well. This is creating a huge challenge for sales people, who need to keep up with what these products do, don't do, why they are of value to customers, and so on.

Some firms have tried to deal with this problem through technology. Perhaps a company has installed an intranet or sales portal. Unfortunately, this 'boil the ocean' approach to the problem often results in the return of 25 whitepapers when all a sales professional really needs is the answer to a question.

We are also in the era of mergers and acquisitions (M&A), which is creating two more challenges. The first of these is that sales people now not only have to worry about keeping up with a flow of products from their own development groups, they also have to contend with learning everything there is to know about completely new product lines that are coming from the companies they bought, or who bought them.

These exploding product lines are getting way beyond the scope of management. For example, there is a California-based medical products reseller firm whose product line now encompasses 30,000 products from 300 manufacturers. What mortal human being is going to be an expert on 30,000 products, or even 3,000 or 300? The answer is no one.

The second byproduct of the M&A activity is a whole new set of human resources—engineers, marketing managers, product specialists, and the like—that sales people need to rely on for assistance. If it is a hard enough challenge to keep up with who to call in our own company, imagine how much harder it is to find and develop relationships with all these new people as a result of a merger or acquisition.

Today's Brute Force Solutions

To understand the impact of all of this, one simply needs to look at what is in the hands of a sales person when they walk out of a customer meeting. It would be great if it were an order, but that is rarely the case. More often, a sales call results in a list of tough questions:

- How does your product function at sub-zero temperatures?
- What other customers do you have in our industry and how are they using your products?
- How do you compare to Competitor X?
- We also have operations in Japan and Africa; how will you support us there?
- What would be involved to modify your product to fit our quality standards?

These are all questions that need to be resolved for the sales process to continue. So how does the sales person get those answers today? Most likely he or she goes back to the office, picks up the phone, and starts dialing and e-mailing all over the company trying to find someone who knows the answer. We have all been there and we all know how painful and ineffective this is.

First, if I am new to the company I probably have no idea whom to call. I haven't had time to develop my personal support network. A veteran can also have problems here, because people change jobs or responsibilities so often that the person who could help last year cannot help today.

Even if I do call the right number, what are the chances that I will reach that person on the first call? Slim to none. Instead, I get the bane of existence for a sales professional—voice mail. And if I leave a message, what are the chances that it will get returned? Less and less everyday, because product experts are inundated with calls and very likely only have time to get back to a fraction of the people who ask them for help.

And even if I do get the answer I am looking for, while that is great for me, what value does that represent for the dozens of sales people across the company with similar questions?

So what else could I do to get the answers I need? I could attempt a 'Hail Mary' e-mail across the company. We have all seen those, where the universe is copied in the 'sent to' address field. The message that follows is a desperate call for help from a sales rep looking for a reference, a technical answer, some financial documentation, etc. How many of those requests do you think are deleted out-of-hand?

I review this scenario with sales executives all the time and they always agree that 'yes,' that is how it is and 'no,' it is not effective.

Traditional CRM Shortcomings

There has been a lot written and said about how technology should take over the task of giving sales people access to the information they need to do their jobs. There has also been a lot written and said about how technology has failed to live up to that expectation.

The skeptics point to how opportunity management systems (OMS) and marketing encyclopedias have simply not worked in harnessing the expertise of organizations to solve customer problems. Primarily, an OMS is a tool for tracking what is in the pipeline. It may provide some basic capabilities to access customer, product, or service information, but it was never designed to function as the primary method to deliver contextual expertise-based solutions to sales people from the rest of the organization.

When marketing encyclopedias, sales intranets, and sales portals hit the market, they were each promoted as the answer to the shortcomings of OMSs. Conceptually, they each allow you to index every piece of content you have created and make it searchable via the Internet. For a large, Global 2000 firm, this can exceed 1,000,000 pages of information.

While good in theory, these 'corporate filing cabinets' have proven impractical in real life in two areas. First, the search engines are still not powerful enough to be able to discern exactly what you are looking for. A typical search may result in a sales person being presented with 15 to 20 documents that 'might' fit his or her needs. The responsibility is then shifted back to the sales person, who must wade through all of the identified items, to see if they in fact do contain what he or she is looking for.

The second shortcoming is that what you are presented with is often out of context with what you are looking for. A search may lead a sales person to a data sheet that says, "Our product does A." However, that does not suffice when the question was, "How does the way our product does A compare to Competitor X?" Or, "How does our product function under these specific conditions?" Because of this disconnect, the sales person's real information needs go unmet.

While these tools have failed to meet the information needs of sales people, all of the technology building blocks are available to overcome this problem. At Participate Systems, we have been working with a broad range of companies such as ACE Hardware, Cisco, Wrigley's, and AT&T to implement technology-enabled sales communities and optimize the process of knowledge exchange across the enterprise.

Technology-Enabled Sales Ecosystems

Let me share with you a real-world scenario about overcoming the knowledge exchange dilemma. The sales people at Wm. Wrigley Jr. Company, one of our customers, successfully leveraged our Participate Enterprise technology to create what they call a Sales Web Center.

The objective of this project was to provide sales people—whether they have been with Wrigley for two weeks, two months, two years or 20 years—with a tool that they could use to get the answers they needed quickly, easily and cost effectively.

Today, when Wrigley sales people leave a customer meeting, they will most likely leave with a list of client-generated questions just like any other rep. The difference is what they do to get their answers.

To obtain the information they need, sales people, whether they are traveling, in the office, or at home, simply access their e-mail account and type in the questions they could not answer for their customer. This is how they have always worked, so they are not being asked to do anything extra. The only difference is that they address their e-mail to the Wrigley Sales Web Center.

When the Sales Web Center receives the e-mail, the first thing the software does is categorize the questions based on content and context. When we initially installed the application, we worked with Wrigley to create an expertise map that identifies all the subject matter experts across Wrigley worldwide, and what they are experts on. Based on this knowledge, the Sales Web Center automatically routes the e-mail to the right individual(s).

When the experts receive the question, they in turn structure their response as an e-mail and send the answer back to the Sales Web Center, where a copy is then forwarded to the appropriate sales person. The sales rep is also given the name of the expert who answered the question. If need be, he can access an online profile on that expert through the Sales Web Center. He can find out where the expert resides within Wrigley, what other questions or contributions he has made to the system, and how to contact him directly if he needs more help.

Another important aspect of the Sales Web Center is that it saves a copy of each answer in its core knowledge bank. If a day, week, or month later, a different rep asks the same question, the answer is immediately sent back to him.

Overall, this is a very frictionless process. Sales people are not asked to keep up with who knows what within Wrigley; the system handles that task. Sales people are not asked to learn any new tools, just to use e-mail. Experts know that if they answer a question once, they won't be bothered with that topic again. Because of this, it is very easy to get user buy-in on both sides: sales and the functional area experts that support them.

The adoption rate at Wrigley proves this point. Since January 2002, when the system was unveiled, 99% of Wrigley's North American sales force has used the Sales Web Center. Fifty percent of these users now leverage the application at least once a week.

Another interesting fact about the Wrigley experience is how fast the knowledge bank can grow. In March 2002, just a few months after the system went live, Wrigley hosted an online event to launch one of their latest products, Eclipse 'Flash Strips,' which are high-intensity, dissolvable breath films. During the course of the event, 42% of the field sales force's questions were answered by Wrigley's customer marketing managers, and the remaining 58% were handled by the Sales Web Center.

Throughout the system's first nine months, 60,000 requests for information have been answered. You can imagine the value that has been created during this time.

Bigger Enterprise, Bigger Benefits

This method of handling sales ecosystem expertise probably has the biggest benefit to the biggest firms. For the first time, Global 2000 companies can gain a competitive advantage through the sheer size of their sales force.

Up until now, having a huge sales force was not necessarily a plus. With size came complexity in terms of training, communications, ensuring consistent messages are delivered in all markets, etc. We probably all know of cases where a small, focused competitor outperformed a giant because of their detailed knowledge of their products, their ability to coordinate all the resources necessary to put together a strong business case, and their ability to respond quickly to customer questions or issues.

Now size becomes an asset. This experiential knowledge base will be broader and more complete for a company with 5,000 reps and 500 engineers than it will be for a company with 50 reps and five engineers. Furthermore, based on the way we implement these systems, the geographic disparity issue associated with global firms disappears. If sales people have access to the Internet, they can get answers regardless of where they are in the world, 24 hours a day, seven days a week, 365 days a year.

Somewhere in our companies lies the answer to the challenges our sales teams are encountering that are significantly impacting their performance. Like Wrigley did with their Sales Web Center, we need to identify, harness, preserve, and nurture the sales ecosystem expertise. Accomplishing that objective will determine the winners and losers in all markets going forward.

GARY LUTZ

Gary is Senior Vice President and National Sales Manager for Wells Fargo & Company's National Commercial Banking Business Development organization. In this capacity, he and his group of financial services sales professionals are responsible for achieving Wells Fargo Commercial Banking's overall growth objectives in 21 states. His 18 years of commercial banking experience have been with four banks: United Bank of Denver, First Interstate, Norwest, and Wells Fargo. Though he's only changed companies once, the horse keeps changing under him. In addition to bringing a sales orientation to the banking industry, Gary also brings a deeply human dimension. He's active in the Denver community through his involvement as past Chairman of Junior Achievement's Board of Directors, and is currently Board Chairman for Big Brothers Big Sisters of Colorado. Among other activities and awards, Gary was recognized by The Denver Business Journal as one of 1997's 'Forty Under 40' Outstanding Business Leaders, and has been listed for the past five years as one of The Denver Business Journal's 'Who's Who in Banking & Finance.'

BT

Focusing on the personal win side of Win-Results, being clear on sales process, and keeping sales management's ego in check are key components of a winning formula. Ensuring open communications, providing supporting technology, and removing obstacles to sales productivity help, too.

Let's start with what keeps me up at night. We talked about this at the Insight Technology Group CSO Summit (Colorado Springs, June 2001). Almost every one of us said, "Keeping good people." How do we keep our people charged and energized and fulfilled and happy? What components of the compensation plan matter to them? What are the components of management behavior that make a difference?

My efforts keep zeroing in on keeping and adding the very best people. The thing that seems to matter most in my view of the world is being very clear on an individual's personal wins.

Bringing Win-Results To Life

Although it may seem like jargon to say this, 'sales excellence' to me is when a sales person is able to identify a prospect's need, match it to a solution, and in doing so, receive the necessary reward. Otherwise, what motivates him or her to go to the trouble to do it over and over again?

There needs to be something that speaks to both sides. There has to be the personal win for the customer and for the sales person. Our representatives have to feel good about the company and the products they represent; they have to feel, hopefully, a sense of pride in what they do. In addition, for the sales person *there has to be a business result*. To spend time and effort on a sale, there must be a specific business achievement.

To be a sales professional rather than a vendor, you also need to find out what speaks to the prospect side. CFOs or CEOs don't work for free, but they also don't work just for the money. There's something personal that makes them feel good about going to their board or to their management team and saying, "I recommend making a banking change from XYZ to Wells Fargo." When you think about what it takes to change a personal banking relationship, it's a pain in the neck.

For a business, it is much more complicated and in-depth. So, there has to be a very good reason for them to do it. They need to feel good about sitting in front of the board, management team, or their staff and saying, "We're going to go through everything associated with changing the banking relationship, and this is a good decision because..." And then there's the business result—it must make sense for the business. There has to be a good improvement in expenses, or cash flow, or whatever the situation is to justify the business side of the decision.

In their *Strategic Selling* program, Miller Heiman presents this concept as Win-Results. This is exactly what I'm talking about. To make Win-Results real we consistently reinforce these strategies.

Commodity Versus Relationship

The classic mistake a lot of commercial bankers make, and a lot of bankers for that matter, is that we have commoditized ourselves. Think about what questions the traditional banker asks a prospect the minute he walks into the office. "How do we get your business?" "How much are your payments?" "What's your structure?" People think they are avoiding price by talking about structure, while structure is nothing more than a different component of price.

They prepare some lowball, marginally profitable bid to get a piece of the transaction. And then, a year later, everyone is crushed when they're sitting around trying to figure out why that same customer went to XYZ National Bank down the road for a tenth of a basis point. Well, there's no loyalty because there's no relationship, and there is nothing that suggested that *that* customer's business was anything more than a transaction.

In commercial banking, the only way we make sustained money is to build annuity strength over time. This means having as much of that business' opportunity, both with the employees of the business and their corporate business, as possible. And you just can't do that if you don't have a relationship—if your customers don't have the sense that there is trust.

Sticking Through Thick And Thin

One of the areas I'm most proud of about Wells Fargo Commercial Banking's business is over the last 20 plus years, we've proven to our long-standing customers time and time again that, in the good times and the bad times, we are going to stick by you. Our business has shown record growth for the last three to five years. But it did not grow as much as some of our competitors because we are within a pretty narrow bandwidth of what we do well.

In our current economy, contrary to what Greenspan says, we are not seeing much improvement in the middle market. It's plugging along at a very anemic pace. Even so, we don't have huge, unjustifiable loan write-offs. Our business isn't substantially shrinking. Once again, it's the same bandwidth because we are sticking with people we know; we know the managers and they know us. The only way to build these relationships is from the start. During the sales solicitation process, we reinforce the point that Wells Fargo is about people.

By and large, the middle market businesses we pursue are owned and operated by families or individuals, not millions of shareholders. And that business is their life.

Our definition of the middle market for commercial banking is somewhere between $10 million and $400 million in annual revenues. The key to any bracketed population, given the standard bell curve situation, is making sure that through our distribution channels, those companies are given the right products and services. We find that, by and large, companies in that revenue size generally have the same kinds of needs and situations that we're best able to address.

Excellence In Sales Management

I think sales excellence is intuitively simpler than a lot of people want to make it. Sales excellence is the ability to consistently and professionally solve problems. As a sales person, excellence is about the prospect. Excellence is about understanding what's keeping the prospect up at night.

For managers, sales excellence means the exact same thing. It's about me understanding my sales people and their needs so well that I ought to be able to articulate what keeps my sales people up at night. What is getting in the way of them doing their job?

My job is to ask them every year, "What keeps you from having your goal doubled?" and not have it be taken as a threat or a joke. My intention is to continually discover what's getting in their way. What's keeping them from being as productive and as fulfilled as possible? And how can I help them keep as healthy as possible?

This isn't the stuff of annual performance reviews. The key is to talk to our Business Development Officers (BDOs) regularly. I look to create a meeting that addresses everyone's objectives. The shareholders need $X\%$ growth. What does commercial banking need? What does each individual office need to meet the business objectives? At the same time, what's in it for the BDOs to accomplish those goals? I'm interested in understanding the answers to these questions.

CRM That Works

For our field people, I want to know the unique factors of *their* marketplace. I constantly ask the field sales managers, "What tools do you need to succeed?" We spent a lot of time at our last meeting talking about CRM. The question was asked, "Is CRM good and important and necessary?" And the answer was—Yes! But if it's going to be successful, and if it's going to be valuable, then the first question has to be, "How do the sales people need to use it?"

And always, behind everything is the question about comp plans. Does the comp plan have something to help motivate behavior, or is it a mechanism to control costs? I believe the comp plan needs to motivate the behavior necessary to achieve the shareholders' objectives. But, at the same time, a good comp plan and a good CRM system should take into account the issues that sales reps face in their markets doing their jobs every day.

One example is the examination of how we provide reps with data in their markets. It wasn't all that long ago that we would go to a standard source—Dun & Bradstreet—and provide our sales reps with information on their markets. A couple of the BDOs that were industry experts said, "You know, all this information you give us is great, but there's too much. We don't want to have to go through the process of sorting it by SIC code."

This issue seems obvious, easy, and intuitive to address, but in the past, for whatever reason, it never happened. Now we contract with someone and put together data that deals specifically with agriculture, dairy, or a specific sort order, and give it to our team in a totally different format. Did it cost money? Yes. Was it different for every other BDO? Yes. Did it change how we got our management reports? Yes. But, our BDOs were no longer spending X number of hours every day of every week trying to figure out how to sort a particular aspect of their data.

In another example, a past internal accounting mechanism tracked where the BDOs' smallest expenses went and determined who approved travel and expenses. Across the board, we found that approvals were happening on a decentralized basis and were wildly inconsistent. This was handicapping a lot of people whose expense reports were being approved by people who perhaps didn't have the same philosophy of sales as I do.

We realized that a lot of time was being spent on this expense dollar issue, rather than dealing with closing business. We changed the process. Currently, one of four people approves BDO expenses. We say, "Here is a budget. It's your budget and your business. You manage it and deal with it as you see fit." It was an easy thing to fix once we understood what was the problem, what was its magnitude, and the misplaced emphasis on the legacy approach.

Now our expense approach is totally consistent. It is consistent for two reasons. 1) Everyone has the same guidelines. 2) We are sending the message that, on behalf of their efforts and on behalf of our company, here is what a reasonable sales person can spend. Run your business.

▶ Run It Like You Own It

One of our mottos, one of the creeds in Wells Fargo Commercial Banking is 'run it like you own it.' You're a bright person; you know what you need to do. Manage your budget. Manage your time. Essentially, the message is: we trust you.

'Run it like you own it' is definitely not just a catch phrase; it plays out in the way we manage these folks. Whether it's expense dollars or the amount of time they spend doing certain activities, the common thread is that I want them to spend their day running their markets as though the expense dollars were their own and the profit dollars that make up their goals were their own.

In my opinion, the key point for a group of fully commissioned sales people operating within the somewhat conventional, traditional parameters of a commercial banking group is that you have a ton of risk, and a ton of upside. It's your risk, your upside, and you are best suited to manage it. That being said, what tools do you need in order to deliver? What issues do you face? These issues need to be addressed, and only then do you have a confident, empowered, professional, and excellent sales person. Are you going to be able to go out and gain the respect and the absolutely necessary trust of a business owner, a CEO, a CFO who is running their business like they own it? Because most of the time, they do.

Our people have a very small base salary, which operates functionally a lot like a draw. Above and beyond that, they are paid on a quarterly basis to generate specific business objectives that are directly tied to profits for the shareholders. As the shareholders profit, so do the BDOs.

Continuing with the notion of running it like you own it and maximizing profits, facing the officer/owner of a company also means being able to make commitments. It's important to note that our BDOs can commit resources. But given the number and complexity of products they have to sell, they have people to help them for certain things, such as the extension of credit. They are not able to commit themselves to extending credit.

To support them in this area, they have people in each and every market who can extend credit. The BDO's job is to serve as a problem solver for that business and that prospect. He or she needs to understand what resources, what tools, what people, and what processes are needed to be able to commit to the prospect.

Let's say you have a BDO who is responsible for getting an answer to a business owner who may be requesting an extension of credit in a certain area. It may be that the owner hasn't provided all the information that an expert would need to say, "Yes, we can do that." How do we ensure we get consistency and that good judgment is exercised? There are two challenges to doing this.

First, as Jim Dickie would say, there is the training of the 'tribal customs and rituals.' Second, while all that is well-intended, it doesn't mean anything if we don't get back to the Win-Results statement. One of the biggest challenges of the job, and one of the biggest payoffs for those who do it well, is applying those same, basic principles to the people they are dealing with internally.

There are plenty of cases you can think of where, at the end of the day, if we commit and fund a particular loan, Wells Fargo & Co. has more invested in that particular company than the owners do. And insofar as that is the case, as well as asking people to commit their time and their resources, it's an opportunity cost. What's in it for them?

Let's say a BDO is approaching someone who deals with the extension of credit inside Wells Fargo. That person has many other conflicting priorities on her mind. Think Win-Results: why should she stop doing what she's doing, drop her other tasks, and pick up the BDO's prospect to look at that particular deal?

This is not a trivial question. The BDO had better understand the needs of that location and the needs of the people processing this request. What's in it for them to support this credit? How does supporting this credit help those people achieve their goals? How does it help Commercial Banking achieve its goals? The constant training we are giving them is to understand what these other people, who are integral to our business, need to be successful too.

How many times do you hear people from marketing, production, or customer service talk in generic terms about arrogant sales people? If you look at the critical numbers of our cash flow and the time it takes us to turn a closed deal into profit, that key area often hinges on how we manage our internal relationships. These have an opportunity cost.

In getting an order filled, it's the very same issue. All of these people have multiple implementations to perform. Does sales understand customer service's issues well enough to deliver to them a closed prospect that's neat, tidy, and with expectations properly managed? Or, is sales marching in with an untidy, messy, ill-conceived deal that someone else has to try to clean up? It is very important that the sales people are respected internally and are seen as members of the team.

To manage this, we contact the internal groups working with our sales force and ask, "Is sales giving you consistently complete packages?" This is **Point #1**—constant feedback. It's crucial to understand that in each of these markets, there is a team of people who have to function together and help each other out, because if one team isn't doing its job, other people are going to suffer.

Point #2—reinforcement. There is a component of the comp plan that very specifically states, "From the time there is a commitment from the customer, there are X number of days to get the thing up and running."

The key is that it's not the BDO's job to do all of this, otherwise they'd never have time to sell. But it is their job to understand very specifically the customer's needs and what specialists need to be involved to meet those needs. And if we can't meet their needs, we need to figure that out well ahead of time. That's part of the training.

Process Versus Internal Issues

I'm always looking for barriers to our sales productivity. The BDO says, "I'm having trouble with XYZ product in getting A, B, and C done in 30 days, or 60 days, or 90 days." Is this a process issue or an internal issue? My job is to go back and find out from those involved, are they getting incomplete information from the BDOs? Are we selling something we can't provide? Are we getting them involved too late in the process? If the answer to those process questions is no, then is something going on in their internal world? Are they having processing issues? Are they short on people? Understanding the internal issues is key to improving the process.

Focusing on the process is the only thing that will make it work because there is so much involved in every product that we sell. Within those products, there's so much that has to go on behind the scenes. If it takes two months longer for a customer to generate profits, that's a hollow victory because, until then, we're still susceptible to the competition. We've lost deals because a business owner says, "Yeah, I said I'd do it but I never thought it would take this long to execute."

Sales People Are Management's Customers

As important as training, programs, CRM, and all of the products are, it still comes down to a handful of questions: How do you treat your people? How do they feel? How do you set the right example? Other than a comp plan, what can you do to demonstrate to them that they are valued? Do we understand that, as managers, our sales people are our customers?

I travel two to three days every other week. I expect sales people to go out in the market to understand their customers' needs. I have that same expectation of the sales managers. And they ought to have the same expectation of me, as does my management.

Understanding what will allow the BDOs to function to their best ability is the sole purpose of my trip. For example, we've got a great sales person in

Minneapolis. Assisting this person is a whole team of Minneapolis Wells Fargo employees whose job it is to support the BDO in selling the business, approving the loans, funding the loans, and doing treasury management. Our job at Wells Fargo is to build relationships. 'Relationship' implies that you are going to be interacting with people that add value to your life.

If I were on a call, the customer would look me in the face and say or think, "So what? Why do I want to meet with you, Gary from Denver? Are you going to approve my loan? Are you going to help me with my lock box problems? Gary, are you going to help me when I have too much inventory on my balance sheets and I'm out of covenants?"

And, of course, the answer to all these questions is—No.

They might think, "Well, Gary, is this a performance appraisal for the person who is calling on my business?" Or, "Is this a performance appraisal of me as a customer?" If I said anything other than yes, I would be lying. There is no reason for me to be there, unless I can help that prospect.

Why would they care about a National Sales Manager from Denver? On prospect visits, I want the BDOs to take with them our decision makers: for example, the person who is approving their loan. Who is their customer service rep? Who is going to be there for them when their business needs change? It isn't me.

I think a lot of times sales managers go on calls out of insecurity. And if they think they need to be involved in every sale, then they are hiring the wrong people and ought to feel insecure.

The Hiring Process

This brings me to the other area I want to cover. We're looking at people and our process for hiring them. We're overlaying that through the form of a test for all of our new hires. This is something we have worked to refine over the years and we are learning more about it as we go.

One of our issues in the past is that we hired these great sales people who were supremely confident. They could take rejection, they could live on an incentive comp plan, so on and so forth. But they were mean as hell to the service people. And what happened with these people is that they were booking a deal and 120 days or 190 days would go by and we still would not be generating any profit. Why? Well, no one wanted to work with the sales person because the person was a jerk.

We have changed all that. One of our requirements now is that every manager needs to take candidates out to lunch or dinner and see how they treat the waiter or the busboy. Are they rude? Do they make eye contact? How do they treat people? There is nothing we can quantify; there is nothing we can measure. But I couldn't work with a better group of sales managers than my current team, and they all have great instincts.

Because the team concept at Wells Fargo is so important in terms of cross-selling and everything else we have talked about, we now have many more people in the interview process than we had in the past. In addition to the Regional Sales Manager and maybe the senior person in the local office, we now have the candidate meet with some of the relationship managers, customer service people, and/or Product Partner Specialists. These interviewers don't get to vote, but they definitely get to give us really important feedback. And the feedback is, "I really liked her. She was really nice; I could work with her." Or, "What a snob!"

We had a situation very recently where someone came in with a platinum resume. However, all of our team members felt uncomfortable with this individual, so we said, "Thank you very much," and didn't pursue him further. Instead, we went out and found somebody with a 14-karat gold resume. Maybe the resume wasn't as stellar, but everyone on the team said, "Man, we really like him. He's one of us. He's the kind of person we can go have a beer with and play softball with and work with in the office." We hired him in a minute. Without that input, we'd have made the wrong hiring decision.

This gets back to Win-Results and the team concept. What better way to feel like you have buy-in when a new person walks into the office the first day, and you've already met him and given him your seal of approval; rather than, "Here comes this stranger—what are we going to do with him?" It sets up a whole different feeling.

One of my hobbies is reading biographies. I love to read biographies of great leaders. I don't tend to read a whole lot of specific management books, but I love history. One of my favorite quotes is from Theodore Roosevelt, who said, "The best executive is the one who has sense enough to pick good people to do what needs to be done, and self restraint enough to keep from meddling while they do it."

In the middle of the night, I wrote that quote down on a little scrap of paper. I keep it with me because, to me, this summarizes what is my job and what is the sales manager's job.

JOSEPH BATISTA

When I first met Joe Batista at a sales effectiveness symposium where we were both speaking, I was immediately intrigued with his title: Director & Chief Creatologist—Compaq Computer (now Hewlett-Packard Corporation). As a 'creatologist,' Joe is responsible for the growth, strategy, and implementation of creative enterprise and Internet businesses. He concentrates on building value by leveraging capital, labor, market, and technology assets. He actively works with emerging companies as a business advisor, formulating innovative ways to leverage technology, marketing, and strategy to create a competitive advantage. Many large corporations seek his 'creative application theory' of applying real world technology and strategy to business domain challenges and business value creation. Joe has been recognized by many organizations for his innovations, including being awarded CIO Magazine's TOP 50 Web Awards for building a leading edge corporate portal to leverage internal knowledge assets. Joe holds a Masters of Science degree from the University of Pennsylvania.

JD

> *Organizing to create value in today's economy, firms must extend beyond delivering excellent products and quality services; we also need to offer our clients expertise and insights. We need to leverage all our intellectual capital—market position, supply-chain of contacts, and technology and process portfolios—to create 'net new' value and tangible results for our clients.*

What does a Chief Creatologist do? My responsibility is to act as a resource to our valued clients and the HP Field Account Professionals. Our focus is to live at the intersection of business and technology domains and uncover or create competitive advantage for our clients. We do this by bringing to the table all the available HP resources and assets necessary to create and deliver 'net new' value streams that accelerate a new market reality for our customers.

What we do is triangulate our experiences, any number of different assets in HP's technology and business portfolio, and dialogue with the client on real business challenges. Our passion for our customers is an HP mantra.

The outcomes include a variety of projects, innovative alliances, partnerships, technology solutions, and new business concepts that really impact our clients' businesses.

For instance, we are working with clients to understand what the office-of-the-future—what we call Smart Spaces—would look like. How do you begin to optimize your knowledge workers' environment? By providing 'context' to space, some interesting value propositions begin to evolve for the healthcare, services, and retail firms looking to coordinate and leverage staff and assets within that context.

Creatology Begins With A Dialogue

Our primary objective is to fundamentally enhance the client process. We know we will have to have traditional conversations with our clients. We will have to understand what they are looking to do technology-wise, what are their requirements from an IT perspective, what types of products have they already installed, what additional solutions have they budgeted for, etc. These are all very predictable conversations with our clients, and we at HP are fortunate in having an excellent and extensive set of product offerings to meet the most demanding of needs. But at HP, that is just the beginning.

▶ Pools of Knowledge

I recently traveled up to Buffalo, New York, to visit a banking client. I was initially invited in to have a technology-focused discussion regarding how the bank could leverage or enhance their intranet as a tool for their knowledge workers.

While HP has a number of hardware and software products to meet this need, we also have extensive practical knowledge from having built intranets inside our company, and from being a pioneer in the whole concept of Business-to-Employee (B2E) portals. So, rather than continue with an agenda targeted towards technology, we shifted the conversation towards the lessons learned, what works and doesn't work, return on investment techniques and best practices, etc., that we at HP have uncovered in solving this business challenge for our own company.

By having these types of conversations, we enhance the working relationship. Customers do not view us as someone who is just trying to sell them something, but rather as a partner with a wealth of knowledge that they can leverage around a particular business domain, such as optimizing the performance of their knowledge workers. Building or inventorying these 'pools of knowledge' and sharing them with clients creates a 'net new' value stream.

I believe most sales executives would agree that this is the selling model of the future. We cannot just rely on delivering excellent products to the marketplace and expect to be successful. Even bundling or repackaging products into solutions is not enough. We have to go beyond that and help our clients see how the solutions can be successfully integrated into their organization to solve their real business challenges, with a sensitivity that each company's DNA (technology, culture, people, markets) are different.

Identifying Your Portfolio Of Assets

To apply this concept to your marketplace, you first need to understand all the value you can bring to the table, and then unleash that on your clients. When you move to the mindset of thinking, "How can we impact the business of our clients using our complete portfolio of assets?" only then does your journey begin.

First, you have to begin defining what are your traditional assets. For a company like HP, these include hardware, software, communications, and services. Cataloguing these assets is relatively easy to do. But we cannot stop there; we then need to explore and really understand our intellectual capital. Let me offer some suggestions of where to look.

▶ **Untapped or Re-oriented Knowledge** — Part of our intellectual capital is the knowledge that resides in the minds of our employees. Maybe some individual down in Florida has developed a unique approach for handling certain internal processes that could be reoriented for a customer. Understanding these assets becomes the key challenge. We need to determine ways to find those insights, collect them, repurpose them, and then share them with customers.

▶ **Supply Chain of Contacts** — Another part of our intellectual assets could be our Rolodex. On any given day we are involved in innovative work with our suppliers, our business partners, and our customers. By simply being aware of all of the things going on in these three areas, we could provide significant value to customers by putting them in touch with people working on problems similar to theirs; resources they never even knew existed.

▶ **Linking** — This idea explores the ability to link two or more organizations or business units within a corporation to build something 'net new.' For instance, we could leverage an internally developed algorithm, software application, or business process and bundle it with a piece of equipment. We could link any given product group with R&D to develop a new offering. Or, working with an alliance partner with a new product, we might develop an innovative co-branded service. There are any number of linkage options to create new revenue streams.

Now that you have this portfolio of assets, what do you do next? Many companies have a huge portfolio of assets that go way beyond the traditional products they sell; the problem is that not many firms invest the time and energy to figure out how to reorient those assets to benefit their customers. That is a shortcoming.

M x V = MO CREATING MO...

You often hear executives speak about wanting to create momentum in their marketplace or momentum within their firms. Let's explore that. What is momentum? Remember Physics 101? Mass times velocity is what creates true momentum, or what I call 'MO.'

What I am advocating is for companies to understand their true mass, which is represented by their total portfolio of assets. They then need to develop innovative methods to reorient those assets in ways that create velocity in terms of the speed at which customers can solve problems. If they do that, then they will achieve their maximum momentum in revenues and customer satisfaction.

▶ Client Conversations

How do you do that? From our experience, there are three essential ingredients. First, we need to create a forum to openly dialogue with our clients about problems, not products. Based on work we have done with our client base, I developed a program called iVelocity: a not-so-structured format designed to help our clients express their business challenges, competitive threats and market expansion plans.

To optimize this client conversation, we need to assemble a collection of knowledge assets and people from both the customer side and the HP side. The customer's team could include business people, IT professionals, financial analysts, etc. HP might contribute people with expertise in technology, process flow, business innovation, etc. The goal of this phase of the project is to develop a clear and well-rounded understanding of where the customer is and where they ultimately need to be.

The second ingredient is a little more difficult to explain. Here is where Creatology comes into play. If we are going to help our clients extract new ideas and value out of these sessions, we want to involve people who effectively examine and understand things as they are, but then think outside the box and explore brand new ways of dealing with an issue.

That is why, from an HP perspective, we focus on contributing people who have a real passion for innovation. Re-orientation and an awareness of our portfolio of assets form the basis for new and powerful combinations. Adding this to a very talented array of individuals who can test and explore business theses during the iVelocity session will create a 'net new' impact.

The third ingredient that helps a team develop innovation is access to the complete library of assets their company has at their disposal, and the ways those items have been previously oriented or deployed. When this knowledge base is added to an understanding of where things are, then creative people can develop solutions that generate significant momentum.

Many sales executives may think that this is the type of work their sales force should be doing. But the program I am suggesting goes far beyond what we can expect from our talented sales professionals. Today, tremendous demands are placed on our selling teams. On a daily basis, they have numerous customer issues to deal with, a flood of e-mail and information requests to read and respond to, plus they have to keep up-to-date with an ever-expanding product line that changes every couple of hours.

Even if they had the time to do it, training sales professionals to perform this function becomes a challenge. In many cases these conversations fall outside of a traditional product-services dialogue. They end up being very detailed business conversations that require a lot of expertise to carry on at the depth the customer wants to take them. We have found that a blended team approach where each individual contributes significantly to the process is a winning combination.

Creative Process In Action

Here is a real world example. Global services organizations—auditing firms, healthcare institutions, manufacturing firms—face a significant challenge regarding how to certify the thousands of people working for them worldwide on a yearly basis. They are looking for innovative ways to train a highly mobile work force on issues surrounding such things as OSHA certification and testing.

When we have discussions with these firms, we center on ways to accelerate, track, and leverage the knowledge assets within the firm, either for competitive advantage or to meet regulatory issues, or both. This is not a conversation about what types of servers you might need, how many terabytes of data will be involved, what type of maintenance contract you need for your hardware, or anything along those lines. We are not anywhere near caring about those issues at this point; we are looking for how to generate a 'net new' impact on business.

During our discussion, we may zero in on the fact that everyone requires mandatory training of approximately 15 credit hours, the delivery mechanism requires video broadcasting, and professionals will have to take time from their busy schedules to physically travel to their company's office locations to receive training.

I think you're getting the picture of the business issues. Our challenge became, "How do we service the training needs of the highly mobile professional in a way that leverages a media-rich learning environment, and that is flexible enough to enhance the learning process without requiring travel? And how do we build a sound ROI case that supports the new approach?"

We came up with a whole collection of ideas, but immediately began to converge on four themes: 1) Product Assets—existing mobile computing appliances; 2) Business Relationships—emerging technology market entrants; 3) Intellectual Capital—a pool of talented people to integrate and design the solution; and, 4) Business Mechanics—the ability to build a solid ROI model.

▶ Existing Product Assets and Emerging Technology

We created a centrally developed courseware strategy that would be distributed and executed on a mobile handheld computing device: for example, HP's iPAQ. The learning module could be conducted anywhere—at home, in the airport, during lunch. The mobile appliance delivered on two promises; first, it allowed for the richness of content and learning experience, and second, the instant-on capabilities allowed the learning module to be used anywhere.

▶ Intellectual Capital

Now, the important part. Since we needed to know and track who successfully completed the certification or training, linking the courseware on the mobile appliance to a corporate Learning Management System (LMS) was very important. By providing knowledge and functionality on how to accomplish this, we allowed the training team to track and report who had successfully completed the training. This functionality was very important because it was mandatory for reporting purposes to complete certification.

▶ Business Mechanics

Implementing this type of strategy requires expertise in needs assessment, design, deployment, risk mitigation, collaboration, and business case development. By bringing our knowledge to those areas, we were able to help deploy a mobile strategy for delivering a closed-loop learning process that created a new model for learning success. We now call this m-Learning.

Through this process, we were able to tap into relationships HP has with other companies; our experience with enterprise integration and creating learning systems; our product leadership in mobile appliances with the iPAQ; and our idea generation and business sensitivity to an economic model and deployment strategy that made financial sense.

Bottom line, we built a new market category environment called m-Learning that not only met the needs of our existing client, but quite honestly could become the next killer app for knowledge-intensive enterprises, especially those requiring regulatory certification or rapid learning deployments to mobile staff.

Ultimate Goal: Creating Net New Value

If we fast forward a few years to 2010, powerful new transformations within enterprises will occur with those companies that take advantage of new technologies and combine them with legacy assets to create 'net new' value streams.

Our charter is to create differentiation and value in the eyes of the customer. To do that, you have to dedicate resources to identify, understand, and create sources of innovation. You cannot just mouth the words 'out-of-the-box thinking;' you have to do the work to make it real and tangible. Our group is a collection of very talented professionals across the HP enterprises that live an HP mantra of passion for customers. It may sound corny, I know, but it's our culture.

Clearly, the center of gravity in the marketplace is shifting from product leadership to a customer intimacy model. This is a new marketplace, and we need to play by new rules. The solution providers that win in this environment will be the ones that can deal with the complexity of challenges their clients are facing by bringing together a variety of assets to create something that is 'net new.' That is what customers will ultimately want to purchase: business impact and competitive advantage!

INVENT....

RICK COBB

When I interviewed Rick, he was Vice President of Worldwide Sales and Strategic Alliances with Intraspect Software. Rick's background includes graduating from the U.S. Naval Academy and an eight-year stint at Cadence Design Systems. The latter half of his Cadence stay was in Asia Pacific; his last position was in Singapore as Vice President and General Manager of APAC. With 15 years of experience in high-tech, Rick has seen the cyclical ups and downs of the business world. We talked about how things have changed and the new 'sales truths' that apply to these challenging times. I've gotten familiar nods when presenting these 'truths' at sales meetings in 2002, and indications are that 2003 will continue the economic doldrums. I think you'll find Rick's comments and observations especially relevant.

BT

> **From a leader's perspective, it all comes down to the quality of the people in your organization. Do you have extremely high-quality, ethical, hard-working, intelligent, well-trained, professional people? People who are able to set the right kind of expectations in a win-win fashion and deliver on those expectations on an ongoing basis. And, do you have a well-defined process around how you work as an organization, how you engage customers, how you compete, etc.?**

The Key Sales Truths

Let me introduce what I've been presenting to my team for the past two years as the Key New Sales Truths.

1. If you're lucky, last year's decision maker is an influencer this year.

2. As a result of #1, triangulation is essential.

3. You will do three to five times the work to get 20% of the results.

4. People are spending money infrequently on themselves but when they do spend, it's in response to:

- a key customer they've got to win
- a product they've got to launch
- the need to support existing strategic initiatives

I'll add a fifth observation a bit later but, for now, let's consider these four.

Decrease In Influence

The first sales truth may shock and dismay you and your high-level customer contact(s). As the economy has slowed, companies to a surprising extent have withdrawn the authority of individuals to make or approve purchasing decisions. Vice presidents of sales, CIOs, even company presidents often have to take their recommendations to higher levels or their board for final approval.

If you're lucky, your contact is still credible and retains some influence with this higher authority.

Triangulation

My second sales truth is the importance of triangulation. The level of involvement of your management team and the visibility it needs into deals are much higher today than they've ever been. Getting proper triangulation within business and IT means that both organizations need to be aligned. In the past, it seemed that there were some business folks that could spend whatever they wanted and jam it down the throat of IT. There were some IT people that could spend whatever they wanted and turn around and tell businesses what to do. We are seeing much less of either of these today.

Triangulation is important because there may be competing projects that you may not even be aware of. Or, the team you are working with may be fully budgeted with millions of dollars to be spent, only to have the CFO decide, "We're only going forward with two of the three projects."

The way that you identify holes in your strategy is to have a strategy in the first place. This is another aspect of triangulation. Having an account plan and an account strategy is really critical. For this reason, during the past year I've increased our focus on developing targeted account penetration plans.

You must have some process whereby in a collaborative environment you can test your plan, triangulate on things you're hearing and seeing, and plan your next action item. Without that, people are just flying blind. This is something that I've always used in my career as a manager and as an individual contributor because I thought it would help me to win more frequently. And, the funny thing is that the more I reinforce this, the more we win better and bigger business.

There are some people that either refuse to use a process like this or they just don't get it. They've been relying on the fact that there was abundance out there. If they made enough calls in a day, they would find several people that would end up being customers whether or not they understood how the customer bought. That doesn't work anymore. So, we've really increased the focus on management visibility and the coaching process using a structural format.

Working Harder To Get 20% Of The Results

Along the lines of working three to five times harder to get 20% of the results, we have tried to slim down the number of things we are working on. So, the first thing we've done is cut back considerably on the vertical markets that we are pursuing. Also, we want repeatable messaging. We want markets that are real markets, where our people have structured avenues to communicate from one prospect company to the next and throughout an industry.

We have channeled our team efforts on very specific marketplaces where our references would provide the largest impact. We've also increased the coaching and planning on our account management requirements. Those are our two biggest accomplishments. In focusing on the vertical markets, we have relied more than ever on reference selling. Having solid success stories about someone in the same vertical space and leveraging those materials has been our most successful sales approach.

Return On Investment

A notion that comes up a lot with respect to the fourth truth is return on investment (ROI). Regarding ROI, some decisions that people make are absolutely necessary, like having tires on their car. However, even with essentials, today somebody will ask, "What's the ROI on having those?" Nearly everybody today has the required essential products to operate a business.

It used to be that you had e-mail or a web browser 'because everybody else had it.' That whole feeling extended well into the bubble phase, but those days are over. People spent bazillions of dollars on products because everybody else had them. After-the-fact ROI was frequently measured from a CYA standpoint, because all of a sudden people were saying, "Well, gee, what did we get from that $150 million we spent on the web or CRM?"

We've seen sales reps going back to justify additional consulting that was twice the cost of what was originally proposed. Maybe the original proposal was to spend four times the amount of the software, but the sales reps now have to justify another four-times increment. Some of that after-the-fact ROI is just, "Let's just do a little to cover your butt here."

Today, people have to make at least some estimation of ROI. It doesn't have to be measured in a grandiose, strategic sense; it can be very tactical. For example, I may want to shut down 12 servers that carry a company solution we built that's costing me X number of dollars on a yearly basis to maintain. ROI can be measured very easily along those lines. People frequently try to measure ROI on the strategic side as increased revenue. But when you get into that level of ROI, everybody is going to claim some piece of the increase in revenue, so it becomes more of a positioning game.

In talking about ROI, there are different levels: business-based ROI, personal-based ROI, strategic and revenue-based ROI, and very tactical, cost-saving ROI. While I believe we deliver a lot of strategic return on investment—customer retention, increased revenue, profits, etc.— I think we have the ability to show really strong cost savings.

Clearly, we can demonstrate productivity per head; you can do more with less. But, we can also address the tactics around the question, "How are we doing this today and what is it costing to support those systems?" When addressing this issue, people come back and say, "Well, you know, I've got e-mail that I am using extensively in my organization. I archive everything and it costs me hundreds of thousands of dollars a year to keep these e-mail archives. So I need a better way to capture e-mail in its context of use. And I need something that doesn't cost me an arm and a leg from an IT or hardware standpoint."

Frequently, people have built custom file sharing systems that they try to brand. They then try to include customers in some web-based sharing of files and folders, which gets expensive. These things end up being an IT nightmare that costs a lot of money. If you can show savings there, it's fantastic.

A Fifth Observation

I mentioned earlier a fifth observation about the current economic environment. I've seen companies in which sales people really want and need to concentrate; yet they find themselves pursuing anything that moves. They rely on early adopters and visionaries to get across the 'chasm' to the 'bowling alley' (terms from Geoffrey Moore's *Crossing the Chasm*). A major recession and the implosion of the dot-com era have had a tendency to push a lot of companies back over the chasm to the starting point.

So, people who might have thought they were across the chasm suddenly found it necessary to resell their company and their vision because they had once again fallen into the group of untested companies. When deciding who gets their business, the pragmatists of the world now review more criteria: viability and size of the company, cost and customer list.

More than anything else, this trend has caused the failure of a number of small companies. The same referenceable customers they'd been selling to were suddenly reevaluating them against a new set of criteria they didn't anticipate. For example, an existing customer might say, "Regardless of our earlier purchases, if your gross revenues are under a certain level, we can't do business with you." That's a nasty surprise for smaller firms.

Narrow Your Focus

Now more than ever, even if you have already crossed the chasm, you've got to narrow your focus. In our case, we not only narrowed our focus on vertical markets but we also went to an assigned account list. We assign each sales person 20 focal accounts and direct all outbound activity to those 20 accounts.

Inbound leads are qualified by a manager. We decide at that level whether a lead warrants sales attention. Rather than at the sales person's level, rather than it being based on a zip code, we put managers in the role of deciding whether this is something that should be pursued, and if so, by whom.

In assigning accounts, it's not so much about availability. It's about closing business—who can do it best? I always say it doesn't help you to wound a grizzly bear. If we're going to attempt it, we better make sure we've got the right number of shots in the magazine and that we can bring it down. So, when a lead comes in, we look at who is available and make a decision based on the people most likely to close the business.

By the way, the number of people available for hire that can actually be successful in an environment like this has decreased by a large factor. In all markets, at all times, we have some people that are doing really well. And we have some people that did really well a year ago and are bouncing back because they are refocused and re-energized. They've taken our sales principles and applied them.

We've also seen some people who never got it together again and could not make the appropriate changes. These people couldn't focus their efforts even though in words they said, "Yeah, we get it, we get it." At the end of the day, they weren't able to apply the principles. And today they're gone.

Our sales process works as follows: once we have qualified an inbound lead, whether it's through telemarketing or telesales, we forward it to sales. If the lead represents one of our top 20 accounts, it goes directly to the sales person. From there it is entered into a lead tracking system, where it begins as 'below the radar' in terms of probability. As the opportunity moves through the sales cycle, our forecasting system maps it accordingly: 25%, 50%, 75% and 90% in terms of probability.

Having a 25% opportunity means there is a real initiative that has some sponsor and some budget behind it. We've met the customer and believe that we have an opportunity to win, or have won opportunities like this in the past. Here, somebody has a real program, a real budget assigned to it, and a team of folks to conduct an evaluation.

An opportunity moves to 50% probability once you have a validated internal champion. At this stage, you have identified at least part of a compelling ROI directly to the customer. You have identified at least the beginnings of a compelling event; and the customer has intimated that you are a finalist in their decision.

Basically, the customer has narrowed his field down from a large number of vendors to three vendors, and you are part of this select group. To get to a 75% opportunity, you need verbal acceptance from the customer, you have figured out the ROI, you have the compelling event well defined and agreed to by the customer. At 90%, you are going through contracts. As you can see, all these steps are cumulative.

It Has To Be Part Of The Vernacular

To make this process happen for us, the first thing we did was to train our people. The second step was to make the process part of our vernacular. Every vice president of sales has a process. The ones that don't are absolutely worthless in these difficult times. If you don't have a way to evaluate a deal and talk about it, then you are going to get wiped out. You must have a common vocabulary. Without it, you can't communicate to your management team, your sales people, and your systems engineers; you can't ask questions and get consistent answers that everyone understands.

If there is a common vernacular, then when I ask you something, you'll know exactly what it is that I am asking you; if not, we are going to fail. Just as there are sales people today who have found themselves in a slightly different environment than they've experienced in the past, there are vice presidents of sales who must be struggling like crazy right now. At the beginning of the downturn, I heard stories about companies that didn't close a single deal for a year. That's pretty hard to imagine.

Targeting Your Accounts

Some companies totally lost all ability to close business and, of course, blamed it on the product, or the market, or the customers. But sales execution plays a role in any environment, and having that ability is absolutely critical. Equally critical is giving our people the tools they need, including a well-defined sales process.

We've built our sales principles into our forecasting, as well as how we talk about and reinforce the deals, and so on. We have a weekly update of our top 20 accounts. We use an e-mail-based template system that rolls up into our own collaborative solution. The system takes the top 20 deals across the customer base, and we evaluate the progress checklist on a weekly basis. It takes a sales person about 15 minutes to write an update on the progress of one top 20 account. Each top 20 account encompasses the entire firm, and one sales person might have one deal at any given time. This keeps a really tactical focus on moving deals forward.

There was a time when people said that, if you use the same standards that you used two to ten years ago, you will close a third of your business, you'll lose a third of your business, and another third will be lost to a 'no decision' or to a delay. Today, if you look at the early part of the funnel for any quarter, you probably have to double your pipeline amount. You could adjust either your measurement or your criteria and better define what a qualified opportunity is.

I'm not saying that in today's environment you need 25% more opportunities to start with. You need almost twice as much. In the past, to achieve a $10 million quarter we needed $30 million in the pipeline. In today's environment, we might need $50 million. This means I have to do three to five times the amount of work for 20% of the results. That is a bit facetious, but if you haven't changed your pipeline measurement or qualification mechanism, you need to start now. You need to estimate a much larger pipeline to get the same amount of business that you could have gotten a year or a year and a half ago.

On the one hand, you need two-plus times as many opportunities, and on the other hand, you are looking at fewer deals and are qualifying them more rigorously. At Intraspect, because we've cut out some verticals, we're not spreading ourselves too thin across the board. But pursuing fewer verticals means we have to pick the ones that are big enough to yield sizable volume—that is key.

The other thing you have to do is make sure the expectations are lowered. How much a sales person can achieve is going to be less than in the past. In my view, you have to set expectations within your own company and build these into your model. I heard about another company that used to assign $3 million to $5 million quotas per head and fire a sales person if he missed two quarters in a row. I think that company is in very poor shape right now because they never adjusted their expectations. They turned over everybody regardless of real talent. There was no qualitative measurement of their people; it was all quantitative.

Incremental Buying

In today's environment, people are buying in increments. One of our customers was recently quoted as saying that they are reducing the number of things they are investing in, and are also making sure that whatever they buy works before they buy more of it. The days of the $5 million quota and the drive-by sale are gone. Today, customers begin with a limited pilot. They want to prove it out, and then they want to buy more, but they don't want to buy any more than they can deploy. If you don't readjust expectations in your company, then you are going to have some very disappointed investors and executives.

You'd better make sure you are tracking what's really going on in your marketplace; you may not be able to hit the growth rates that you were hitting, or you may not be able to hit the probability numbers that you were hitting. And then, if you can't get to those numbers, you need to ask yourself, "Well, how could I do that? What are my alternatives? Is a merger or acquisition appropriate to increase the breadth of my product? Should we open up alternative channels to increase the productivity of my sales force?"

Week-To-Week Tracking

Regarding the top 20 accounts that I talked about earlier, we have a company-wide update via a system we've developed that provides a week-to-week progress report on the factors that make for a qualified opportunity. Have we identified the coach and champion? What was accomplished at the last meeting? When is the next meeting? Who's our competition? The whole picture is on an e-mail template, and people just open it up on their desktop. It's pretty simple and accessible.

This system is useful and powerful because the e-mail gets reviewed in our executive staff meeting every week. That e-mail is much more compelling than someone coming in with a number and saying, "Here's what it is." The e-mail review includes the dependencies and issues; these things are so interrelated it's unbelievable. If you're late by a couple of months with a product, or you have bugs that can't be fixed, it's definitely going to affect your top and bottom lines. It's critical for people to understand that *the objective of a company, of all the functions, is to sell.*

All the factors that make a sales organization great—high quality people, referenceable customers, etc.—aren't just the sales organization's responsibility. The number should be owned by everybody. This isn't as much a problem in a small company because so much of the company is built around customers. But, even if the company is small and everybody's really involved with customers and deals, you still need to make sure you've got the processes in place to communicate productively. People want to know what's going on and how their area of responsibility makes an impact.

Hiring Great People

I started off by talking about having great people, so let me end on that subject as well. The market is starting to settle down a little bit now. I've been with Intraspect approximately four years, and can tell you that during the bubble, I interviewed and hired some people that I wouldn't touch with a ten-foot pole in today's environment. It was a supply and demand issue, and the sense of entitlement with some of these people was so great. In a way, it didn't feel good, but it was a booming market. The fact was that people were making big money for very average performance and that's what you had to pay. It hurt. It hurt people who had been doing this for 15 or 20 years and could remember their first $100,000 year—an awesome memory, right?

For now, I think the days of average performers making big bucks are over. I believe in some principles around the hiring process. The number one thing I look for in a candidate is purposeful behavior. There are very specific ways that you can measure purposeful behavior. Give me a person who has actually demonstrated that she can choose a path and execute on that, rather than someone who has tripped through life and kind of happened to be wherever she was.

The next thing I look for is accomplishment and a consistent track record of success. It's not enough that people try things. They also need to accomplish those things. These are critical factors to me. Also, I like to see that in the business world, even through the dot-com era, these people didn't have a new job every 12 to 18 months.

This is another critical factor. There is nothing you could possibly do to convince me that you were the performer you described on your resume if you were only at a company for a year. The first six months, you're getting your hands around things. Your next six months, you're basically trying to close some deals that maybe were already in the funnel. When people give me resumes of 250% of quota every year in their whole career and every year they went to a new company, that tells me that they were just floating along the top of the bubble.

I want to see a minimum of one job that lasted more than two years. I used to look for one job that lasted more than three or four years, depending on the experience level required for the position I was trying to fill. The duration of a job is very important. I also look for increased responsibilities in roles. I like to see people who have been promoted at a company. If you've been there a couple of years, you've probably been scrutinized at very close quarters, and someone has found you worthy for promotion. I think that's an excellent sign of legitimacy.

In summary, the key things I look for include purposeful behavior, success, consistency, and legitimacy so that a) you're able to really get down and dirty and contribute in a big way, and b) other people recognize and promote you. I don't mind a little bit of adversity, either. Through the successes and positive aspects of life, there are also times in people's careers when they were challenged and overcame those challenges. I look specifically for these circumstances. I like the idea that someone actually stuck through some tough times, made it through, and yet is not carrying a chip on his shoulder about it. Discovering this helps me get multiple perspectives on an individual.

In my company, several people interview candidates. I try to have them test for some of the same things I am, but from different angles. We conduct interviews individually and in pairs. We don't usually go larger than two; otherwise it feels more like an inquiry board from the military.

As we talk now (June 2002), there were some massive fires burning in the West. I think the tough economic times we've been in the past two years and continue to face are like a forest fire. The difference between this forest fire and previous fires is that every now and then, you have one that rages to the degree that it takes down even the big trees. I think the fire we are in right now has taken down some trees that would have survived most of the other ones. I agree it's healthy, but it would be easier to be a lifeguard than a firefighter right now.

KEITH RAFFEL

In 1996, Sales Force Automation (SFA) had not yet morphed into Customer Relationship Management (CRM). It was a time in this nascent industry when people were trying different approaches, each with a vision and passion of their own. One of the pioneers I met then was Keith Raffel as he was launching UpShot Corporation. In a client-server world, populated largely with technocrats who had never sold anything telling sales people how to sell, Keith was a breath of fresh air. He had a unique vision (web-based ASP) but was also a guy who had sold. Obviously bright and articulate (with advanced degrees from Harvard and Oxford), Keith remains down to earth while maintaining his passion for leveraging technology to make sales reps more effective. Prior to founding UpShot, Keith served as a marketing and business development executive at Echelon, a leader in networking everyday devices, and was general manager of the International Telecom Division at ROLM Corporation. His company's website address is www.upshot.com.

BT

> **You have to put basic building blocks in place. This starts with defining the sales process and then getting timely performance metrics. Lots of companies have a process that's broken, or people are dealing with opinions rather than information. Technology and CRM are not magic answers but they can be tools to provide the right information to the right people, right now.**

Individuals Versus The Sales Team

There are different aspects of sales excellence. One thing that's interesting to us is that when you start talking to sales reps about a sales team, they seem confused. "What do you mean, 'sales team'?" Then they thump their chest a couple of times and say, "There's no sales team—I make the sales."

Well, of course they do. But when you ask them how sales happen, they'll reply, "Oh, someone in marketing generates the leads. That person passes a lead to someone in telesales who qualifies it, and then the sales coordinator schedules a meeting for me. When the customer asks technical questions, I have a Sales Engineer call, and then I set things up to bring our VP of Sales in to help make the close." Right, so it's a sales team. "Oh, yeah," they say.

So then we ask how this process is working. Their response is, "Not very well. The leads go to the wrong people, who don't ask the right questions to qualify them; the people answering technical or more in-depth questions, or supplying literature, don't know exactly what the customer asked for. And when the VP finally gets on the phone to close the sale, he doesn't know what we've previously been talking about."

Technology Can Help

When we suggest that technology might help with some of these issues, sales reps at first say, "Oh, you want to watch what I'm doing." Then after a while, the light goes on and they realize, "No, this is a way for me to leverage corporate resources. This way, I no longer have to haul around dog-eared corporate presentations. Instead, I can just press a button and have the literature coordinator send something out for me. When it comes time for the VP of Sales to do something, I can look at the VP's schedule and actually have the call added so that he or she can call right away. And I can see when he or she is traveling in my area so that I can take advantage of that."

We focus on this process to make sure it runs smoothly, so that everybody understands what's going on and picks up the ball quickly. First, it's much more efficient, and second, the chances of closing a sale go way up when everybody knows what's been happening. It's providing more efficient and effective sales.

Early Warning

At UpShot, we have eight steps in our own sales process. Generally, it should take two weeks to move from Step 3, which is completely qualifying a prospect, to Step 4, which is the face-to-face meeting. If at some point we suddenly realize that it is now taking eight weeks, it's clear we have a problem. The entire sales cycle might be three months, but if that one stage is moving to eight weeks, we're going to be in very bad trouble in the next couple of months. Fortunately, if this happens we will have had an early warning.

There are a couple things about early warnings. First, there's the public market aspect of it, of just letting people know what's going on. You don't want to be the CSO going in to talk to the CEO, saying everything's fine and then having the bottom fall out right at the end of the quarter. We have seen a lot of this lately. Second, you can do something about a problematic situation if you discover it early on. You can adjust prices, you can pre-announce a product, or you can increase advertising. You can also make sure that you're not ordering more materials for the factory. You can focus on running your business more efficiently and do something proactive.

Getting visibility by managing the sales process and by being able to see what's going on in real time is critical, especially in these times.

Quicker Results

We had a conversation with a VP of Sales a couple of months ago. She said that the last CRM people who came in to see her said she could be up and running in nine months. Her response was, "That will be great for my successor." People are in a hurry right now; they need to see results and they need to see them quickly.

I also think people don't have the luxury they had a couple years ago, when sales reps were making $300,000 and a company would say, "Oh, I'm going to spend $5 million putting in a CRM system. It's going to take a year or two, but it's going to make us world class." We feel that, a) that's been shown to be baloney, b) they don't need to spend that much, and, c) they can't wait that long anymore.

So there's not only an effort to run things better, but to run things faster, and to see results immediately. It's funny because the whole dot-com thing was supposed to be about the real time enterprise and everything being fast and in Internet time but, at least in this aspect, we're seeing an urgency now that wasn't there earlier.

Improvement With Existing Systems

Of course, there's an arithmetical advantage that people listen to now that they didn't listen to then. If you're enforcing processes and putting best practices into effect that increase sales productivity—say, by 10% or 20%—it makes a big difference. And if you get a one-year head start on your competitors it also makes a lot of difference, not just in the first year but in the second and third years.

We're not pushing a particular process or system and saying to people, "Use this." What we're saying is, "Take the system and process that you're using and we'll accommodate it." So we're a tool, we're a facilitator, but we're not pushing a certain methodology. We have a cadre of consultants who will help you get up and running and deployed in a short amount of time. In some cases we'll even guarantee that you're up and running in 15 business days.

But it's a contract with mutual obligations; there are things that we do and there are things that the customer has to do. And we can always tell in that first call whether they're going to be able to uphold their end. We say, "Please give us the steps of your sales process." And they say, "Steps? Process?" Then we know: whoa, this might take longer than we thought.

Process Can Benefit Sales Reps

We certainly see cases where the VP of Sales thinks they have processes and steps, while the people in the field don't think so. He doesn't understand exactly what's going on and the discipline that's required isn't there. People in the field don't see why they should follow the process or follow the procedures. They don't see any benefits for themselves. However, the key to making any of those processes and procedures work is that there has to be a benefit to field sales reps.

There was a guy who managed Southeast Asia for a previous company I was at and he had a lot to do with why I started UpShot. He reported to the Asia guy, who reported to the worldwide sales guy, who reported to me. I said to him, "You didn't fill out your sales report last month." And he said— I think he actually said, "Go jump in the lake." I went back to my office because he was at 220% of quota. What the heck are you going to do? He's not filling out reports and he's at 220% of quota. Are you going to fire your top performing guy? Of course not. The problem was that he wasn't getting any benefit. The report was for me; it wasn't for him. It was a pain in the neck for him.

And so I think you have to make sure that you're giving field sales reps something, too. It's not just for management, and I think that's some of the problem with the big systems that are out there right now. The message is along the lines of: "It's 11:00 p.m., do you know where your sales reps are?"

We've been in a lot of companies where sales reps just fill out their forecast once a month. That's the only time they ever use the system, because it doesn't do anything for them. In contrast, we want to try to make sure that you have something that's easy to use, something that allows sales reps to leverage resources and sell more, faster.

We conducted some research last quarter. Often cited was UpShot's ability to adapt to a lot of different methodologies and processes. Many prospects named flexibility as a key influencing factor in their decision to choose us. Whether people have or don't have a well-defined process, it seems important, at least to the people we're encountering, that there is this flexibility to adapt to their current system.

It's About Methodology and Ease of Use

Certainly one thing that has changed over the years is that most CSOs have had a bad CRM experience, either firsthand or through a peer, whereas a few years ago, CRM was seen as or hoped to be a magic bullet. They thought, "We'll just install Siebel or Pivotal or whatever, and sales will go up." But that's not the way it works. It's not just buying a piece of software; it means having processes, procedures, and a methodology in place. It especially means providing benefits to the field sales person for using them, making more resources available to him or her, making sure that he or she gets leads faster, and those kinds of things.

Of course, the system has got to be easy to use for those people. Look at how customer support representatives are trained. Typically they sit with a "Y" connector on the telephone and just listen to another rep for a week or two. They look at and use the system, get trained, and practice using the system.

These reps are making $60,000 a year and you just spent two weeks doing training. So what? That only cost you a couple thousand dollars. With a field sales rep that's trying to sell $2 million a year, if you say it's going to take two weeks to learn to use the system—forget about it. It's not good for the company, and there's no way someone's going to give up two weeks of selling time to learn how to use a system.

▶ Today's Reality: More Revenue Now

The tough environment that we're in right now reminds me of the 1992 Clinton presidential campaign where James Carville put up that sign, "It's the economy, Stupid." Now, I don't want to use the word 'stupid' to describe people who are working hard to do a good job selling, but right now, "It's the revenue!"

A couple of years ago, people were saying it's e-business, getting everything up on the web. Now, to use another quote, Dr. Johnson said, "The prospect of a hanging concentrates the mind wonderfully." Today, every CSO looking outside the window feels he or she is seeing the gallows being built. With that kind of pressure, CSOs are saying, "I have to do something and it's not e-business. I'm not going to do something that could eventually do everything for everybody. My focus is right now, starting now. Nine months from now will be too late for me. That means I have to be more efficient. I have to target better, I have to have a higher win rate."

In terms of the market for CRM, what we're finding is that people are going back to first principles. They're going to do something that's focused on sales processes, procedures, and effectiveness, because what's really important to the company is more revenue—*now.*

To a certain extent, smaller- and medium-sized companies have felt this way for some time. What's striking to us is that larger companies are now falling in step, too. They're focused on getting something up and running quickly, that is cost-effective—not something that's going to cost them tens of millions of dollars.

And today it's not just the CSO who's involved. There's usually a CIO saying, "I know you need help right now, but I'm not going to let you buy something that doesn't integrate with anything else. We might not integrate it now, but we're going to later."

Daily Examples Using Technology

In sales management, some key questions are, "What's happening? What's changed?" A favorite example of mine involves a sales manager who was given weekly sales reports printed in the form of spreadsheets. In an effort to see changes from period to period, he would hold up the sheets to his window with the light coming through, and look for areas where figures didn't align. Today, that manager can see what's going on three weeks sooner than he did before. And he doesn't have to hold spreadsheets up to the window! Is this revolutionary? No. Is it a matter of excellence? Absolutely.

▶ Telesales Effectiveness

Recently, I met with an UpShot customer who was tremendously excited that finally, he could see how efficient and effective all his telesales reps were. They were running a controlled experiment where they had field sales people doing telesales, as well as people who were paid a lot less. The job was to qualify leads, and the people who were paid a lot less were making a lot more calls by a ratio of at least 2:1. In this particular case of qualifying customers, the answer was quantity over quality. Quantity was actually better than quality, which might be counter-intuitive. I can tell you these people were sure excited to figure this out. In other words, to get someone qualified early in the process, they didn't need the same kind of sales skills they needed later in the process.

▶ Analyzing Wins and Losses

In my world, using our own system has played a big role in establishing metrics for what we do, from the marketing department all the way out to the selling of the service. We have all our win/loss records. We can see why we're winning and why we're losing.

Recently, we noticed a certain factor that was showing up in our loss reports. People were concerned about buying from nonpublic companies because they couldn't see their finances and resources. So, we went to our Board of Directors and investors and raised $27 million to strengthen our balance sheet. We can now show prospects that we have a strong balance sheet and have plenty of cash. We're in good shape because that was actually the number one reason we were having problems. It wasn't a competitive reason; it was because companies have just been burned by the dot-com crash.

In summary, our analyses in Q1 showed us why we were losing deals. We looked at our options and within a couple months we raised $27 million to strengthen our financial picture. And it helped. That's the power of getting information and not just opinions.

▶ Finding Key Metrics

We also changed our marketing mix. We looked at the seat opportunity per lead and realized that some of our more prolific lead sources were getting us only small seat opportunities. So we shifted some things around to get leads from larger companies.

When you don't know what's going on, or when it's just somebody's strong hunch, resentments and finger-pointing can start to develop. However, armed with the right information, you can display it for all, identify potential solutions, and decide on a corrective course of action. The key is figuring out what the key metrics are for each company and measuring them. We have several reports in our application that I call semi-custom. How long does it take to move from stage to stage in the sales cycle? Who's selling the most? What kind of customers are the best for you? Which partners are most effective in which industries? All of these metrics come with our application but we've got to talk to the customer and understand what their key metrics really are.

Peace, Love, And Understanding

Marketing is actually a big part of sales. When you're part of a corporate effort to generate revenue, there's a good reason why there may be both a VP of Marketing and a VP of Sales. The slogan we have around here is, "It's marketing's job to turn dollars into opportunity, and sales' job to turn opportunity into dollars."

And, of course, the reason this works at all is because there's leverage throughout the process. You take $10 in marketing and you're supposed to turn it into $100 in revenue.

I think that happens, but I think that in most companies the process is not optimal, and in a lot of companies it's just plain broken. Leads are being generated. The VP in Marketing is patting him- or herself on the back, while the people out in the field think that they're getting diddly.

At UpShot, I feel we're doing well because we a) spend time getting the leads out, b) have a feedback loop to figure out how good the leads are and where the good leads are coming from, and, c) continually hone and target what we're doing. We just started a campaign based on feedback and everything we've learned, and after a month or six weeks we'll go look at the data and hone it some more.

▶ Lead Follow Up

We're pretty pleased with how quickly leads are now being followed up on. I'll tell you, though, when we started this process 30% of our leads weren't being touched! Now we have zero leads going untouched because we're watching lead follow up. Our marketing module lets us do this.

We introduced UpShot marketing at the DEMO Conference in February 2002. The first question I asked, which was a lot of fun, was, "How many of you have ever heard a sales person say that he or she has enough leads?" Everyone just roared because no one has ever heard a sales rep saying that. I don't know; it's like Liz Taylor saying she has enough diamonds or something. It's not going to happen.

If you were to talk to all of our sales people, I think every single one of them would say that UpShot does a better job at getting them leads than any company they've worked for. In comparison to other companies, I think we'd get the highest marks. But if you asked whether or not UpShot marketing gives enough leads, I don't think the marks would be as high. So more isn't enough.

▶ Getting Rid of the 'Bad Feeling' Component

Finally, I think there's a component of culture that's hard to calculate but is essential to make this all work. There's an openness that comes from people being willing to get and deal with measures of their performance. When we talk to the folks on the sales team about leads, follow up, and so on, the 'bad feeling' component is out of it. It's gone away.

If Rob Reid, president of UpShot, and I were beating people up about their performance, we'd never learn anything. Everyone would be spending all their energy in CYA mode. The way it is right now, each member of the team *wants* to know the details. Sales people go down to marketing and ask, "What did you find out? What is the conversion rate to high quality? What is the rate of lead follow up in my region and the others?"

Our people are not sitting on opposite sides of the building letting certain funny rumors and feelings build up. Everything is really out in the open; people kind of embrace any given situation and work on it together. A lot of our people report that for them it's been a really nice change.

I agree with this entirely and I feel it goes beyond attitude. You could have the right attitude, but the wrong information, or a lack of information. As we've gotten better at delivering the information through our own system, we become truer to our culture. It's been great in terms of getting people to work together. As Elvis Costello said, "What's so funny about peace, love, and understanding?"

Looking Ahead

I think that 10 years from now, when we have a little bit more perspective, we'll see that there was an inflection point in the Fall of 2001 in the way software's delivered, its message, and in the way that CRM works. When the history of software technology is written, I think people are going to look back at 2001 and 2002 as the time when people said, "Oh, we don't need a boil-the-ocean approach. Delivering software via web applications is a better, more cost-effective, easier to use, and faster way to do things."

DAVID M. GROVE

Long before I met Dave Grove, I had heard from a number of sources what an innovator he was. Dave has over 16 years of sales and marketing management experience and is currently the Senior Vice President of Sales, Marketing and Merchandising for Corporate Express North American Operations. In this role, he has responsibility for all Strategic and Global Accounts, Diversity, Vertical Markets, Sales Operations, Marketing and Segmentation, Marketing Communications, Merchandising Strategy Operations, Pricing Margin Management, and eBusiness.

JD

> **At its most fundamental level, Corporate Express' sales strategy boils down to three key activities: conversion, retention, and penetration.**

At Corporate Express we sell all the things you need to run your business. Every business needs them. Traditionally, we have been a very predictable operation. We could plan on growing our business as long as the economy was growing.

Our customer base is strong in Fortune 1000 accounts, specifically in technology, healthcare and the telecommunications sectors. So as you can imagine, when our customers started to feel the downturn in their business last year (2001), we started to feel it in ours, as well.

This was a big wake up call for us. Over the years we got very good at penetrating accounts. We knew that if we were going to hit our plan in 2002, we were going to have to create strategies to win more new business. Having made that decision, we then stepped back and evaluated our sales force strengths.

What we found was that we were great at penetrating and retaining our customer base, but the majority of our recent sales growth had come from major acquisitions. While this helped grow revenues and expand market share, it also took the focus off our new account conversion activities.

Facilitating Organic Growth

Our new focus is on driving profitable organic sales growth. To help accomplish this we have made several changes. The first thing we did was to implement a new 'go-to-market' strategy, segmenting the market differently than we had in the past. At the time we did this, we were also looking to decrease costs, so we had to look for opportunities to fund our account conversion programs.

It is during economic down times that you really start to question how you are spending your money and how you are doing business, which we should probably do more of the time. For me the decision on where to cut was fairly clear. We drastically reduced our brand advertising budget and focused our resources on account conversion programs and activities.

As I said, we knew we were very good at retention and penetration. Our reps are skilled at building relationships. Our key challenge was focusing our sales force on new account conversion.

To support our strategy, we invested in some ideas that are not all that unique, but they have worked. One of the conversion programs we implemented was literally called 'A Foot in the Door.' It included a direct mail campaign sent to top prospects that offered them a high-end GPS system as an incentive for a meeting.

We did another program specifically for the legal market that included a custom catalog and a direct mail campaign, again to drive face-to-face meetings.

We developed several of these types of programs and they were very successful. Investing money in conversion tools so our reps can get into new accounts generated a much higher ROI for us than a mass advertising campaign ever would have accomplished.

Once we got these customers, we next focused on getting them to order. Consistent and ongoing ordering is the key to success in this industry, and our sales force understands this and they have responded. As a result, we have achieved an increase in the number of customers that become consistently active once they are signed up.

Separating Hunters From Farmers

Another thing we have done is to make a number of changes in the way we manage the sales force. We appreciate that slowing growth is an economic reality. But now we are focused on how to compensate for that slowness by having a pipeline, that's always full, to help us grow in these slow times.

We have high performance standards for our reps, and as part of that we began looking at their activities and natural skill sets.

In every sales organization in any industry, you'll find sales people who naturally excel at winning new business – or conversion – and sales people who are strong at building and maintaining strong customer relationships – penetration and retention. Both are critical skills for growing and servicing your customers.

By identifying these two classes of sales people, we were able to modify the sales compensation plan. We are now using the hunter/farmer model. The hunter model focuses on conversion, which is a higher risk, higher reward plan. These reps have 90 to 120 days to prove to us they can open new business. During that time we do everything we can to help them.

The farmer model focuses on effectively penetrating existing accounts with new products. These reps also receive plenty of training to support their activities. We also made additional compensation changes that reward performers who are ahead of their revenue plan, or sell more profitably, or both.

In addition, we also made major non-compensation related changes. We segmented the market. We put people in the right job roles. We've put the measurements and accountabilities in place. And we have the compensation plan that supports our business goals.

This was a radical move for Corporate Express and it is driving dramatic and positive behavior changes in our sales organization. We're focusing on the right things: converting new business, retaining it and penetrating it. That's all we're talking about.

Optimizing Sales Management Effectiveness

We did not just stop at the sales rep level; we put programs in place that are aimed at improving the effectiveness of our sales management as well. Internally, we call this 'Operation Mustang.' It goes far beyond introductory sales management seminars that teach sales managers the basics of helping reps with their sales presentations and closing business.

At Corporate Express we had done sales management training before, but effectively what we were doing was conducting what I would call 'Common Sense' seminars. We needed to spend the time certifying our sales managers. To accomplish this, we put together a sales management certification curriculum.

Sales Management Certification 101 focuses on the minimum things we expect sales managers in our industry to know to be effective. It covers topics like finance, margin management, bid strategies, procurement process, how to do a business review, how to penetrate an account, how to sell our eBusiness model, how to orient a new rep, what is a sales rotation, what's our marketing and branding plan, etc.

This is a three-day class with a modular-based training design so that a manager can easily share the information with his or her sales team when they return from training. We do all the work for them. As they get every single one of their reps up to speed on these topics, their job as a Sales Manager becomes much easier.

As part of the next phase of Operation Mustang, we built a brand new competency model, validated by an industrial psychology firm and a sales performance firm. We then compared that model against our existing sales management personnel and what we found was they were great at closing business, but they were not always good at developing their people.

Through this process we identified the next stage in the Sales Management certification process – coaching, mentoring, training and employee development – which became the basis for Sales Management Certification 201.

In 201 we focus on how to be a good sales manager; how to do the right things to lead, train and develop your people. We also cover more advanced topics such as how to do territory planning, how to do sales strategy planning, how to do talent development planning, how to take corrective action, how to do performance coaching, interviewing, recruiting, etc.

201 training is a three-day course as well, and it ties in with the tools we give them to set and manage their quotas.

We're currently developing our 301 course, which will focus on advanced finance, presentation skills and negotiation skills. Another aspect of the training will focus on how we 'de-commoditize' our product. Our marketing team is working on defining all the value-added services we offer and making sure our reps are getting credit for those in the eyes of the customer.

We also have put in place a leadership succession plan for sales, which guides us in making decisions regarding who to promote from managers to Vice Presidents of Sales.

Leadership succession planning helps us identify people we want to develop and those that may need some support or a back-on-track plan.

We also keep track of all the people that did not make our leadership succession planning at the senior level, but who are people we want to continue to develop. These are the people who still might get in a leadership succession plan, but they were not considered now for one reason or another.

New Employee Support

Lastly, on the training front, we are investing a lot of time and attention on our new hires. Even in today's climate we are continuing to build our sales organization by bringing on up to 50 new reps each month. After these new reps spend 60 to 90 days in the field, they spend ten days in intensive sales training at our headquarters.

As part of this ten days of training, all new reps go through procurement process training, Miller Heiman *Conceptual Selling* and three or four days of specific training on how to sell individual product categories.

By the time they go home, they have really increased their effectiveness. After tracking their performance versus new hires that did not complete the program, we see a dramatic increase in productivity, because they're motivated and they really know how to do the job.

It is a significant investment on our part, but these new hires get to meet the senior management team, the sales support staff, etc., and they get excited about the company.

We are making changes in our marketing area, too. We want to continue to build and tailor our marketing programs around segmented customer needs. We have divided our market into four segments: strategic accounts, large accounts, mid market, and small market. We have the physical distribution infrastructure that allows us to play in all those areas, but in each one we are going to compete differently and we are going to sell product categories differently.

Leveraging Technology

We are also moving as fast as we can toward building more and more self-service applications into our Internet solution. Today, more than 35% of our business is through online ordering, and by the end of next year it will be higher than 50%.

In the future we will start looking at more technology to support sales, but we will focus on tools that provide key things. For example, lead management. We're in a target-rich environment where everybody needs our products. We intend to do a better job of managing our contact with prospects.

Another thing we're looking for is a sales automation tool that tracks all the programs a sales rep has presented to a customer or prospect. If we could have a picture perfect sales force automation system, it would include compensation, lead management, territory planning, quota setting tools, the program tracking tool, a comprehensive customer record and business intelligence tools integrated in it. Unfortunately, today there is no single tool that does all that; you've got to buy three or four different packages to get that all bundled.

Recommendations

What advice would I have for my peers? First, I would focus on marketing right. When I say marketing right, I mean do not try to build one size that fits all. It doesn't work. We are making changes in our marketing area. We want to continue to build and tailor our marketing programs around segmented customer needs.

Another thing I would do is continue to build or buy tools that truly make your sales people more effective and maximizes the use of their time. Third, I think we need to continue to invest in training, and not just for the reps but for the managers as well.

Finally, I have a firm belief that if you are really a great sales and marketing executive, you have to manage your company through influence. We rarely mandate things. I would never mandate that everybody on our team had to sell a certain way. What I do focus on is convincing our people that this is the right sales program because we designed it based on their input, and they will be the ones to sell it to the rest of the reps.

We have also found that if we are not on our revenue plan, we don't need to play heavy handed with the reps. In fact, we need to be better listeners during these times and be a great marketer by building on what they say. So, get your people involved along the way; that's one of the ways we have successfully built credibility.

TOM SCHMIDT

Tom Schmidt's family bought their first automobile franchise, Pontiac, in 1937. It was a car dealership and a blacksmith shop. They acquired a Chevrolet franchise in '38, then Tom's father and uncle split the franchises after the war. Tom became president in 1980 and the dealerships were recombined under his leadership in 2000. Today, The Ed Schmidt Automotive Group handles twelve franchises in all. They are a seller-servicer of cars and light-, medium- (including SUVs) and heavy-duty trucks, making them unique in serving all those market segments. Gross revenues have grown from $37 million in 1987 to over $220 million today with 310 employees. Tom is active in a number of business and community groups including the Toledo Symphony, Rotary, Young President's Organization, and the Boys and Girls Club of Toledo, to name just a few. Tom also sits on the Business Council for the College of Business at the University of Toledo and is a frequent presenter in their School of Sales.

BT

Buying a car remains the second biggest purchase most families make. Yet today, buyers want to complete this purchase in minimal time, with minimum hassle. They want immediate gratification and long-term satisfaction. The Ed Schmidt auto dealerships look to consistency in their sales and service culture and commitments to meet these dual objectives.

Everything Starts With A Plan

▶ The Importance of Market Research to the Plan

Everything starts with a plan and plans are meant to be followed in some ways, and to be broken in others. However, if you don't have a plan, you don't have a roadmap of where you want to go. In 1987, we strategically looked at what product lines we had, what market segments we served, what market segments we didn't, and then made a conscious decision about what we wanted to be.

For me, this exercise was very personal. I looked at the market and said "Jeez, I think truck sales are going to really pick up and I don't think General Motors is very well positioned in the truck segment." At the time, they weren't. In fact, Roger Smith had made a comment that trucks were going to be a fad, and yet here we are, almost 15 years past his tenure, and the market is still going in that direction. So we decided we really wanted to lead in trucks, and that's what we set out to do.

Minivans had taken off in the mid '80s and Chrysler had done very well with that. It was clearly a growing segment. At the same time, we were beginning to see some initial activity in pickup trucks. To give you an idea with GMC, in the early and mid-'80s, we sold 50 light-duty trucks a month. By the end of 1988, we were selling 100 a month. So there were clear indications that the market was really going to be heavy into trucks.

It may have started with the minivan craze, but today, who wants to drive a minivan? There are so many other choices and it's such a mundane vehicle to drive. There were going to be some spin-offs of minivans and we wanted to be the primary provider of trucks in our market.

Having said this, our first acquisition wasn't truck related. We hadn't done an acquisition before. My dad had never done one, and I had never done one. There were some car lines that became available that were in a European luxury segment that we didn't serve. So we moved into that to test the waters and to answer the questions, "How easy is it to do an acquisition? And how easy is it to integrate it into our dealerships?" Our first acquisition was Volvo.

Coming back to the truck side, we did a market analysis of the local market and asked, if we could have one truck franchise in addition to our GMC, what would it be? We ran some sophisticated market research and the results showed us that if we could at some point pick up a Jeep franchise, that would be a winner.

Coincidentally, within six months, the individual that had Jeep in Toledo, Ohio, came to me and asked if I would like to buy his franchise. Had I not had the data and really looked at where we were going to take our business, I probably would have said, "Well, I don't know." As it was, because I knew that was the number one franchise on our hit list, we bought it.

▶ Elements of the Plan

I started with a five-year business plan which was as much for external consumption as internal. I wanted something that I could show to lenders that included segments on financial profitability. It was to be a document that consolidated historically what we had done, who we are, where we think we're going. It included customer survey information—what our customers thought of us. And market share information: where were we strong, where were we weak, where were there opportunities? Were there segments that we should look at getting out of? Were there other segments we should look at getting into?

It's very much an updating process and an operational document as well as a strategic plan. I'm in the process of going through a revision on it right now. While we're in the course of everyday business, the plan helps us lift our heads up, take a look around, and see how the landscape changed. Also included in the plan are our accomplishments and areas that we need to improve.

▶ Elements of Change

We did a lot of surveying on the no-dicker-sticker approach. One-price selling became very popular in the late '80s. I think a lot of that came on with the advent of Saturn and their one-price approach. What we found with our survey results was that 80% of the customers really preferred the traditional buying process because they perceived that they had more control. We decided not to make the shift to one-price. There were several dealers in the Midwest that tried it, but I know of only a couple groups still selling that way today.

We did a survey on the Internet, too. Eighty percent of our customers shop our Internet site before coming to the dealership. We do not sell many cars online, but customers like to shop our inventory, check the value of their used car or look at what their financing options are prior to coming in. And I like it because, when the customer comes in armed with facts and figures, it makes it really easy for us to compress the buying time. People today are under such a tremendous time crunch. They don't want to spend four hours buying a car. They want to be able to buy it on their lunch hour and we have to be able to accommodate that.

Also, they want to find something on the lot. This is a tremendous change in the automobile business since I've been in it. In 1980, a good 60% of what we sold was ordered. Today, I would say it's 3%. People want to walk on the lot, see what we have, and make a choice—and they want to drive it home that day.

That's a tremendous change from when you would order your car, wait eight to 12 weeks, the car would come in, and then you'd take delivery of the vehicle. The selling is completely different than what it was in 1980. We're a society that in so many different ways wants to enjoy life and have instant gratification. People want to be gratified right now, and it's our job to see that they are.

To do this, inventories have to be meticulously maintained. We do trade with other dealers, but it's preferable to sell out of stock. Trading is very expensive and the quality assurance that you get back is not always 100%, so we really prefer to manage our inventories as closely as we can. Every week, we look at what's selling: what are the colors, the models, all the way down to which equipment packages, wheels and tires. We're constantly monitoring and trying to anticipate what is hot and what is not.

Your Reach Can Exceed Your Grasp

There have been several things I've done that have worked, and a lot of things that haven't. One that did not work for me, and has not worked for a lot of automobile dealers, is extending our reach beyond what we can control closely. After we'd done a couple of local acquisitions, I took out a map and drew a circle around part of the state in about a three-hour circumference. My theory was, if I can get to it in a day's drive, I should be able to manage it. And I proved that theory false. Three hours means yes, it takes three hours to get there; then you have to put in a day, and *then* you have to get home. That turns into a 14-, 15-, sometimes an 18-hour day.

So I brought my focus a lot closer to home and our holdings now are all in the Toledo area. Staying close makes managing inventories and assets a whole lot easier than trying to do it from far away. And I think a lot of business owners have discovered the same thing. I was fortunate to learn in a three-hour experience. Other car dealers had stores in Kansas City, Florida, Texas, and Michigan, and spent a lot of time going from place to place to place. I looked at that and decided that wasn't something that I really wanted to do. Now all of our companies are held locally.

I've gone through my own maturation. I don't have general managers on site because I'm interested in developing a management culture and not a culture that represents the general manager of a particular store. So we have two people onsite at each store: one heads our service operations and the other heads our sales operations. These two individuals report to a management group.

Consistent Culture, Consistent Experience

▶ Consistency of Experience

We're looking for a consistent culture across all the stores. And it's amazingly hard to provide a customer experience that is consistent across all sales people and all locations.

The difficulty can be one of a few things: training, individual management biases, and systems. You can train people and still have a management bias where an individual manager may look at corporate policy and say, "Well, I can to it better." It's his interpretation of what we would expect, and you wind up with different interpretations by location.

For example, with a high-line European import, customers expect a certain experience. They get it from Lexus, they get it from Mercedes. It's care, it's time, and it's the sales process that a customer goes through. I believe that the same sales standard should be deployed to a Chevrolet buyer. The customer may be different, the expectations may be different, but the quality that we give him in the sales experience should be absolutely the same.

The buyer that buys the Chevrolet and a guy that buys a Mercedes share something in common. Neither one of them has very much time—we know that. Our customers tell us either their buying experience is too long, or we're meeting their expectation in the time that they have allotted to buy a car. So we know that's a common thread. How a customer goes through the process and how we can condense that becomes very, very important.

It may surprise you to learn that regardless of the make, margins across the board are generally pretty thin. All manufacturers try to cut out the negotiating and haggling. The best way they see to do that is by reducing margin. What we have done, and I think where the industry is clearly trending, is toward multiple dealerships. There are cost savings based on how much we can streamline and cut out from back-office operations. And that's what we've been able to accomplish.

The other two areas where I think dealers make money are in financing and service. Is that something that also favors multi-dealer owners? Sure, because as we negotiate with insurance companies who are providing us a product, we're able to negotiate better rates for the company and, by consolidating all that, for our customers.

Service is a back-end operation. You have all the things that a customer would be familiar with, such as talking to a service writer, explaining what the problem is, and having a technician work on the car. But behind that, you have a parts department, an inventory behind that parts department, and people to serve that parts department. You have people that process warranty claims. Our ability has been to streamline those processes and consolidate them.

▶ Training to Improve Consistency

We accomplish this by providing sales training. We also provide service support so that the customers are getting the kind of support that would make them want to consider us again. We have an entering-training module that we put everybody through. We also have outside training assistance from Jim Moran, the distributor for Toyota in the southeastern U.S. He has a tremendous company and they provide us tremendous sales support, which translates into some service training as well.

The third component is that we provide all these wonderful tools for our employees. In the past we never bothered to follow up on the training piece to see how well our people used these tools. Now we have a certified Microsoft trainer in our company and he has his own lab. He runs classes and, in order to access an application, get into our CRM system, get onto our network, or even get an e-mail address here, you have to have successfully completed the training.

▶ Technology Lags Behind

Still, technology lags behind in the dealership world. If you look at the world in general and ask, "What's the cost of a piece of data today versus what it was ten years ago?" It's remarkably lower. Yet, in car dealerships, it really hasn't changed much. It's down a little bit, but not as much as it should be. This is primarily because, in a lot of dealership settings and in the automobile realm in general, people are working with old technology.

If you'd asked me a year ago, I would've said, "Wow, technology is really going to take us into some phenomenal areas!" And I think technology has its uses, but I don't look at my laptop as this new vista of opportunity the way I did maybe two or three years ago. I think a lot of companies are looking at that now and feel that the technology promise has been broken.

Am I an anti-technology person? No, not at all. But I'm now being very careful about how I deploy technology in our company. I still feel that this business and all sales-related businesses are people businesses. People start a transaction, people continue it, and people maintain relationships. Technology has a role in supporting that, but it is not going to be the primary method of getting orders and selling products.

Acquisition is always something that I'm interested in, but now I think that operations and creating a consistent customer experience are really the focal points of where we're headed in the next five years.

We've gotten through it, but most dealerships are operating on antiquated platforms. Reynolds + Reynolds is my supplier, but they're moving from a very antiquated technology that's 25 years old that they really have never updated. They put a new happy face on it, but it's really the same old stuff.

From a manufacturer's position, what Reynolds + Reynolds provides us has not really helped us move forward.

The innovations in IT that we've done have been driven internally. We put in our own network. We put in our own CRM solution that was independent of Reynolds + Reynolds. We did things beyond what they offered.

Recognize/Remember/Respect Your Customers

▶ Step 1: Consolidating Customer Information

Great personal experiences and relationships have been key to our success. When we were small this was much easier but, as mentioned earlier, the multi-dealer model is also becoming key to future success. This poses a unique challenge as we've gotten larger, which is to continue to provide people that one-on-one experience—even in a large company environment.

I don't know whether this holds true in other industries but we tend to operate in silos. Our silos are called the new car department, the used car department, the body shop, the service department, and the parts department. These are all little fiefdoms in and unto themselves, and when a customer walks in the front door of a dealership, he gets the opportunity to create first time impressions five different times. I don't know of another business that puts customers through that kind of torture.

One of the things I looked at first was, do we have a system? Can we get all of our data, consolidate it, and learn something about our customers by doing that? And so we've spent two years putting that part together. The next piece now is asking, "How do we reorganize our business units so that we can really put one person in charge of managing one customer relationship?"

When I said that Reynolds + Reynolds has done a very effective job holding us back, they create data files for every single department and those data files don't communicate with any other data file. Well, that was great technology back in the '70s but it's not great technology today. The notion of a relational database is still completely foreign to them.

What we wanted to do was take all of the purchasing behaviors and all the customer information from all of our departments—what they bought, when they bought it, what's the cumulative value of a customer. Up until a year ago, we didn't know this information. Today, we do. But it required taking all of those files from all the stores, from all the departments within all those stores, and then creating a unique customer file where all that information was held by customer.

So if a customer owns a Jeep and a Volvo and a VW Jetta, we know that. Knowing this is important because we can determine the value of our customers. Even if you bought the Jeep before you moved to Toledo but were now bringing it in for service, that's all in our record. And it's the same for business accounts. If a company buys 20 separate cars from us, we can manage that as an account.

▶ Step 2: Consolidating Operations

Consolidating everything was step number one. Step number two is where we are right now. How do we get out of this traditional automobile model of running five separate departments and go to managing our customers with one customer contact?

Let's say you buy a car at one of our dealerships from Chris. Chris would manage every aspect of that. When you came in for service, he would be the guy that would take care of you. I think the biggest challenge we have in our business today is that a customer comes in, forms a relationship with the salesman, buys the car from him and, hopefully, at the conclusion, feels good about it.

But now the salesman says, "Well, I've had that experience with you. Goodbye." And he turns it over to his service writer, somebody you've never met before. Now *you* get the opportunity to meet a whole new person. Right after you've made a significant investment and you're bringing it back for the first time, it's to a guy you don't know. Doesn't that just kind of fly in the face of developing a good customer relationship?

I think it does. And so the whole issue becomes, how do we change the internal structure of our company to accommodate that one customer-to-one employee relationship? How do we do that?

▶ Step 3: Redefining Roles and Relationships

Changing our structure is what we're struggling with right now. I'm looking at other companies. There's a company here in Toledo that manufactures doors and windows and they've figured out how to do this all over the world. I want to see how they do it. There are a couple of car companies that I'm familiar with in other locations that I'm going to visit. There are people that are thinking the same way I'm thinking, but it's not universal in our industry.

Some folks push back and ask, "Do you want your sales people doing service writing?" Well, I guess it depends how you look at it. Let's look at it with a couple of statistics. For a cold customer, somebody that walks in the dealership maybe because he saw our ad in the newspaper but has never done business with us, industry average tells us that we stand a one in five chance of closing that deal. If the customer has purchased from our dealership before, we stand a one in two chance of closing the deal. So the issue becomes, where do you want to spend your time and resources? Instead of advertising, maybe we should divert some of those funds to, say, hosting owner receptions/workshops.

Making One-On-One Relationships Work

Ten years ago I started reading Don Peppers and Martha Rogers's concepts on one-to-one marketing. Those concepts seemed so distant back then and some of it still seems distant today. But I think the hardcore reality is that, if you don't look at developing a relationship with your customers, they're going to find somebody else who will.

Let me say that one-to-one relationships are a lot easier to talk about than they are to do. After all the things I read about one-to-one relationships, an article in the Harvard Business Review summed it up the best. The first element is data consolidation: what do you know about your customers? There are some fundamental questions asked in that article and if you can't answer those questions, it's kind of pointless to go on to the next step.

The second part is, who are your customers and who aren't your customers? We now know that piece. And I think now the segmentation is, how do I find more people like the people that are our best customers, and what kind of an experience do they expect? That's the piece I'm working on right now.

I guess everybody uses a different definer. I use Claritas' *Prism* as a lead indicator to identify good customers and bad customers. It's a set of 400 different predictors by household. I like things to fit into neat little boxes. *Prism* defines each household by 52 different categories. Seemingly weird things like kids and cul-de-sacs are one predictive cluster. Others are country families defined by income, spending habits, kind of car they drive, where they live, all of that.

Prism clustering is something built into our database. I look to put things together for customer segments that we want and not market to people we don't want. If they happen to come in and buy a car, I'm not going to stop them. But there isn't any rule in the book that says I have to market to them.

Summary

The Ed Schmidt Automotive Group has seen enormous change in the past 20 years—not to mention the last 73. We have and continue to update our five-year plan. We're exploring new ways to organize ourselves, communicate, and maintain solid relationships with our customers. We're putting the tools and training, the strategy and tactics in place to continue our growth and accommodate future changes.

ROGER KOENIG

Roger Koenig is a leader in the communications and electronic equipment industries, known for his expertise in business leadership, executive management, product development, and building successful companies. Roger is CEO and founder of Carrier Access, a communications equipment manufacturer which he guided to a successful IPO in 1998. Carrier Access has delivered more than 2.5 million access lines to over 1,800 telecommunications companies and users. Prior to Carrier Access, Roger founded Koenig Communications and he also held engineering and management positions for ROLM and IBM Europe. Roger has won many awards, including the 1998 Esprit Entrepreneur of the Year, the 1999 Ernst & Young Entrepreneur of the Year, and a seventh place ranking among the 200 Best Small Companies as selected by Forbes magazine in 2000. Roger has a Master of Science degree in Engineering Management from Stanford University and a Bachelor of Science degree in Electrical Engineering from Michigan State University.

JD

When you are selling through a channel, you need to understand that your 'sales in' is a result of your channel's 'sales out.' If you want the channel to sell, you have to go beyond providing them a great product and value proposition; you also have to make it easy for them to sell.

At Carrier Access, we manufacture equipment that enables our customers, including many incumbent carriers and wireless service providers, to expand service revenue, lower operating costs, and extend capital budgets. By reducing capital expenditures, customers are able to deliver more network functionality and service for the same amount of money. As you can imagine, this has a very positive impact on capital constrained telecommunications businesses.

To give you an example without getting too technical, a major component of a wireless carrier's operating expense is the cost of connecting cell sites that are all over the landscape, back to the switching offices so it can in turn route calls and connect people.

We're in the process of delivering new equipment for nationwide deployments in the wireless business that consolidates the number of transport lines—T1s, DS3's, etc.—needed to make those connections. Providing the same service with fewer lines will result in a significant improvement to that wireless service provider's bottom line.

Since we started in 1995, our company has consistently raised the issue of capital savings. We promised our customers that we would provide systems that did a superior job of communications service integration, at a lower cost.

We delivered on that promise and then waited for the orders to come in. To be honest, the volume was not what we expected. We went back to our customers and said, "We delivered a killer solution for digital Centrex desktop services. We overcame a huge capital expense challenge. We overcame the operating cost problems of actually getting this installed. Why aren't you selling a lot more digital Centrex subscribers?"

We felt we had delivered a solution to a universal problem, but our concern was that the only markets that seemed to be getting any traction were government applications, such as the state of Pennsylvania, and federal government agencies. We wanted to know why they were not taking this offering out to a much broader user base.

The answers that we got back from our customers were surprising in their consistency. While the products we delivered were great, they were too complex for our telecom service providers to easily sell to their end user business customers.

When Value Proposition Is Not Enough

We're proud that our solutions can handle a multitude of situations, but we found that the flexibility of our offerings were often intimidating to the sales people working for our telecom customers. For them to effectively represent our products to their customers, they first needed to determine what the needs of that individual client were, and then work through a network proposal. Once that was defined, they then needed to develop an accurate quote for the cost of the system.

So, while we offered a strong value proposition to the firms we sold to, in the end that was not enough. We were expecting the channel sales people to invest too much time and effort to get to the point where they could close a deal.

As a result, we realized we had a critical training problem that we needed to overcome. Up to that point, the focus of our sales process was on the steps that we needed to go through to convince our customers of the value our solutions represented to them. We decided we needed to go beyond that and determine ways we could help their sales people translate and apply those value propositions to their customers.

The Realities Of Your Channel's World

Yet, at the same time, we knew we also had to work within the realities of today's marketplace. The first reality was that end user customers, the people ultimately using a telecom service provider, really want solutions to their specific communications needs. They want to communicate with other people—not all other people, just the business associates, colleagues, or family members they choose—when they want to talk to them. And if that person is not available, then those customers want to be able to leave a message, so the recipient can call back at his or her convenience.

From the end user perspective, this appears to be a simple objective. But as you start to view the whole world of telecommunications you quickly realize that ours is a very technology-encumbered universe. End users find they need multiple phone numbers: office, cell, even home. Each has its own voice mailbox, and each mailbox may have different methods for retrieving messages. They don't want to deal with all of this; they want to purchase services from a provider who can make the complexity go away.

The second reality was that these end users work for all different sizes of companies, from Fortune 1000 firms spending millions per month on services, to mid-sized companies spending thousands or tens of thousands a month, to very small firms spending just hundreds a month. Obviously, solutions for a Fortune 1000 company will need to take into account many more variables than those for a ten-person firm.

The third reality was that the sales people calling on these accounts are often much more product focused than solution focused. Over the years we have created silos of sales expertise. Today, there are sales people who are great at selling voice, but are weak at selling data, or vice- versa. This situation is in direct conflict with the goals all carriers strive for today, which is to blend a combination of voice and data services that work on a variety of software and hardware systems, so they can create a differentiation in the marketplace.

A perfect example is Virtual Private Network voice services, where companies put their enterprise voice connectivity on their data networks.

For an end user firm, this saves money; it provides better efficiency and has great bottom line value. But for the service provider, it is still a specialized craft to sell and deliver these solutions. This product orientation will change over time, but in the near term we cannot count on these sales people to be able to single-handedly manage the entire front-end of the process for a solution sale.

It would be great if these sales people could turn to their systems engineers (SEs) for help. But the fourth reality of the marketplace is that those people already have more than they can manage today. In our current soft economy, and the subsequent cost cutting atmosphere, the ratio of sales people to SEs has gone from two or three sales people to one SE, to as high as 15 to one. To expect a fewer number of SEs to learn all the intricacies of selling more complex solutions is simply too much to ask.

Focusing On Your Channel's Sales Process

It became clear that in order for us to grow more quickly, we needed to enable a service provider's sales team to simply and quickly analyze the needs of their customers, then communicate what a solution would look like and how it would benefit them.

We focused our thinking on ways we could take responsibility for the front-end of the sales process for our customers. Ideally, it would have been great to have a Carrier Access person available to go on every end user customer call, but for financial and resource availability reasons that was impractical. Yet that idea did help set the stage for our initiative to reengineer the sales process. Our task was to determine how we could provide our customer's sales people with access to the wealth of knowledge our company had, so they could easily do the front-end sales tasks themselves.

The answer we came up with was to create a web-based expert sales facility that would focus on two goals. The first would be a detailed needs analysis capability. Our objective here was to enable any sales person, with a minimal amount of training, to leverage our sales support system. They would walk their customer through a structured series of questions that would identify the end user firm's communications needs, and match those needs to one of our service offerings.

Our second goal was to have the system generate a detailed proposal based on those end user needs. This would start with a plain English description of the problem that needed to be solved, followed by an overview of how we were going to deal with those issues. Our objective here was to take over the responsibility for generating the proposal, building a detailed view of how the network would function, spelling out all the hardware and implementation costs, and so on.

We felt that if we could achieve these two goals, we could take out a lot of the pain and frustration associated with selling our solutions, and also help the service provider's sales people become much more productive at delivering digital services. As their 'sales out' increased, our 'sales in' would go up correspondingly.

Technology Enables The Channel's Effectiveness

To accomplish this, we first started looking at the complexities of the detailed business discussions taking place between the service provider sales person and the prospect. To do this, we actually sat down with our customers and jointly walked through the process.

Through these discussions we realized that during this customer interaction several steps needed to be completed in order to determine the client's needs. We also needed to educate them on the idea that new solutions may exist to meet those needs and then motivate them to do something about those issues now.

The needs analysis was the first hurdle to overcome. Today, when you walk into a retail store and start to talk to the owner about their communications needs, they'll say, "Well, we have a point-of-sale network, and we can't impact that because it is backed up and is redundant. Then we have this for our voice communications, we have that for sales people, and another system for the warehouse." As you can see, things start getting very complicated, very fast. But this is typical in business environments today.

We really took the time to understand all the issues that could come up in these customer conversations and then looked for ways to optimize that process. Our goal was to provide a tool for service provider sales reps that would guide them through a simple, easy process for conducting a comprehensive needs analysis.

What we came up with is a very streamlined process that is based on 14 questions at most, in plain English, that the sales person needs to get answers to in order to cover all of the cases that could come up. Behind these questions is a sophisticated model that understands all the implications, co-requisites and prerequisites for dealing with the prospect's communications environment.

The system is designed so that the rep could record the answers during the conversation and enter them into the system later, or actually use the system interactively during the call.

The next step was to have the system take the customer's input and build a comprehensive proposal for the sales person to present. Based on the answers to these questions, the system creates network diagrams, overviews on all the equipment and part lists, and all the relevant pricing data. The proposal also covers the implementation plans.

Optimizing The Sales Call

Now, compare this selling approach to how these sales people *had* been working. Prior to this, to ensure they got all the information they needed, they would often have to conduct the needs analysis process through multiple calls that could take hours. Now they can do it in minutes, with a single call.

Next, in the past, lacking the full product line knowledge themselves, the sales person would have to farm out parts of the data to various expertise silos within their company to attempt to understand what the customer told them, and then what they could do to improve that communications environment. Again, this typically involved getting access to those SE resources that were already stretched to the limit.

Now that expertise is available to the sales person literally at his fingertips, and that knowledge base is always current. As things change—prices, features, compatibility issues, etc.—those new data elements are updated in the central system. This process ensures that sales people are working with the most current information available.

Finally, again looking at how things were once done, when sales reps had an idea of the various technologies that needed to be integrated, they then faced the task of translating those concepts into a business language that the customer could understand. They needed to create proposals that translated technology into plain English answers for their customers. They also needed to spell out the business value that would be created by making these communications changes.

Today, our system completes that process automatically. When channel sales people use the system, it creates the proposal verbiage, network diagrams, and the implementation plan for a given customer's situation. Since this information is based on the knowledge elements in the centralized sales expert system, the consistency and accuracy of these documents is significantly improved as compared to the past 'one-off' proposal approach.

We named the system **WICK (WAN Integrated Connection Kit)**. It is actually an application we developed in-house and is very cost effective because we built it using generally available web-based software development tools.

The response we have received from our customers has really exceeded our expectations. The first thing they say is that they have never seen anything like it. The next thing they tell us is that they feel appreciated and that their success really matters to someone else. Because we developed this tool for their use, we've demonstrated that we understand the sales challenges they are facing.

To maximize the acceptance of the system by their sales people, we have designed the application so that it can be integrated directly into the service provider's existing Internet site or sales portal. It can also be branded with their company name, versus appearing to be a separate program from Carrier Access.

The Value Of Optimization

The value of **WICK** is evident the very first time you use the system. When we demonstrate the application to service provider sales people, their jaws drop open. They see that they can go through the needs analysis, solution creation, and proposal generation steps of the sales process in 10 to 15 minutes, and actually can leave the customer with a very detailed 35-page proposal at the end of the call.

This changes the entire sales process. The first benefit is that it facilitates the sales person in making the transition from selling products to selling solutions. And, sales reps do not have to spend months becoming experts on all the intricacies of the technologies involved. This shift increases the value of these reps in the eyes of the end user, because they are now more knowledgeable and professional compared to their product-focused counterparts.

Secondly, this system collapses the front-end of the sales process down to its absolute minimum. Now in the course of a day, a sales person has time to see more customers and easily generate more high quality proposals. More times at bat translates into more sales, for both our channel partner and us.

A third benefit, tied to the collapsing of the sales process, is that new markets are now open to the service provider. It has been interesting to watch the telecommunications space develop over time. Most firms segment the market into large accounts (Fortune 1000 or 2000), mid-tier firms, and small accounts.

Because of the economics of sales—cost versus revenue potential—most companies target their selling activity towards the larger accounts. So you have thousands of sales people targeting the Fortune 1000, and only a few calling on the rest of the world.

However, if you are able to make a single call on a mid-tier or smaller firm, and complete a full sales process during that call, now you change the economics and make those accounts more attractive targets. If you dedicate part of your sales force to this portion of the market, you are tapping into a much less competitive environment, where often your sales person may be the only rep that company encounters.

The fourth benefit, which we achieve jointly, is the movement towards becoming stronger business partners with our customers. When they see us come in the door, they don't automatically see us as a vendor. Instead, they see Carrier Access as a company who is genuinely interested in their business, and willing to make the investments needed to help ensure they are successful in the marketplace.

Creating A Win, Win, Win Environment

Ultimately, to be successful in sales today you have to understand what the 'win' is for all the parties involved in the process. Make no mistake; our objective at Carrier Access is to sell more products. But that need has to be blended with the objectives of others.

The service providers we sell to want to get beyond commoditization of telecommunications services and create real value-added solutions that will meet the needs of the marketplace and create more customer loyalty.

Their sales people need to be able to achieve the sales volumes their companies expect. In order to achieve their goals, they need help and services that fundamentally increase their effectiveness and also support them in making the transition to solution sales.

Our success depends on our ability to help the service providers we work with, and the sales people that work for them, meet their goals. We think the **WICK** initiative goes a long way towards that, and in doing so creates a final win for the end user firm, as they get the value they really wanted to buy in the first place.

MICHAEL CLAYTON

If you spend any time at all talking to Michael Clayton, you will quickly recognize his passion for increasing the performance levels of sales teams. Mike has over 20 years of engineering, marketing, and sales experience with multi-national high technology firms such as Plessey and GEC. In 1991, he founded OutSource International, a U.K.-based provider of global high-value technology and services to clients such as Cisco Systems, Lucent, Dell Computer, and PictureTel. Mike grew OutSource to profitability through organic growth and acquisition to become a publicly limited company prior to ultimately being purchased by outside investors in 1999. He is currently CEO of Radiant Real–Time, the leading supplier of Sales Process Optimization solutions that provide a guided selling environment for sales staff. Radiant's client list includes leading international companies such as Hewlett-Packard, Nortel Networks, Avaya, Sony Ericsson, British Telecom, and Prudential. His new company's web site is www.radiantreal-time.com.

JD

> **To meet the sales challenges we are encountering, one of the key things we are going to have to continue to leverage is Customer Relationship Management (CRM) technology. These systems have shown that they can improve the productivity and effectiveness of sales teams. However, the tools that got us to where we are today are not the solutions that will get us where we need to be tomorrow.**

Let me start by stating that a part of what Radiant delivers to its customers is a set of software solutions that could be classified as CRM applications. With that being the case, I feel I can speak from experience about the changes we have to make in the CRM marketplace.

If I were going to grade the overall performance of the CRM industry over the past few years, I would probably give it a 'C+' or possibly a 'B-' in terms of delivering value to sales people. We are seeing an increasing number of cases where companies that have successfully implemented these systems have reported some improvements in sales productivity.

The reason I cannot grade this any higher is that we achieved these improvements by helping sales teams solve some of the simpler issues they were dealing with. Up to this point, what we have been doing is increasing the efficiency of sales people.

The vast majority of sales professionals using CRM systems today are leveraging the contact management, office suite, opportunity management, and forecasting functionality they provide. These are useful tools for tracking activities, communicating across sales teams, allowing sales people to create mailings or presentations, and so forth.

If users become proficient at using these applications they can in fact increase their productivity, which will free up more time for them to sell. But to hit our numbers today, making more calls is only part of the solution, and it is the easier part. The harder half of the equation is making more 'effective' calls.

The Sales Effectiveness Challenge

Sales today is an increasingly challenging profession. The environment we sell into is one of constant transformation in terms of buying attitudes, product innovations, global competition, economic trends, etc. Dealing with this never-ending change is not a matter of making sales people more efficient, it is making them more effective.

There have been several studies that have come out over the past two years, including the one by Insight Technology Group, that highlight the effectiveness challenges we are facing. The problems sales executives are encountering are issues such as getting new sales people productive more quickly, introducing new products more successfully, improving cross-selling and up-selling, selling value to avoid discounting, adequately supporting channel partners, improving customer loyalty, and so forth.

Perhaps a part of accomplishing these objectives may have to do with helping sales people find more time to sell. However, I would be willing to bet that virtually every Chief Sales Officer, if given a choice between increasing the time a sales person has to sell, versus fundamentally improving his ability to sell, would take effectiveness over efficiency in a heartbeat.

To achieve significant improvements in sales effectiveness, several challenges need to be overcome. The first and most important of these is that we need to understand and define a science for the manner in which we sell. The only way to do this will be to bring process management to sales.

Since no two companies sell alike, this will not be a one-size-fits-all solution for the world of sales. Even within a company, we find that there is not a single process, but multiple processes that need to be implemented depending on which products, geographies, economic buyers, etc. upon which you are focusing your selling efforts.

To create these processes, we need to start by motivating top sellers to share their expertise. Once their input has been synthesized, and those processes are defined, we then need to develop methods to reinforce, and enforce, that our sales teams use them. We need to find ways to motivate sales people to embrace these new approaches to selling. They need to be able to quickly and easily see how these processes will increase their sales effectiveness, as well as their professionalism in the eyes of their prospects and customers.

We need these new processes to be embraced not just by our own people, but our channel partners as well. To accomplish this, we will have to quit focusing on our own wants and needs, and instead find ways to focus on theirs. If we can help them more easily sell to their customers, then our revenue objectives will be easily met.

Finally, we need to drop the 'us versus them' mentality, and start to see sales as an integral part of the overall enterprise. We need to find ways of working closer with marketing, support, manufacturing, distribution, finance, and so forth; sharing information, knowledge, ideas, marketplace feedback, etc. so we are all fundamentally more effective.

Evolving CRM Towards Sales Effectiveness

When you consider a business challenge of this magnitude, you quickly see that technology is going to have to play a pivotal part in empowering the performance levels of our sales teams, not just their productivity levels. The CRM industry will have a key role to play in enabling change. But to accomplish this, we are going to have to see some fundamental changes in the types of solutions we are delivering to sales people.

When I look across the CRM landscape, the gaps between what is available and what is needed are very apparent. Consider the state of the art for CRM today:

- The systems are inflexible and demand that sales people work the way the systems have been designed. We need to make sure that the tools we provide work for the people, versus forcing the people to work for the tools.

- The functionality provided merely helps track sales. We need to provide solutions that assist sales people in generating sales.

- If sales methodology support or milestone management capabilities are available in the tool, they are generally too static in nature to be of any value. We need to provide dynamic guidance on *how* to make the milestone happen for a unique prospect to be truly useful.

- Enhancing or customizing these applications requires expensive support from scarce IT programming resources to make the system useable. Sales operations people should be able to perform that function easily and quickly by themselves.

- To get anything done, sales people typically have to open several different programs to do their work. All the information they need has to be made available via a seller-centric interface.

- Within CRM applications, sales people have to click through dozens of screens, only to find the information they want isn't there. They need to find what they need in three clicks or less.

- Data currency is a huge problem for CRM applications today, often resulting in sales people being provided with inaccurate information. We need the systems to administer themselves to ensure everything that is presented is up to date.

- Most applications merely deliver customer or product 'data' to sales people. We have to go beyond that and give them access to knowledge about their solutions, competitors, and the marketplace in general.

- There is also no intelligence to accompany information delivery. We need to enhance these systems so that they provide 'coaching' into how to leverage that knowledge to accomplish the task at hand.

- Once the systems are implemented, it is hard to go back and make modifications to them. Based on the dynamics of sales, we need to provide massive flexibility to modify the processes and the information content based on the changes that occur in the markets sales people live in.

- While a lot of thought has been given to how to streamline data input into these systems, little has been done to optimize the use of that data. We need to provide insight-focused reporting capabilities so that management and sales people alike can see how they have been selling and can optimize their successes and minimize their failures.

- Finally, CRM implementations have been costing millions of dollars and taking years to accomplish. The sales challenges we face are now – not next year; *now* is when these systems need to be available.

This is the 'Mandate for Change' for the CRM marketplace. If the vendor community adopts this mindset, then the real power that technology can provide will finally be realized. Let me provide a scenario for how this new generation of CRM tools will supercharge how we sell: a concept we have been referring to as Sales Process Optimization.

Sales Process Optimization

The core of these new CRM applications will be a process database. These sales processes should not be confused with the sales methodology support already available in some CRM applications. It is worth taking a moment to explain the difference.

A sales methodology is a framework for the steps a sales person should use to engage a customer. These are available from a variety of sales training firms. They provide value by creating a common culture within sales as to how they sell.

A sales process sits on top of whatever methodology you have adopted and takes the sales person to the next level of detail by giving him or her insights into how to accomplish those steps. While you can have a single sales methodology that spans the entire sales force, you need to allow for extreme flexibility in the number of sales processes. The reason for this is that processes vary depending on the specific sales situation in which a sales person is engaged.

For example, you may have a completely different process for selling new products than you would for selling commodities. Selling to the government will entail a different approach than selling to commercial accounts. Selling to a CEO will obviously be different from selling to a department head. Geographies may influence how you sell; you may have a more relationship-focused sales process for selling in Japan versus the United States.

The initial task to create this repository of sales processes will not rely on having programmers do the job. Instead, these new CRM systems will provide a software wizard that guides any knowledgeable person through the creation process. A sales operations manager, a top sales rep, a sales trainer, or a sales manager who is familiar with how sales are being made today can easily transfer his or her knowledge into the system.

A sales methodology may include a step called 'Educate the Client.' Under this scenario, the process kicks in to define all the actions that should be taken to complete that step. This might include instructing the sales rep to perform a company overview presentation, provide the prospect with reprints of articles advocating your product design, give references that can be contacted to verify your claims, etc.

The wizard will take this a step further and actually allow the sales process owner to link all of the materials a sales person would use for each of those actions. Once the process repository is populated, then it is immediately available to start coaching sales people on how to more effectively sell.

For example, a sales person has received a lead from marketing that the vice president of manufacturing for a firm in his territory has expressed interest in one of the company's products. The sales person accesses the Sales Process Optimization system and assigns that opportunity to the process that matches the prospect's areas of interest. This process then guides the sales rep through understanding who to engage with, why, and then clearly shows him how to be successful.

Leveraging all the knowledge elements about sales that have been previously captured, the system shares the latest best practices as well as highlighting all of the sales support resources available to complete that action. Even before the sales person makes her first call, she can start to formulate a targeted strategy for how to proceed based on the knowledge and insights contained in the system.

After making a preliminary phone call to the prospect and setting up the first appointment, the sales person comes back to the system and shares the additional information she has gathered, such as, "The budget for this purchase is 'X'," "The competitors being considered are 'Y' and 'Z'," "The main evaluation criteria will be product reliability and price," and so forth.

Based on this new knowledge, the sales process may be further optimized. The sales person may be informed that on the first call, she should take a reprint of an article that appeared in a major publication highlighting how the company had just won an award for excellence in manufacturing based on the reliability of their products.

The system now becomes an invaluable aid all the way through the sell cycle. As the sales person tells the system more, the specificity and detail of how to best manage the sales process is continually improved.

For example, let's say the sell cycle has progressed to the 'Generate Proposal' stage in the sales methodology. By accessing the Sales Process Optimization system, sales people will be able to leverage a host of knowledge available across the enterprise. The system informs the sales person that there are five other sales opportunities that have closed in the past three months that have characteristics similar to the deal she is working on, and tells her who the lead rep is on each of those accounts.

Now knowing who to call, she picks up the phone and is able to strategize with one of her peers in Europe, North America, Asia, etc. and gets invaluable coaching on what to do, what not to do, and what last minute pitfalls to expect.

Realizing The Promised ROI From CRM

That is the power CRM should have been delivering for the last decade. What sales professional would not make this type of system an active part of his or her daily workflow?

Once we enhance these application frameworks to support Sales Process Optimization, all the rest of the promises of CRM for sales fall into place. First, we will have delivered on our objective of increasing not just the productivity of the sales force, but their effectiveness as well, by giving them access to the optimal process they should employ to deal with the sales opportunity at hand.

Second, we will give sales management that laser-like view into the opportunity pipeline that they have needed for so long. They will be able to look at every deal and see what steps and actions have been completed, which ones are scheduled, and which ones are yet to be defined.

Based on these insights, managers will be able to easily determine when to coach a rep and when to actively intervene in an opportunity. And all this will be available to management as a by-product of the sales people using the system to meet their own needs, versus relying on sales reps to take time to input data for yet another administrative task we have dumped on them.

Based on the insights into the real status of deals, the current challenge of generating accurate forecasts will be minimized. Senior management will have access to all the details of how many opportunities are being worked on, exactly how far they have progressed, and when deals stall, they will be able to determine where the bottlenecks in the process are occurring.

The emotion of hoping deals will close will be replaced with the reality of what still needs to be accomplished. With this knowledge in hand, a company can more effectively decide how many, of what products, in what color, for what part of the world, should be manufactured by when.

The CRM Vendor Challenge

None of this is fantasy. We are working on many of these projects today where this exact type of performance improvement has been delivered, so I know for a fact it can be done. The issue for the CRM industry as a whole is, how many other vendors will follow suit, and how quickly?

Making this transition will decide the future destiny of the CRM marketplace. The age of CRM 'hype selling'—convincing customers to buy CRM tools just because everyone else was—is over. Going forward, sales teams will make investments only in technology that offer real solutions to the real challenges they face.

How many vendors will successfully negotiate this market shift to Sales Process Optimization, I am not sure. But I can promise you that those who continue to focus on sales efficiency and ignore the marketplace demands for significant increases in sales productivity and effectiveness will soon perish. It is as simple as that.

MICHAEL FIELDS

Michael Fields is a technology investor and business executive with over 35 years of experience. He is a managing member of NewVista Capital, an early stage venture capital fund, and Chairman of The Fields Group, a management-consulting firm for emerging information technology companies. I met Mike in 1989 when he was President of Oracle USA for Oracle Corporation. He left Oracle and founded OpenVision Technologies, Inc., where he served as Chairman and Chief Executive Officer. OpenVision, a leading supplier of systems management applications for open client/server computing environments, was later acquired by Veritas. Mike has also worked at Applied Data Research and Burroughs Corporation. His career in the computer industry began at The Equitable in New York City in 1964 and continued with his service in the U.S. Air Force. I always love to get together with Mike. He has a big laugh and a great sense of humor. And, with his experience and success, I always get great executive perspective.

BT

> **CFOs are taking on more direct operating responsibility within corporations because CIOs are reporting to the CFO again. We went through a period when the CIO was considered to be equal to the CFO, and everyone thought the Internet and the 'whatever.coms' would rule the business world. Recently, a lot of corporations discovered that costs were getting completely out of hand—these guys were writing big checks without proper due diligence. Now we are getting back to basics, especially in sales.**

Looking Back Over The Tech Wreckage

Let me establish my perspective on what I believe has occurred over the past two years. For those of us who have been in the technology space—the true technology space—we went to bed with the devil. What I mean by that is we allowed companies that were not tech companies to be defined as such. They were marketing companies or distribution companies, but they were not technology companies. They were using a form of technology in order to further their particular core business attribute.

However, if these companies had been defined for what they really were, and if everybody had known what they were, they wouldn't have been successful. Pets.com was not a technology company, but we in the industry allowed it to be defined as one. Why? All boats are lifted by a rising tide. Everyone viewed this as an event that would somehow change the world.

So the Webvans, the Pets.coms, and others were defined as part of this rising tide of technology. Further, actual tech companies started to emulate these companies, calling themselves a "Whatever.com." We came up with something called ASP (application service provider) and tried to become it. Technology was supposedly changing the world but, in reality, it wasn't changing the real world.

High tech bought into this cycle for only one reason: the share price and values were going up. This was not about market share. It was about the money, pure and simple. The more money that you could raise, or the more money at which your assets could be valued, the better. And when everyone's focus became always and only about the money, that's when we lay down with the devil.

Now, the business models of these companies have been exposed for what they were. Selling a $5 bag of dog food over the Internet, paying $15 to ship it, and only charging the customer $2 is not a business model that can endure. However, many people became enamored by it.

People raised and spent a lot of capital and, to some extent, it was almost incestuous. I may be using strong words, but companies became awfully close with each other. For example, a new Whatever.com would raise $50 million, with the venture arm of an established tech company investing $10 million in the round. Then, that Whatever.com would buy $15 million worth of that established tech company's products and services. The process added to the buzz of the start-up and the revenue of the established company.

The cycle existed, all the boats were rising, and everyone was happy and smoking from the same pipe. I sat on the Ford Motor Company's Advisory Board, and at the time, they had $20 billion in cash, untold billions of dollars in assets, and about $150 billion a year in revenue. At that time, they were highly profitable and had a market capitalization of $43 billion.

At the same time, Commerce One, which was pioneering the notion of B2B electronic commerce, had a $46 billion market cap. We were saying, "Wow, isn't that wonderful." But the reality was that it was never sustainable.

It was a Ponzi scheme and if you got in early and got out, you made a lot of money. If you got in early and didn't get out, or if you got in late, you're in a terrible, terrible situation today. The bubble was not sustainable, and we've just now started to come through it.

Back To The Future

Where we are now is akin to *Back to the Future*. Right now, it's about 1989 in the tech world. What I mean by that is we are back to having to prove our value proposition to our customers and the marketplace. The technology-buying market is not recognizing unsubstantiated value, particularly in relation to small companies. If you don't have customers, a track record, visibility into your revenue and profitability over the next couple of years, and cash in the bank, you're not going to attract any investments.

We took OpenVision public in 1996. Even then, if you didn't have two or three quarters of growing earnings and revenue, and if you couldn't show the bankers that the next year was pretty much in the bag, you couldn't interest any potential investors. Well, that's where we are now. If you don't have those things, you can't find anybody to talk to. And those that want to talk to you are looking for very low capitalization rates around anything related to technology.

So, it's back to the future relative to what the two markets look like and what the client base is expecting from the providers of technology. It's been reported that General Motors spent nearly $300 million testing different kinds of Internet-based technologies and market solutions. You've probably read that they recently wrote all of that off.

They wrote it off because it never got integrated within their core business. This is just one example of the significant change that's taken place very quickly. The tech world looks a lot like one of those cartoons where the coyote chases the roadrunner; we ran straight off the cliff and only had enough time to look down and say, "Oops," before we fell. There was no getting back to the ledge—which is what I think we've faced as businesses.

What It Means Moving Ahead

The other aspect of being back to the future is we can dust off and put back into use a lot of the sales tactics and strategies that existed before; value selling is back. Customer service, understanding your clients' long-term business objectives, and knowing how to become a value-add to their overall interest—rather than focusing on what you are selling—are all back now.

There was a time when customers wanted only to meet with kids because they thought young people were the only ones that understood what was going on. Now, customers want to see guys with some gray hair because they have stronger business perspective and better business acumen.

What's different now, of course, is customers have found ways to utilize the Internet to their advantage. The Internet as a tool has not lost its purpose. The difference is most companies understand that the Internet itself will not make or break a business. What the Internet does is provide an opportunity; the Internet is another facility or capability that can enhance your position with clients, improve your connection to the marketplace, and improve your profitability.

Overall, the Internet requires and causes other things to happen, just as you would expect from any other business application. The advantage for people with industry experience is that the market today looks like the real beginnings of the client/server computing and database computing business cycles that took place in the 1980s and 1990s.

The interest of late was, "Don't spend any time with the customer. This is a fast-moving, fast-paced world. Decisions have to be made quickly. If you don't make the decision now, somebody's going to make it for you and you're going to miss your business window." That's how it has been for the last few years.

The focus has now changed back to the way it was before: strategic business issues are important. That's not to say that companies stopped experiencing critical issues, but I think more firms are thinking more strategically today. They are asking, "How does this apply to our overall goals as a company? How does this meet our overall strategic objectives?" When it comes to marketing enterprise technologies, I think the sales folks have to realize that they're part of a bigger picture—the value of the company.

We may have returned back to the future, but this doesn't mean that the solution is the same. You have to carry the impact of the Internet and of global communications as part of this package. But we are back to the fundamentals of understanding the business objectives and goals of the company, understanding how you support those with your product offerings, and understanding where you fit into the dynamics of the firm.

Protracted Sales Cycles To Continue

Even with a clear connection between a sales proposition and a company's strategic direction, a high percentage of sales efforts are resulting in a 'no decision' or a delayed decision. This comes from the fact that the tech sector over promised and under delivered, and people and corporations took major hits because of it. If you look at CIOs in the U.S. marketplace today, you see a lot of new faces. In some cases, those new faces are replacing other new faces from the last four or five years.

Corporations have each spent tens of millions of dollars trying to implement strategic programs. We can't expect that just because we can see a definable business objective and the customer also sees it, they'll be able to move quickly to change. Their qualification process is not very different from eight or nine years ago. CIOs two years ago could make $50 million decisions with a stroke of a pen; now they may have to get Board approval. Certainly, they need CFO or Operating Committee approval before they can move.

As a result, companies are implementing justification processes and are vetting proposals. These programs will probably crystallize in another year or two. Deals are going to take longer, they're going to be harder to close, and justification will have to be proven. The value proposition will have to be both articulated and proven. All of these factors will extend the length of the sales cycle.

Companies Focus On Business Value

In the technology space, some companies have recognized the value space that they have to be in. They're trying to find ways to struggle through even as they're hurting in terms of market value. One is my former company, Veritas. They have truly built on their objective of being a full-service supplier for the storage management industry. They are offering services in addition to products and other capabilities to their customers.

BEA is another company whose success was sparked by the acceptance of the Internet for business process. But their roots go back to Tuxedo, an IBM mainframe product. Their understanding of the value potential for enterprise technology within a business was always very high; now, the management team is finding ways to execute on that.

On the buy side, there are some firms that have built on the use of the Internet as a tool, rather than making the Internet their business. Marriott Corporation, for example, has married the Internet to their business, but in ways that add value to their customer service. There are companies out there attempting to implement technology the right way. Marriott is actually using the information that they garner from their technology. Another good example is Safeway, who figured out how to execute the Webvan idea correctly. Overall, the checks and balances that are taking place in the corporate world are having a pretty significant effect.

U.K. Benefits From Skipping Internet Fever

I spend 30% of my time in the U.K. It seems the U.K. didn't get as enamored with the Internet economy as we did. That has proven to be opportunistic for their companies and their tech industry because they stayed focused on true business processes—not just Internet mindshare. Look for this to be interesting competition for new emerging technology in the future.

Economic Prediction

I don't think we'll see a major pickup in the technology world until 2004. I think we should face facts: we're going to have another tough year in 2003; it's going to be difficult to expand; and you have to find ways to get to profitability and hold your position with some modest growth up through the next 18 to 24 months. If you can't, you'll be out of business.

Technology has allowed corporations to reduce their hiring because of increased productivity. Also, when companies merge technology with the business, it puts them in a position where they can actually manage and sustain their sales operations successfully.

If you think about it, there have been companies in the last six to nine months that reduced their staff by 20% to 30%. Going back 15 or 20 years, if you reduced your staff by that much, you were going to be out of business because you didn't have a sustainable company. But we're capable of these kinds of reductions, and the main enabling factor is technology.

Further, I would venture to say that technology bought before the Internet bubble has been the true enabler. This technology is finally an integral part of the corporation. Lots of folks have been hired and let go since that time.

We're back to basics from both the customer standpoint and the technology company's standpoint. For younger companies, early-stage companies that are looking to become bigger, the need to partner for distribution is now much higher than it was before. Building serious distribution channels, even with the advent of CRM technology, is very difficult for most young, small companies to achieve. Finding partners that have distribution capability and could focus on your solution is the future for early-stage companies.

There has been a lot of talk about sales, marketing, and technology. CRM companies seem to have unwarranted faith that their technology will help figure out everything that's needed to identify and connect with buyers. I hate to say it, but it's similar to the intelligence community's misplaced faith in technology. People believed that, through the use of satellites, cameras, listening posts, and telephone interception, somehow all this technology was going to answer our questions. The feeling was that we didn't need people on the ground that spoke the language and were up close and personal with our enemy. Now, we know we need both components.

I expect to see value-added resellers partnering with companies that have another piece of the same puzzle and saying, "Okay, let's work together to maximize our efforts to sell." Traditional 'pure play' distribution companies will also play a role. Remember, it's going to come back to understanding the business from a buyer's standpoint—understanding the customer's business and goals. And having the right solutions in order to meet them.

That makes business pretty personal. If you've got a team of people that knows markets, knows companies within those markets, and what are their needs, they can successfully meld together some solutions in order to satisfy the customer's objective.

Playing Way Ahead

This project began when I was graciously asked to give the commencement speech at the university three years ago. At the event, I noticed that, of the 150 graduates, only eight had majored in computer science. About half were graduating with degrees in public administration, mainly because the government is the largest employer in the Virgin Islands, followed by the tourism industry.

My thesis was that Castro is going to die one day, and when he does, the people taking over may recognize the economic value of tourism in Cuba. If Cuba reopens as a tourist spot, tourism in the U.S. Virgin Islands will drop by 20% to 30%. I asked what would fill that gap. The solution is not more people working for the government. I said, "You can't afford that, so you must look to do something that's going to have an effect seven to ten years from now when this occurs." I'm excited to be part of creating a vision this far in advance and working now to realize change in business and the economy of this territory, and of the United States.

Recently, I've been working with the government and the University of the Virgin Islands. The Virgin Islands has a special status as a territory of the United States, and the major providers of global sea bed fiber have located their maintenance cable heads on the island of St. Croix. We're exploring this as an opportunity to diversify the Virgin Islands' economy by attracting large global corporations to run their ecommerce B2B activity out of St. Croix. By doing that, companies enjoy all of the advantages of U.S. law, intellectual property rights, patent protection, U.S. accounting standards, and maximum broadband coverage because of the interconnects there.

Also, companies can enjoy the kinds of tax breaks available in the Bahamas or the Cayman Islands without being considered unpatriotic. This problem has occurred with companies like Stanley Works and others that have moved offshore. Some people feel that pursuing tax breaks is unpatriotic, but pursuing tax breaks is probably the highest form of patriotism we know. The whole country started with some guys dumping tea in the Boston harbor over a tax dispute. We all try to gain tax breaks legally. The problem occurs when tax breaks come at the expense of U.S. jobs and the Treasury.

When companies decided to move to Bermuda and the Caymans, it created two serious problems. One, of course, is that a foreign government was realizing benefits. Two, the accounting and legal standards in those countries were such that you could hide things a la Enron (note: Enron set up 600 offshore accounts in the Caymans).

However, because the U.S. Virgin Islands are a U.S. territory, they come under U.S. accounting standards. You have to report income the same way you would as if you were in the United States. The governor has signed legislation we drafted in the Virgin Island legislature to grant significant tax benefits to global corporations that offer specific benefits to the island and the island population. These benefits could include school to work programs, internships, jobs—all those opportunities that would arise as companies build out their communication and technology infrastructure on the island. It helps that everybody there is a U.S. citizen.

The University secured legislative approval for a research and technology park that will be managed by the University. The government has set aside 150 acres to build the park, and the communications infrastructure there is unparalleled.

Global Crossing, AT&T, Cable and Wireless, and MCI all run their maintenance hubs to the island of St. Croix for global maintenance turnaround. They wanted a location far enough east in the Caribbean so their European coverage would not have to traverse too many islands, and far enough south so that they could get close to the canal to get the fiber from Asia. The island of St. Croix is the easternmost and southernmost location of the United States in the western hemisphere. The fact that it's a U.S. territory is beneficial because, if there's ever a problem, the U.S. Navy can come in and provide support.

The Sales and Marketing Excellence Challenge

There's still a lot of work to be done to attract companies, but at least we have the legislation now and have started the game. I've launched a campaign to talk with senators and congressmen who have been opposed to offshore accounting activities. We're showing them this is truly beneficial because it's benefiting U.S. citizens.

SHERYL KINGSTONE

Sheryl Kingstone is one of the precious few analysts I have encountered that really understands the issues associated with successfully leveraging technology to optimize the performance of sales and marketing teams. She is the Program Manager of the Yankee Group's CRM Strategies Planning Service. Specifically, Sheryl researches and writes on sales and marketing effectiveness, and her work is often quoted by the major business and industry journals. Before joining the Yankee Group, she consulted with a number of enterprise software companies in the areas of business-to-business e-commerce, e-service, CRM, product acquisitions, and IPO strategies for Blanc and Otus. She has also worked for DataMirror and Praxis International. Sheryl holds a Bachelor of Science degree from the University of Massachusetts and a Master of Business Administration degree from Simmons College. Her company's web site address is www.yankeegroup.com.

JD

> **I find it interesting how many people still think that Customer Relationship Management (CRM) is this switch that you can simply buy, turn on, and say, 'Voila! Now everything is perfect.' That is not how it works. CRM is not a turnkey answer, because CRM is not a system—it is a process. Until you understand that, it doesn't matter how much money you spend; you are not going to solve your sales, service, and marketing problems.**

As an analyst, one of the frustrating challenges I have to deal with is the fact that the term CRM has so many meanings to so many people. Any time I start to talk to a Yankee Group client, I have to start off by establishing what their framework for CRM is all about. They may know a great deal, or they may not know much of anything. So we need to establish a common vocabulary.

I vividly remember one conversation I had with a telecommunications firm. They started off the meeting by saying, "We really want to know what is CRM?" Well, to lay the foundation I started describing how it is an infrastructure that supports collaborative selling and marketing, etc., and there was silence on the phone. After a moment, they said, "That's fine. Now, we really want to know what is CRM?" So this time I started describing it from a technology and process perspective. After a minute or two they said, "No, what is CRM?" And I said, "You mean 'Customer Relationship Management?'" And they said, "Thank you."

As you can imagine, now when people ask me what is CRM, I'm gun shy. I have to ask them a number of questions—at what level, at what stage, what have you done so far—before I can even start to gauge how to take the conversation forward. I hate to even attempt to tell people what is CRM anymore when just about everyone has his or her own definition. If you have an e-mail problem, you can put it in e-mail management solutions, and that might be considered to be a part of CRM. Or, if you have a lead management challenge, you can put in a lead management system. But these are really point solutions.

CRM is much more encompassing, much more strategic that that. CRM is really all about understanding the customer and making better products— better solutions, really—that fit their needs, their business objectives, and their goals so that you can be the next GE of the world. CRM is not about installing technology; it is about embracing a corporate mindset for continuous and evolutionary change.

It's critical to think about CRM from the customers' point of view and re-organize businesses around that process. It's very difficult and not many organizations are willing to make that type of commitment and dedication. Yet without that kind of focus, what we end up doing is implementing a whole series of technology-based point solutions in sales, marketing, and support, and then everyone is surprised when, at the end of this all, after millions have been spent, nothing really has changed in our businesses.

Laying The Foundation For CRM

▶ What Problem Are We Trying to Solve?

I have had a number of discussions with companies that start off with them saying, "We need a CRM system." My response is always the same: "To solve what problem?" If you are going to begin a CRM initiative, you need to understand that the starting point has to be with executive management. Forget talking about technology for a minute. What are the top five business objectives you are trying to accomplish as an organization? Are you focused on building real partnerships with your clients, are you trying to grow the channel, do you need to defend market share? This conversation has to start with the CEO. In a few years from now, how will you judge success?

Once you have those key objectives on the table, you then need to go to the vice presidents of marketing, sales, and support, and ask them what are the top five challenges they are struggling with that are keeping their organizations from doing their part to help achieve those corporate goals. Next, you need to take the conversation down to the people in these various departments who actually do the work and ask them what they think are the issues. Notice we are not talking solutions here; we are talking objectives and challenges. There is really no point talking about solution alternatives until you go through this first level of conversation.

▶ Mapping 'Where Are We Now?'

Once the corporate objectives have been defined and the challenges are understood, you then need to determine why the challenges exist. You need to define the current state process. How are you doing lead management, how are you doing proposal generation, how are you processing orders or answering customer service requests? While you are mapping the process, you also need to get the associated metrics; what is our lead conversion rate, how long does it take to get a proposal out the door, what is our order error level, how long does it take to respond to a customer request?

This is an investment of time and resources, but what is the alternative? Frankly, I am tired of coming in after the fact and being told that a CRM initiative failed. My first question is, "How did it fail?" Most often, the answer I get is, "Well, it didn't meet our expectations." When I then ask, "What were your specific expectations?" I get blank stares. When I get invited to take a look at projects like these, I can't call these failures—they never even started!

Far too many companies are jumping far too quickly into technology before they have done their homework. It is critical that you assess the 'state of the market' inside your organizations before you do anything else. Do some process mapping, get some definitive benchmarks, make some assessments about what is working and what isn't, describe how the process needs to change for improvement to occur, and then set some performance expectations for how you want things to be six months or a year from now.

When I look at CRM success, I see objectives that lead to challenges, challenges that lead to pain points, pain points that lead to process, process that surfaces metrics, and metrics that lead to a clear understanding of what needs to be done next. When you think about it, it is actually a very simple flow, yet it is done far too infrequently.

This all leads back to my earlier comment about evolutionary change. If my end goal is to become superhuman, and I take a realistic look at myself and realize that today I am an ape, dragging its arms on the ground, tripping all over itself; well, at least now I can see that I am not going to get to where I want to go in one generation of evolutionary change. I can now set realistic expectations for what can be accomplished in phase one of change, phase two, phase three, etc. until I reach my ultimate goal.

Creating The CRM Solution Framework

To me, this is the critical starting point: laying a solid foundation for change. So, what do you do next? If people have done this type of analysis, then I often get calls asking me to help them wade through the morass of solution alternatives available in the marketplace. Here again, we are making the mistake of focusing on technology and not on process.

What do I mean by that? Technology to me is a minor piece in the puzzle because there are dozens of perfectly workable options that will fit your needs. When a company comes to me and says, "We really need to do a detailed evaluation of Microsoft versus Siebel versus SAP. We need to understand their architecture, their infrastructure, their code generation and maintenance philosophy," my reaction is, "Who cares!"

CRM success is not about J2EE, it's not about .Net, it's not about XML. No one vendor is going to solve the entire range of customer management problems you face. Your technology framework will come as a result of multiple vendors working together to supply parts of the solution needed to do the work that needs to be done, the way you optimally want to do it. Success is not about Siebel, or Oracle, or any other technology vendor; it is about your company and the way you work.

At the end of the day, CRM technology will be deemed either useful or useless depending on one thing: did people use it? For CRM technology to provide any value at all, human beings first need to gather information and put in into a computer. You can have the most sophisticated, elegant algorithms in the world, but the improvement process breaks down if someone is not willing to feed valid data into the system for it to analyze. If I cannot create an environment that supports people sharing information, what good is CRM technology? What you have without this is 'garbage in, garbage out.'

▶ CRM Under-Budgeting

We are spending a fortune on technology. I don't even want to think about how many billions of dollars in checks have been cut to pay for hardware, software, and communications. It is mind boggling. And what is equally mind boggling is how little we invest in other, more critical aspects of the project.

I have already talked about how we under-budget strategy development, process mapping, metrics gathering, and the like. This is not necessarily confined to money; it is also about time. We are not willing to invest the time to do these things. Another area we are under-budgeting is supporting the people we are going to ultimately rely on to use these technology tools.

When I say 'support,' do not confuse that with 'training.' They are two very different things. I have been in companies that say, "We spent a lot of money on our people." That may be true, but what did you spend that money on, training or support? Let me show you the difference, because it is critical to a project's success or failure.

When you implement a CRM system, you may very well train the users on how the technology works. But what does this really involve? Too often, when I look at the details of training programs I see that they gather users into a room and then put the wrong person up in front of them to walk them through how the technology works.

You may put an accountant up in front of the room to discuss ROI methodologies, you may have a forecast specialist overview how pipeline management is imbedded in the tools, or you may have a configuration expert talk about all the prerequisites and co-requisites that need to be considered for a configurator to function. This may all have some intellectual value, but all of these discussions are focused on what technology can do, and therefore what you need to do to support the technology.

Let's be frank. You have a room full of sales people, marketing people, support people, all of them working pretty hard trying to deal with their own sets of challenges. What did they come to hear? Are they really interested in listening to someone explain what they can do for the technology, or what the technology can do for them? Once again, this gets back to process. The person we want to have to engage these users needs to be someone who can think strategically and relate technology to a business process.

These 'training sessions' need a new focus: what is the impact of users taking the time to accurately enter information into the system to begin with? When data goes in, how does it impact the process going forward? How does it improve communications between them and their co-workers; how does it minimize my administrative burden or the burden placed on another department further down the process; is there a way that my life becomes easier some time in the future based on the fact that I took the time to use the system today?

When people start to understand technology from a process perspective, then they can relate to it. The end benefit doesn't always need to be a personal gain. A customer service rep, for example, can find personal fulfillment knowing that, because he or she entered all of the order information correctly the first time, someone in the warehouse was able to more easily process that order. Adoption becomes a cycle. You train for it, you use it; you use it, you gain from it; you gain from it, you figure out how to make it better; you make it better, then you train for it again, and so forth.

The Myth Of Intergalactic Success

Using this approach, it is never about technology. It is about continuous process innovation. Things keep getting better and better. But be aware that everything, everywhere does not get better all at once.

When you look across the landscape of CRM success, you see these are really pockets of improvement versus enterprise-wide success. There are companies with good pre-sales web sites, other firms have leveraged technology to solve the information needs of mobile reps, still other firms may have developed some innovative customer care approaches. But in these same companies, you might find that while sales is doing great, they have failed in their support of marketing; or marketing's needs have been met, but they have failed to respond to the challenges of the call center.

Clearly, this is ultimately about enterprise effectiveness, and this may be what vendors are promising. But today, that promise is a myth. I do not think there is a company in the world today that is ready to be inducted into the CRM Hall of Fame. But I also do not think that this is a reason for companies to abandon CRM.

To be honest with you, I don't see much that is going to change in the next two years. I really don't. All I can see over the near-term horizon is companies still implementing point solutions within specific functional areas in their operations to solve specific problems. And you know what? That's not necessarily a bad thing. I'm happy as long as there are improvements consistently being made along the way.

If we could accomplish three things over the next two or three years, I think we could make giant strides towards really setting the stage for the concept of CRM to achieve its full potential. First, we need to set the record straight that technology is not the answer to all the problems the sales, marketing, and service worlds face. Second, we need to understand that consolidating everything into one database is not the Holy Grail. Finally, if we are truly going to transform our companies to be customer-centric, then we have to pay more than just lip service to that concept. We need to change our processes to support our customers, instead of wishing our customers would change their processes to support us.

The Business Case For Incremental Change In The Meantime

Now, while all of this is happening, there are still problems to be solved. I would definitely encourage companies to take the time to understand what those problems are, surface what are the process flaws that cause those problems to occur, and then determine what role, if any, technology will play in minimizing or eliminating those problems.

There is one other aspect of CRM that is worth addressing, and that is cost justifying the investments in this area within your company. I think it is safe to say that if a company bought every CRM solution when a vendor promised them an ROI, they would go broke very quickly. ROI is not about the generic gains that might be achieved by a mythical company through the use of a vendor's tools. ROI only has meaning if it can be related to your company, your operations, and your balance sheet.

Ultimately, you have to put the metrics around your own project; you should not look to a vendor to do that task. You have to map out the whole process and then you have to make assumptions that you believe in and can defend regarding how technology will improve the way your company does business.

Investment decisions are now being made at the executive level for every dollar a company spends. It is no longer an issue of going in and explaining your justification for wanting to go with vendor A over vendors B or C. Today, you have to explain why your project should be funded in marketing, sales or service, versus competing projects in manufacturing, finance, distribution, information technology, and so forth.

For decades now, these parts of the organization have gotten very skilled at really understanding their process flow, and when they come to the table asking for money, they can show a CFO or a CEO exactly where things will improve as a result of this investment.

If you are the head of sales, marketing, and support; that is your competition. Realize the playing field is process improvement, not technology. Come to the table with a plan for how to increase the lead conversion rate by X percent, or get new sales people productive in Y fewer months, or reduce the number of service calls it takes to install your product at a customer site because the order entry error rate has dropped from Z to zero, and you will have an even chance of getting your fair share of investment funds that are available. Come armed only with vendor promises of how great the technology is, and be prepared for a cold reception.

THOMAS BLONDI

Tom Blondi is one of those rare individuals who has the business and technical knowledge and experience to wear literally any CXO hat. He has over 25 years of experience in the information technology industry, and specializes in evaluating the effectiveness of early stage companies: their strategic positioning, sales/marketing strategies, and organizational infrastructures to execute those plans. He is currently the CEO for Hard Dollar Corporation, the world's largest integrated estimating and project management software company. Prior to that, Tom held executive management positions at companies such as Cyclone Commerce, Peerless Systems, Software AG, and Informatics. Tom has written extensively and lectured professionally all over the globe on a variety of industry, sales, marketing, and strategic management issues. He is a graduate of Southern Illinois University, with a double major in mathematics and physics.

JD

> **If your sales force is not producing the results you need them to achieve, one of the first things that you need to seriously consider as the sales leader for your company is, 'Are we to blame?' To start this self-exploration, there are three areas you need to examine to see if the messages you are sending the sales force, directly or indirectly, are focusing them on the right goals and objectives.**

Years ago, I came across a saying that has always stuck with me: "An organization elicits the performance it rewards." Most sales executives will tell you that they currently have plenty of external problems impacting the performance of their sales teams, so the last thing they need to do is compound that by creating internal problems as well.

When sales fails to meet expectations, you need to take a hard look at everything you are doing, and I have found that a good starting point is to first assess what type of performance you are currently rewarding. Rewards can come in a number of forms, but they typically fall into three categories: compensation, recognition, and involvement. How we leverage each of these three factors can have a huge impact on our results.

Compensation

How we pay people is the most obvious way we reward and influence performance in sales. We are all aware that the way that you structure commission and bonus plans can definitely impact behavior. I think the thing we often fail to do though is really think through exacting what messages those plans send; what are we really motivating the sales force to do?

▶ Sending the Wrong Message

The absolute worst thing we can do is give sales people the impression that we don't want them to push their limits. You may think no one in their right mind would do that, but I have seen it happen. One clear way to send that message is by putting a cap on how much sales people can make in commissions.

Here I am, telling my best and brightest people to go out and work really hard to close deals, bring in more money for the company, and yet I put limits on what they can make. What an insane idea. We all need to understand that sales people are commission plan lawyers. They take those plans and turn them inside out figuring out ways to best leverage them. You put a cap on earnings, and as soon as they start to approach that number they are going to manage to that level (sandbagging deals) every time.

What is wrong with the concept of sales people making a lot of money? They are only going to achieve that if they bring in a lot of orders in the first place. I use to work for a gentleman named Walter Bauer, who was the founder of Informatics, one of the first software companies in the computer industry. Walt use to take real pride in how much his sales people made. He wouldn't do it publicly, but once a quarter during senior staff meetings, he would read off the names of all the sales people who were making more than he was. He honestly loved that.

That is the kind of message we need to send to the sales force, that we are happy, even ecstatic when they are successful, and we do not begrudge them making a good living.

▶ Smoothing Out Monthly/Quarterly Performance

I think it is a mistake to put in place any type of compensation program that dis-incentivizes sales people. I would much rather focus on motivation. Over the years, I have seen a number of creative ways we can use quota plans to achieve the results we want.

For example, one of the firms I worked for in a past life use to have severe revenue spikes where upwards of 60% to 70% of their sales came in the last five days of the quarter. As you can imagine, this led to some nail-biting experiences when things didn't go exactly as we had forecast them. We were able to reduce the number of times we were surprised, and also the degree to which we were surprised, by making a fairly minor change in our quota plans.

What we did was stagger the month-end closing dates for international and domestic operations. We moved the date that we closed the books for commission purposes for the international sales people to the 15th of the month, and kept the domestic sales force on the traditional month-end date.

What this allowed us to do was get a sanity check early in the month regarding just how sales were progressing. If international met or beat their numbers, then we could breathe a little easier. If they missed their goals, then we knew a couple weeks earlier that we needed to get more aggressive with the North American team. The sales force adjusted to this move without much problem, and the change certainly made operations more manageable.

▶ Avoiding Summer Doldrums

Another challenge for sales management is dealing with the slowdown in orders over the summer months or any 'seasonal' sales cycles. Many sales executives have resigned themselves to the idea that this is a fact of life. But it doesn't have to be. One strategy we tried that worked was moving the quota year-end from December 31st to September 30th.

The way the commission plan was structured, the quota performance numbers we used to calculate commission accelerators, bonuses, and sales club qualification were all based on sales rep performance from October to September, instead of January to December. Our sales people figured out really quickly that they couldn't slide through the summer and then hope to have a great Q4 to bail them out. They needed to find ways to keep selling aggressively during the summer months, which they did.

Another program I've seen implemented was to pay double commissions on deals that closed in July and August. There were a couple of interesting twists to this plan. First, you had to be on or above your year-to-date quota going into July to qualify for the bonus program, and secondly, the extra commissions weren't paid to the sales person until April 1st of the following year.

This accomplished two objectives. It motivated the sales people to push hard during what historically were the toughest months of the year, and it also reduced voluntary turnover. The company had very aggressive growth goals year-to-year, so every January quotas went up significantly. Prior to implementing this plan, they had a spike in sales attrition in Q1 of each year, as a number of reps panicked when they got their new sales targets and left the company to take other jobs.

Under this arrangement, leaving cost the good performers quite a bit of money. Because of this, many decided to ride it out through the first quarter in order to pick up the extra commissions. By April 1st they could now see that, while their quotas were a push, they were not as impossible as they thought they were going to be at the beginning of the year, so their desire to go somewhere else to work was reduced.

▶ Generating References vs. Deals

One of the key messages that we need to send to the sales force is that ultimately what we want are referenceable customers versus orders. We have all seen reps whose main focus was to move product. At times, their aggressiveness generated orders that turned into account management nightmares down the road when products didn't function exactly as they had been portrayed during the sales process. Again, compensation programs can have an impact here.

We need to motivate sales people to structure deals for success right from the start. One tactic I have used to accomplish this is to tie a portion of the commission payment to customer success and satisfaction. I reviewed one program that was structured so that the sales person received only 70% of his commission when he booked the order. The remainder was at risk depending on whether the customer could get the product to work to their satisfaction in a timely manner or not.

Once the implementation of the system took place, the sales team had 90 days to get the customer live and into full production. The remaining commissions were not released until the economic buyer at the customer account went to the vendor's customer web site and filled out a survey saying that they were formally satisfied with their purchase. Plans like that send a very clear message.

▶ Change the Plan, Change Behavior

I am sure you know of a number of other ideas. If your sales people are discounting too much, start paying them on margin instead of revenue and they will quickly cut back on how much money they give away in negotiations. If you need to keep sales people continuously pushing hard throughout the year, then implement rolling 90-day quotas versus annual numbers.

The point I am trying to make is that if we change the plan, we can often change behavior. I think it would benefit any sales executive to take some time each year to analyze and really understand the power that compensation plans represent in helping to positively or negatively impact performance.

One last observation I have on this topic is these plans shouldn't be done in a vacuum. Compensation programs need to be aligned to, and supported by, other corporate initiatives to be effective. For example, it doesn't do you much good to offer sales people a double commission bonus for closing new leads in 90 days if marketing plans to shut down their lead generation efforts for a quarter to conserve cash. When you develop these plans, you should review them with the rest of the senior management team to make sure everyone is working out of the same playbook.

Recognition

Of course, motivation doesn't always have to take the form of cash. Recognition (psychic income) is another powerful tool to accomplish the same objective. We all know that, we all say that, but again I think we underutilize recognition far too often.

There have been a number of studies over the years that point out the fact that generally sales people are very ego-centric. Let's look for ways to leverage that. What are some ideas here? I don't know if they still do this, but one simple thing that IBM used to do was recognize their top performers, those who made the 'Golden Circle,' by giving them personal business cards that had the 'Golden Circle' symbol embossed on them. Sales people felt good about giving those cards out. Being recognized as the best of the best became something to strive for.

▶ Motivating to Help Others

An idea I have used in the past was the 'Respected Reps' program. Prior to our annual sales meeting, we would survey the field sales force and ask them who they felt were the most respected people in the field. You could only nominate someone who achieved quota, but this wasn't just a total numbers award.

In addition to revenue attainment, these people also had to have made a significant contribution to the others in the sales force. Maybe they took the time to pass on leads to other regions or other divisions, maybe they shared collateral they created, or maybe they e-mailed the team to pass on a best practice they uncovered. The message we wanted to send here was, in addition to being an individual star, we also want them to be a team player.

At the sales meeting we recognized all their contributions and gave them a chance to be the host for a major event, like a cocktail party or a dinner. I found this approach to be very effective at motivating people to want to go the extra mile.

On the topic of sharing, I recently saw a software application that allows sales people to share good ideas and best practices. Other companies have tried to do this before, but the shortcoming I saw in their approach was that there was nothing really motivating the reps to take part in this program.

The system I saw solves that problem two ways. The first is that users earn points for sharing a best practice, using a best practice, or commenting on one. I believe these points are tied to prizes, so that would be a compensation issue. But there is also a recognition component as well.

The system keeps track of who submitted each best practice and also how valuable other reps found that strategy or tactic to be. The reps that consistently get the highest ratings from their peers are featured on a rotating basis on the system home page. Every time a user signs on to the system, one of the first things he or she sees is a picture and the name of a sales team member that has been recognized for the frequency and quality of the information he or she shares with other team members.

Involvement

The last leverage point we have is involvement. What do I mean by that? If we have a problem in sales—revenues are down, margins are eroding, expenses are too high, customer satisfaction is down, etc.—I think the message we need to send to the sales force is that we all need to be part of the solution.

I am a firm believer in having sales people take an active role in coming up with solutions to the business challenges we face. As a part of our annual strategic planning process, we have invited the top performing rep to sit in on those sessions with senior management and help define the goals, objectives, and strategies for the company.

Another way to approach this is to create a Sales Advisory Board. This is a group of six to ten top performers who represent their peers and have direct input into any changes that might be considered regarding territories, channel management, new product ideas, training, sales compensation, incentives, or benefits.

The Advisory Board works with sales management to define the sales policies and procedures that the sales force lives by for a given quota year. Under this approach, you do not dictate change to sales people; you involve them in the process from the start so, in the end, they don't see this as management's plan for sales. Instead, they see it as the sales team's plan.

Once these programs are put into place, if problems arise, then the Advisory Board reconvenes and comes up with recommendations or changes. This is not a one-time activity, but rather an ongoing endeavor. Each year you add or remove members based on who currently are the top performers. This ensures that you get a continual flow of new blood and new ideas.

You may not want to start off with a program this sophisticated, but there are a number of other ways to get the sales force more involved in problem identification and resolution. You could tack an extra session on to a national sales meeting to collect people's thoughts on the strengths, weaknesses, opportunities, and threats that they see in the marketplace. If costs prohibit you from bringing everyone together, then you could do web-based surveys to collect their insights and opinions.

The objective is to get the sales force more involved. These are the people who are living and breathing the sales challenges we face on a daily basis. Who else in our company is in a better position to come up with solutions?

Keeping One Eye Focused Internally

There is an old Chinese toast that goes, "May you live in interesting times." Some days I feel that things are a little *too* interesting. I could probably stand a few more mundane days myself. But based on current market conditions, I don't see that happening any time soon. I think 2003 is definitely going to be a push and 2004 may well be too.

We absolutely do need to change how the game is played going forward, and we ought to utilize every lever we can to do that. The best thing about compensation, recognition, and involvement is that they are all under our control in sales. Optimizing these three areas will not solve all the issues we face, but it is a good starting point.

RICK CRAMER

Rick Cramer is president and chief executive officer of Veridiem Inc., a Massachusetts-based software and services company that is leading the emerging Marketing Resource Management (MRM) category. An 18-year veteran of the high-tech industry, prior to joining Veridiem, Rick was vice president of sales, marketing and business development at Centra Software. Establishing Centra as a leader in Web-based collaborative solutions, Rick helped to define the product and target market, raise capital, and drive strategic relationships with 120 Fortune 1000 customers. Before Centra, Rick served as a founding member and an executive vice president at Avid Technology where he was instrumental in Avid's successful 1993 IPO. Throughout his career, Rick has held executive-level sales and marketing positions with companies such as Apollo Computer and Xerox Corporation. Veridiem's web address is www.veridiem.com.

JD

> **Today, every CEO and CFO wants to know how marketing investments are impacting sales and profits. Therefore, every CMO must be able to determine what the optimum spending levels and marketing mix should be for his or her company. In the past, this has been an incredibly difficult task, because there was no way to get to a single version of the 'truth.' Fortunately, now that is changing.**

The global mass-media advertising spend for this year should be in excess of $400 billion. When you add to this the funds allocated for direct marketing, promotion, and other activities, that number is probably doubled. In the companies I have talked to this past year it is not uncommon to see the total cost of marketing, programs and the people that run them, come in at between 15 and 35 percent of revenue for Fortune 500-sized firms.

That could change though. As the 'revenues in' have slowed for many companies the scrutiny of 'expenses out' is much higher that ever before. Senior management teams are very focused on determining exactly what the best use of funds is. This is creating a highly competitive environment within companies, as each operational area has to vigorously justify their expense levels or face significant cuts in the funds they are allocated.

Based on this trend, we have entered the era of 'hard data.' In the past marketing has often relied on feedback from attitudinal and impression studies, or customer comments from focus groups to back their claims of effectiveness. While still valuable, analysis at this level does not go nearly deep enough.

For marketing to defend their expenditures they are going to have to make three fundamental changes: they need to determine the return on their investments, based on that insight they then need to optimize their marketing mix, and they need to do both of these in a much more dynamic manner.

The New Realities of Marketing

▶ Quantifying Return on Marketing (ROM)

Marketing has been, and always will be an art. When you are dealing with human perceptions and behaviors, you have to accept that fact. But today that art needs to be complemented with a healthy dose of science. We cannot just track user attitudes and say we have done our job. We need to start to track how that attitude translated into action and how impressions turned into sales.

Take the automotive industry for example. Let's say you are a major car manufacturer. It is nice if your marketing efforts make a consumer positively disposed towards your company and even a specific model of car. But the ultimate objective goes way beyond that. You need to motivate the buyer to go into a dealership, test drive a car, and buy it. That is success in the eyes of an automotive CEO.

Generating this level of insight will mean that CMOs will have to instill a whole new level of rigor in their organizations. To calculate the return on marketing (ROM), we cannot just look at individual programs. Instead we will have to look at all the various times during the customer's buying process that marketing touched the customer, and be able to determine what parts of the marketing plan were most effective in creating buying actions and which were not.

▶ Mastering Marketing Mix Management

We have all heard the oft-quoted claim that at least half of the dollars marketing is spending are wasted. If we are going to correct that situation, then the second thing we are going to have to do is a much better job of marketing mix management. In fact we are probably going to have to reinvent this whole process.

Currently, there are a host of marketing levers; various types of advertising, promotions, events, direct marketing campaigns, sponsorships, incentives, etc. available for marketing teams to utilize. At a gross level, most organizations have some sense of how effective those various elements are, but rarely can they quantify the exact impact those individual programs are having on revenues, margins, customer retention, etc.

Based on the pressures to measure 'true' success, this is the minimum level of understanding we need to move towards. But ultimately even that is not enough. We need to go beyond having a broad based understanding of the impact that marketing is having on consumer behavior, and get down to the details

Every market behaves differently; and because of this every product requires a different strategy. When people think about all the various combinations of marketing levers at their disposal, they need to be able to determine how best to take advantage of those by market, by product, by channel, etc.

To optimize your marketing mix strategy, you need to start by looking at the specific questions that need to be answered. These are unique for each organization, but in general they are related to understanding how each component of your marketing mix impacts key business metrics.

For example, you may want to determine how is your brand advertising driving unit sales? Or how is your investment in interactive marketing and web-based initiatives driving market share? And I don't need a single answer to these questions; I need several.

Going back to the automotive industry example, here you are dealing with companies that have fairly broad product portfolios. There are a variety of car and truck models within their stable. Because of this, they need to not only understand how their various marketing vehicles are working together to drive results, but also how do investments in individual models impact one another.

If we are doing a campaign to advertise a four-wheel drive sedan or station wagon for example, and that campaign is well received in the marketplace, I want to know if there is any kind of positive effect pull-through when I launch a new SUV or promote a compact car at a lower price point.

Companies need to get to the point where they can quantitatively determine how much marketing investment is required by product and by market in order to hit their goals.

▶ Dynamic Change Management

We also need to deal with the fact that the answers to these questions are changing all the time. Alterations in buying habits, competitive announcements, general economic trends, the availability of newer, more focused marketing vehicles, etc. can positively or negatively impact marketing effectiveness.

Because of this, it is no longer acceptable to put together a 12-month marketing plan, let it run to its completion, and then take a one-time snap shot of what happened to use to help optimize your planning for the next year. As the effectiveness of the various components of your marketing mix change, you need to know how they are changing, why, and what to do about it.

If programs are no longer working we need to kill them early. If other programs are generating world-class results, we need to optimize the 'spend' in that area. Speed to change, in response to market dynamics, will have a huge impact on the return marketing generates for an organization.

Marketing Resource Management (MRM) Systems

Well, very few organizations today have the ability to do this type of analysis, but that is quickly changing with the advent of Marketing Resource Management (MRM) systems.

Other parts of our companies have already been leveraging enterprise software systems to enable them to more effectively respond to the volatility of the marketplace. Sales, manufacturing, and supply chain are utilizing closed-looped applications from software firms such as Siebel, SAP, and i2 to track how their investments are translating into completed sales, faster time to market, more effective inventory management, improved customer retention, etc.

Marketing is now in a position to take advantage of this same level of insight into their operations. MRM systems provide timely access to all the information marketers need to intelligently plan, execute, evaluate and then optimize their programs and investments. For the first time CMOs will be able to track the specific impact marketing campaigns have on sales, margins, customer retention, market share, and all the other key metrics that are critical to our success.

With this new understanding, marketing with be able to determine their ROM and then use that knowledge to accurately predict how increases or decreases in marketing budgets will directly impact short-term and long-term business results.

▶ Marketing Efficiency versus Effectiveness

MRM software is a relatively new and evolving category, so a bit of background might be helpful. At the highest level, there are two types of MRM systems; those that increase the efficiency of a marketing organization and those that increase effectiveness.

MRM efficiency applications are primarily collaboration tools. They include project management, knowledge management, and project workflow functionality that help increase the productivity of individual marketers and improve communications across the marketing organization. While this class of MRM tools provides some basic measurements and reporting capabilities, they have generally been found lacking when companies have tried to deal with the issues we have been discussing.

This has led to the development of a newer generation of marketing effectiveness MRM solutions. These systems are much more analytical in their design. They have very robust integrated data management and automated modeling capabilities to support very detailed marketing program effectiveness analyses and forecasting. It is this class of systems that will provide CMOs with the insights into their operations that they need.

Turning Information Into Insights

Today, the issue is not that we don't have access to marketing information, the problem is we often have too much of it. Companies are collecting an increasing amount of data on business results, customer buying trends, sales channel effectiveness, competitive analysis, and the like. We are drowning in data in many cases.

The challenge is effectively assimilating and processing all those data points so we can synthesize it down to the critical insights we need in order to make decisions regarding how to optimize our marketing operations. That is the challenge that effectiveness-oriented MRM solutions are designed to address.

The new-generation MRM systems utilize software agent technology to understand all of the various marketing plans and programs we have in place, determine the impact that market factors are having on those programs, collect market research on how are customers and prospects perceiving and responding to our positioning messages and various product offers. With this information in hand, we can now triangulate towards the truth regarding the business impact that has resulted from our efforts.

Using a goal-oriented approach to data gathering, the systems can extract much of the key business elements necessary to monitor, analyze and optimize marketing performance from existing data warehouses and marts. As the technology matures over the next few years, it will all but eliminate the manual data collection challenge that has been making measuring marketing effectiveness difficult and expensive.

Successfully Harnessing The Power Of MRM

The robustness, scalability, and stability of MRM applications are here today to allow marketing to make revolutionary advances in how they measure and manage their effectiveness. But there are a number of issues to consider when you start to harness that power.

While CRM, ERP, and SCM enterprise software systems are clearly providing many companies with a competitive market advantage, a lesson can be learned from looking at the high initial failure rates these types of initiatives experienced in the early stages of those markets. Solving this class of business problems is not simply a matter of buying some technology; there are people and process issues to contend with as well.

Success for marketing going forward will be dependent on an organization's ability to plan, manage, measure, analyze and optimize marketing investments. In order to do this, we will need the support of many different stakeholders across the enterprise. In addition, because we tend to rely on a variety of service providers to help us create, produce, implement and track these programs, we need to tie them directly into the process. If we can do that, then we will finally be able to compare apples to apples in determining how to optimize our marketing effectiveness.

Over the last several years, through working with our clients to understand the unique aspects of the marketing ecosystems they operate within, we have developed a number of insights into how to manage these types of initiatives. Having worked hand-in-hand with marketing organizations, we have found that the best way to achieve revolutionary change is to take an evolutionary approach.

What does that mean? Let's consider this from the people side of the equation first. Marketers are experts in marketing, not information technology. If you expect these people to become skilled in programming, database design, report formatting, etc. in order to utilize MRM applications, you are asking them to make a revolutionary change in who they are and what they do. No matter how powerful the tools are, that approach is doomed from the start.

What you want to do is find MRM systems that are designed by marketing professionals for marketing professionals. The interfaces should be totally intuitive. The entire complexity of the technology needs to be transparent to the user community.

From a process perspective, the flow of the applications needs to be an evolutionary extension of the way these users already work and think. If we cannot achieve this we will either experience an initial loss of productivity and effectiveness as marketers take the time to learn foreign ways of working, or worst case they will reject the tools outright because they will fail to understand the value.

▶ One Model, One Market, One Measurement Rollout

If you pick solutions that support this evolutionary type of change, you next need to ensure you roll them out in an evolutionary fashion. By that I mean you do not want to attempt to eat the elephant all in one bite. You need to create a scenario whereby people can apply these applications to key, but manageable problems and prove the value of the tools so that you obtain their buy-in going forward.

Once that is accomplished, you can then expand the scope of the project in terms of the breadth of products you are analyzing, and the complexity of the analysis you do on a product.

What we do when working with our clients is to pick a very high profile brand; say a single model of car. We then want to pick one or two key markets to look at, versus having to pull data from all across the nation or the world. Then within that environment, we initially focus on just one or two key measurements. For example, we may start by analyzing how marketing investments, both national air cover as well as regional investments made in a market such as Minnesota, are driving unit sales of luxury sedans.

When you take this approach, you minimize the demand on your own internal resources. This is a manageable task now and allows you to prove the value of MRM while your people are adjusting their thought processes to better, more precise ways of dealing with an old problem.

Once the value is clearly seen, the users themselves accelerate the speed of the project expansion, as they start to come up with more and more ways these insights could impact the effectiveness of marketing planning and execution.

▶ Continuous Optimization – The MRM Competitive Edge

The ultimate challenge we have to address is how do you make marketing improvement a repeatable process? Go through back issues of AdWeek, BusinessWeek, AdAge, Fortune, etc. and you can find many instances of marketing effectiveness success. But the vast majority of these tend to be focused around a given win, or a given campaign. There are precious few case studies about organizations that are able to put together wins back to back, to back, to back.

That is about to change. All the building blocks are there to allow us to apply more science to the art of marketing. We have the data and now we have the tools to turn the data into knowledge, knowledge into insights, and insights into action. Because these new MRM systems will give you near real-time views of the markets you are selling into, today's annual or semi-annual planning cycles will be replaced with much more dynamic reviews, allowing program optimization to take place continuously.

By surfacing their poor performing marketing investments early, killing those programs and then reallocating freed up funds into the campaigns that are generating real sales, marketing will be able to have huge impact on business success. As soon as any player in any market achieves the type of performance we have been reviewing, they are going to fundamentally change the balance of power in that industry segment. When that occurs, marketing effectiveness will no longer be about competitive advantage; it will be about competitive survival.

GERRY MARTIN

Gerry Martin is a noted veteran in the pharmaceutical and biotech industries. Presently, he serves as Chairman of Milkhaus Laboratory, a biotech company researching unique technologies based on cellular signaling. Prior to that, Gerry spent 30 years at Abbott Laboratories in a variety of sales and marketing executive positions, including Vice President of Corporate Hospital Marketing from 1986 to 1996 and Vice President of Corporate Licensing and Technology Alliances from 1996 to 2000. In those last two roles Gerry had the unique opportunity to see how business is changing worldwide, not just for drug companies but health care providers and insurance firms as well. I have always found Gerry to be a very forward thinker, continually looking at new ways to create innovation. He has a Bachelors degree from the University of Connecticut.

JD

> **Today, the cost of bringing a new drug to market is north of one-half billion dollars and is on its way to $1 billion. For companies to even begin to recoup that expense, they are going to have to fundamentally change the sales process, and it appears the tools to support that may be here.**

When I look across the landscape of the pharmaceutical industry I currently see a lot of troubles headed our way. We are a marketplace destined to have to make significant changes over the next few years, because what worked for us in the past will not serve us well in the future.

Traditionally, pharma has been a safe haven for investors. Historically, whenever the economy hit a downturn, people have parked spare cash in the stocks of the major drug firms because they felt these companies would always continue to grow. That assumption is being shaken to the core these days, in part because of external factors and in part due to internal issues.

The New Marketplace Realities

Externally, you have to deal with the reality that our regulatory agency, the Food and Drug Administration (FDA), has made the hurdle harder to get over when it comes to getting approval for a new drug. So we are just not able to bring enough quality products to market fast enough to sustain the old revenue growth rates, which have typically been about 10%, year-over-year. At the same time, companies also have to deal with the explosion of generics which is chipping away at the sales of drugs we already have in the marketplace.

Another external consideration is the wholesale change in the way physicians operate. The number of independent practitioners has dropped dramatically to the point where now the majority of doctors work for groups. In addition, because of managed care, which has reduced reimbursement fees, physicians now have to schedule more patient visits per day in order to generate the same amount of revenue. So every minute of every day in the physician's office becomes more and more precious.

Those are just some of the realities of the marketplace we have to sell into. Internally, we have structured our sales process around the concept of having our reps call on doctors in their offices and explain all the intricacies about our products. Depending on whose numbers you use, there are anywhere from 60,000 to 70,000 pharmaceutical reps calling on physicians today. That's an army of people all trying to reach the same population.

These reps are not only competing with each other to get mindshare, they are also competing with sales people representing everything else that might be used in that office. This situation is creating a Catch 22—we need to see as many physicians, as soon possible, if we are going to make a new drug successful in the market, or maintain sales of an existing drug, and the physicians we need to influence don't have the time to see us anymore.

In all too many cases, the sales process has been reduced to the mere act of sampling. By that I mean having reps drop by the physician's office to drop off free samples of a drug. The government requires that the rep get the doctor's signature verifying that he or she received the samples, but that process only takes 20 or 30 seconds. That in no way qualifies as a true sales call.

Specialization

So how are we dealing with this challenge? From an organizational perspective most companies are now turning to specialization of sales forces. As opposed to expecting reps to become experts on dozens of products, they are being assigned to promote two or three.

This is a positive step, because if you are going to influence a physician, you are going to have to develop a very deep understanding of the products you are representing. You will need to know at a very detailed level what studies have been done on what drugs, what were the results, what are the best uses for that product, what are the side effects, how your product compares to competitive alternatives, etc.

With specialization, we now have the potential for putting someone in front of the doctor who can actually serve as a resource for them. I say potential, because you still have to overcome the time limitation.

If you actually do get a chance to talk to a physician, you need to be able to make your points and answer their questions in minutes, if not seconds. If you don't have all the information with you during that call, and you have to say those dreaded words, "Let me get back to you on that," you have lost the opportunity.

New Sales Systems

I have been looking for ways to solve this problem and one of the more innovative tools I have seen recently is the new tablet PC. Up until now, about the only tools we have given pharma reps to help them when they meet with doctors are limited-function computers they can utilize to capture signatures when they give out samples.

Why don't they use the laptop computers they have often been given? Think of your laptop and why it is unusable on a sales call. First, it is heavy; those devices can weight up to six or seven pounds. Second, to input information into the systems, you have to use a keyboard. Well, that makes it very impractical to use if you are walking down the hall talking to a doctor. Third, if you want to retrieve information, you have to focus your attention on menus and windows, which takes your attention off of the physician.

The tablet PC removes those limitations. It is hard to explain what these devices are if you have never seen one. However, most of us are familiar with the handheld PCs, the so-called PDA (personal digital assistant). They are computers that you interface with using a pen. The tablet PC is a PDA that has been super-sized; whereas the screen on a PDA may be two inches by three inches, the tablet PC screen size is probably closer to eight by eleven.

I had a chance to see one of these units recently, and I was immediately intrigued by the impact the tablet PC could have on improving the effectiveness of a sales call. The first thing that strikes you is that these devices are fairly light; they weigh in at a couple pounds. The second thing you notice is the interface; just like a PDA, you use a pen to interact with the system.

If you want to record some notes, you just write on the screen and it captures your handwriting. The real power of the system is that it is a full-function PC. You have access to all the applications and all the presentations, documents, financial data, etc. that you have on your PC when you are working in the office.

Knowledge At The Point Of Selling

Let me give you a scenario for how I would see these units being used out in the field. A pharmaceutical rep takes the tablet PC with him when he goes out to make calls. Before he walks into the office of, let's say, Dr. Smith, he accesses a contact management system on the tablet. Using the pen, he then taps on the screen next to Dr. Smith's name, and up pop the notes from all the past meetings with this physician, so the rep can refresh his memory of previous conversations.

Upon entering the office, the rep catches Dr. Smith in the hallway where he has a couple of precious moments between patients. He quickly engages Dr. Smith in a conversation to detail a new drug for which his company has received FDA approval. If the rep generates any interest, the next thing that will happen is that he will be peppered with questions by Dr. Smith. With the tablet PC, he will have at his finger tips all the information necessary to immediately address Dr. Smith's questions and concerns.

The doctor may want to know what clinical studies have been done on the drug. By simply writing the letter 'S' anywhere on the screen, the rep can access a list of all studies that are available on that drug, and then by tapping on any of those studies, he can access the details. Using a similar short-hand notation, he could also access information of side effects, answers to frequently asked questions, comparisons of this drug to the competition, etc. All of this would now be accessible as the rep stands with the doctor in the hall.

Using this type of approach, a rep will be able to significantly increase the quality of the time he or she spends with the physician. I can actually envision instances where, once doctors see how much information the rep can access, they will voluntarily opt to spend more time talking about various medical conditions.

Collecting The Voice Of The Customer

In addition to knowledge sharing, the tablet PC will also be a superior way for gathering information. Today, the bane of most sales people's existence is filling out paperwork. Due to the huge administrative burden that has been dropped on them, it is not uncommon for reps to stop calling on accounts at 3:00 in the afternoon so they can spend the rest of the day filling out reports.

If they were using the tablet PC, all of the forms they are being asked to fill out today would also be accessible during their call. Using the pen, they could check off boxes as they record doctor's answers to questions. They can also write notes on the screen in their own handwriting and the systems could, in turn, convert that to text. So, the requirement of aggregating responses at the end of the day or typing up notes in customer files for the most part disappears.

This capability could be especially valuable to companies running drug tests. One of the issues that delays approval is the challenge associated with collecting and processing clinical data from patients. If this task could be more automated, it could speed up the development process and lower the cost of bringing new drugs to market.

If we can solve the challenges of information access during the call and paperwork processing after the call, not only will reps be able to make better calls, they will have the time to make more of them. If we are to accomplish this though, we have to arm our sales people with the tools that can make them more productive and effective. I see the tablet PC being a must-have for not just pharmaceutical sales forces, but any rep that is highly mobile.

Reaching The Customer

Another tool that will transform the sales process in our marketplace will be the Internet. Today, what you have is a huge industry that gains it revenues not by selling to a consumer, but rather by influencing a doctor who has the power to prescribe. In fact, up until a couple years ago, the physician was the only one that pharmaceutical companies could focus their sales and marketing efforts on. This was considered to be a safeguard for the patient.

But recently the federal government loosened the constraints on consumer advertising, so the biggest growth factor in pharmaceutical companies today is the marketing budget. We can now do direct to consumer (DTC) advertising. This has become a much loved and a much hated concept in the industry.

On the positive side, we can now take our messages directly to those who will be personally impacted by drugs we manufacture. You cannot watch TV at night and not see an ad for a product such as Celebrex. DTC clearly is having an impact. Once the patients become educated, they proactively initiate dialogues with their physician and are asking about these medications.

These physicians are now challenged by their own consumers and so the need for them to be knowledgeable about these drugs is increasing. Hopefully, this will translate into them choosing to spend more time with reps when they do come into the office.

The negative side of this issue for the industry is the huge expense involved in implementing these advertising campaigns. Here though, I think the Internet will take some of the sting out of these costs. Making information available to consumers over the web is much more cost effective than traditional advertising, and people like using that medium to obtain information.

I talk to doctors all the time who share stories about patients coming into their offices with printed-out web pages highlighting medical information that they want to discuss during the appointment. This is a positive thing; people need to take a more active role in the management of their health, and the number of people choosing to access information through the web will only increase over time. If we leverage this trend, we can again change the sales process to our advantage.

Selling In The World Of Managed Care

Another factor that is impacting the sales process in the industry is the role of managed care. Here, you have a number of interested parties. You have HMOs who want to provide good service, but do so at a reasonable cost. You have insurance companies that want to get their arms around how much they reimburse for drugs. You also have employers who are very concerned about managing the spiraling cost of offering health care benefits.

To help deal with these issues, you have a legion of new companies that are emerging who assist in determining the most effective way to manage the dispensing of drugs, the indications for various diseases, and the procedures that go with them. All of these new firms represent new selling opportunities and responsibilities for pharmaceutical firms.

Calling on these organizations is a highly sophisticated sell because you are dealing with both very complex business and scientific issues. To influence things at this level, often you are interfacing with a committee.

For example, a company like Kaiser could form a team to select what compound they will use to treat a given type of infection. In the end, they will only choose one or, at most, two from among all the various options they have available to them. So this is very much a winner-take-all situation.

In response to this new shift in the market, we are seeing the formation of smaller armies of senior representatives who are managing the selling efforts to these accounts. To be successful, the support these reps need tends to take the form of advanced training in negotiations, large account management, strategic selling, etc. This will be a critical battleground going forward. A win at this level can have a noticeable impact on a company's future revenues, as can a loss.

The Game Has Changed

As you can see, we are facing our fair share of challenges in sales and marketing in the pharmaceutical industry, and we have to change with the times if we are going to remain competitive. The strategies and tactics we have employed to get us to where we are will not meet our needs in taking us to where we need to go.

From a sales perspective, we need to find a way to be of value to a physician so that they want to see us for more than the few seconds it takes to get samples. We also need to find new and creative ways to engage the end user consumer and make sure that they know what we can do for them.

We will also need to change from a marketing perspective. The industry trade association, Pharma, is leading the way in starting to force the issue of change in this area. They have published a code of marketing ethics that is challenging some of the marketing excesses and practices we have previously used, such as offering trips to Super Bowl games, taking physicians on scientific cruises, etc.

The companies that innovate the most effectively in terms of how they market and sell going forward will likely be rewarded with increased revenues, higher market share, improved margins, and lower costs. Not everyone will successfully make this transition. It will be interesting to see who those leaders turn out to be.

STEVE PRATT

When I caught up with Steve to conduct his interview, I was impressed with his rapid fire delivery and sense of organization. He would tick off key points on a topic, and then expand upon them. Mostly, though, I was impressed that this Final Four consultant continued to talk about measurable results and quick deployment of applications—neither has been a hallmark of the CRM movement. Steve is the global leader of the Deloitte Consulting (soon to become Braxton) Customer Relationship Management Practice. This practice helps companies build better relationships with their customers. The practice is seen as a global leader in helping clients improve how they do marketing, sales, and customer service. Steve has over 18 years management consulting experience and over the last eight years has led the formation and evolution of the firm's CRM practice. Steve is frequently published on the topics of Customer Strategy, CRM, and Web-based Sales and Service. He has Bachelors and Masters Degrees in Electrical Engineering.

BT

> **The days of annual planning and 18-month projects are over. We developed the concept of the '100-Day Win' where there's something to celebrate and something to measure every 100 days. You should also look at 'torch points' so that customers who have been badly burned aren't lost in averaging techniques that yield bland customer satisfaction scores and few insights.**

Information: The Key To Sales Excellence

Sales excellence means having a deep and current understanding of what is and is not working in the marketplace. It means being able to execute against what's working and change what's not working very rapidly. And it means having a sales capability, whether on the web, field sales, or channel sales. Sales excellence means having a real pulse on the marketplace and being able to react quickly. All of this is from a sales management perspective.

From a sales person perspective, sales excellence means having the best information possible provided by the company to create as much value as you can for the customer, and to do that at a fair economic value for the company. It is about getting information to the sales person. This information could take the form of an open service item that hasn't been resolved, or the fact that another part of the customer's company bought something and really liked it. However, in most cases today, there's a tremendous lack of shared information between an individual sales person and the rest of the company.

If you look at Pitney-Bowes, their sales force has done a very good job of maintaining a pulse on the market and identifying what's working and what's not working. They were able to install a pricing configurator because they realized pricing was a problem. They rapidly adjusted to the market and put in a solution. They took a key dissatisfier—error prone orders—and dramatically improved it so there is rarely an error on the order side. Pitney-Bowes has also done a good job of providing customers the ability to order routine items online.

Nokia is another impressive company. Nokia is able to make decisions rapidly and act on what they need to fix. A lot of companies get caught up in yearly cycles and launching 18-month projects. As I said, I think the days of annual planning and 18-month projects are over. Things are happening too quickly to do things in those big time chunks.

The '100-Day Win'

At Deloitte Consulting/Braxton, we like to think that we've pioneered the concept of the '100-Day Win,' which says that companies should lay out a road map so that every 100 days, they achieve some result(s). That's not to say everything can get done in 100 days—some things take 150 days, or 200 days, or 20 days—but you want to line up the end of each project so that every 100 days there is a result. For one 100-day period, we will drive X much more revenue for the company. In another 100 days, we will reduce this much cost from the organization. In the next 100 days, we will really transform the way we segment our customers and the way we align our sales model with them.

Every 100 days, there is something to celebrate and something to measure. Don't put up an 18-month project and say, "Trust me, some day this is going to be great." There are always things you can accomplish relatively quickly, so laying out a program that is a mix of short term and long term projects is very important.

In CRM, the probability of an 18- to 24-month project succeeding on its own is relatively small because the planets absolutely have to align for it to work. There are a couple of reasons why this is so.

First, and probably the most important, is quarterly pressures on sales. When you're three quarters into the project, and you're digging this big financial hole, and you haven't produced any results, people tend to lose patience. Second, is the personality of the sales executives; specifically, they are typically impatient, hard drivers. Their mindset is that when projects take too long, they generally don't work.

Now, you could say, "I want to consolidate the European call center and go from 70 call centers down to four, and I can't do that in 100 days." To that I'd respond, "Absolutely. That will probably take 200 days, but you can figure out some other wins to achieve in the meantime."

When I talk about 100-day wins, it's not about addressing random things as they appear. This is about laying out the road map. We usually create a three-year road map that outlines where we are going and includes the major milestones that need to be met. For example, a milestone might be consolidating the European call center, or integrating web service with the call center, or implementing automated knowledge management.

All of these things are major undertakings. We lay these out on the map and say, "Let's organize the projects so they have 100-day timelines." This gives us something to focus on and measure. But it needs to be laid out in such a way that, over time you're marching toward a strategic end—so projects dovetail.

People tend to view these as mutually exclusive; they say it's one or the other. However, it's not one or the other. There are long term strategic things that are on the road map, but there are also opportunistic, short term, common sense things that can get done.

The 100-days concept is a tremendous management tool because it tends to focus one's mind on getting things done. It helps you meet the management expectation that you will have accomplished something. The 100-day win also makes things visible and tangible. The opposite would be a project with deadlines that continue to slip month, after month, after month.

In these cases, you get into the project and say, "Gee, if only we did this a little bit more, it would be so much better." Then 20 months go by, and you get to the testing phase and say, "Wow, this thing is a lot more complicated than we thought," and it becomes 24 months. And then you get the catastrophic blow-ups. That's how you achieve the $100 million project that delivers nothing. How often have we all heard about projects like this?

Let's face it; this is not good for anyone. Having a plan that is shorter term and managing to a deadline is very, very powerful because it's contained, encourages you to make hard decisions about scope, and allows you to actually get it done. It's much easier for people to say, "Not on this phase," or, "This is all we are doing now." Designs are frozen earlier and people are focused more clearly.

Satisfied Customers Or 'Crispy Critters'

At Deloitte Consulting/Braxton, we have a concept called 'torch points.' Most companies treat their customer experience as one homogenous entity. They'll say they provide a mediocre customer experience, or a good customer experience, or a lousy customer experience. And that's the way they talk about and interact with their customers.

I believe it's very useful to think of the customer experience as a distribution of experiences, rather than something that always happens one way. My favorite bad example is when consulting firms plot the current customer experience and then the future customer experience. They try to have a very methodical process to change the customer experience, and meanwhile all hell is breaking loose. Customers are leaving in hoards due to one easy-to-fix issue that is really ticking them off. So the lesson is this: don't get so clever that you lose common sense.

Looking at customer experience as a distribution rather than as an average addresses the old line, "If you have one foot in a bucket of boiling water and one foot in a bucket of freezing water, on average you are comfortable."

When people ask, "How is customer satisfaction?" and, in response, hear, "Well, on average it's pretty good," they wonder why they are losing customers. In actuality, the ones they are losing are torched, crispy critters who are telling a lot of other folks about their experience.

In every company, some customer interactions are unbelievably great. Some are so lousy you can't believe it. And a bunch are mediocre. What happens is that people try to move the average. And they forget about the tail ends which are their really horrendous interactions—the torch points. So, while you are figuring out your torch points, fix them.

There are certainly individual customer experiences where, if you can fix them, they make a huge difference. But there are also systematic torch points. One example is the call center that transfers you to a busy signal. Or, the web order form that doesn't actually get submitted. A torch point could be the customer service rep who can't answer your question. Or, the sales person who comes to you without addressing your critical service delivery issue. These systematic process issues can generally be fixed very easily.

The Sales and Marketing Excellence Challenge

In sales and marketing analytics, it would be great if you could determine statistically where the biggest problems occur. For example, of last month's 10,000 interactions, we had 420 torch points, 80% of which fall into these two categories. This is too sophisticated for today's tools. But you can still identify problem areas by asking the people in the call center who know.

But, companies don't ask.

Generally, people do not go to their contact center and ask, "What are the things that are most upsetting to our customers?" An innovative approach I've seen is a torch point SWAT team. The team's job was to find really terrible customer experiences and figure out what to do in the short term to fix them. Generally, if you ask the call center supervisors, they will know exactly what makes their customers very happy and what makes them unhappy, but they don't feel that they have any ability to make changes.

I'm not talking about making people feel better after a crummy experience; I'm talking about eliminating the torch point source. Make sure the call doesn't transfer to a busy signal; make sure that when customers order something on the web, the order actually happens. When customers call the call center and ask a question, make sure they get the answer. Make sure that the sales person knows about any critical open service issues before she goes selling to someone.

The solution doesn't need to be a terribly elegant or technical one. It could be a faxed piece of paper. Or, it could be an agreement that is kept with the sales person that, if there is a critical issue on somebody's account, you will let the sales person know. You may say, "We don't have that many critical customer service issues, but when we do, we need to let the sales person know." It's amazing how many times this does not happen.

This inaction can happen because the middle of a company is disenfranchised—they feel disempowered. The executives have great ideas that are positive and hard-charging; they come in full of ambition and ready to take on the world. But they encounter people in the middle who don't want to change.

Maybe it's because the people in the middle have been there for a long time, or their promotions have been slower than they wanted, or the pay has been lower than they expected. Especially in today's economy, they've probably tried to fix things several times, only to be told, "We don't have the budget," or, "Just do your job." So now, when you have a very disillusioned middle, they may say, "Hey, I'm just doing my job."

I think people in the customer service centers genuinely want to do a good job. But, in a lot of cases, they know what is upsetting the customers and yet don't feel as though they're in a position to do anything about it.

Even under these circumstances, I've seen companies engage their people and turn things around. A healthcare company I worked with actually did a great job at that. A big part of the turnaround occurred simply because management started paying attention. They actually had executives go down to the customer interaction centers and say, "Hey, this is important," and ask, "What can we do to serve our customers better?" That involvement and interaction made a huge difference.

You'd be surprised at how inexpensive are some of these common sense fixes. In the past, people said the only way to solve things was through technology. That's not the case anymore. It's more about doing—doing smart things to make the business run better. The companies that are going to do the best are the ones that have a very practical, common sense view to making their companies run better.

Visibility, Accountability, And Shareholder Value

I think the strict linkage to shareholder value is another tool that sorts out bad ideas quickly. Is it going to increase revenue? Is it going to increase margins? Or, is it going to increase productivity of assets?

The project has to do one of these three things. You can then rank projects by the value they will create for your company. You should do this instead of implementing some terribly theoretical framework.

One of my favorite examples is a framework that plots the level of enterprise connectivity versus level of customer intimacy. Everyone wants to be in the upper right hand corner and be an intergalactic collaborator or something. The implication is that you should spend every penny of your cash becoming an intergalactic collaborator, but it's meaningless. The framework gives bad advice and wastes a lot of money.

The true north of CRM should always be shareholder value. How are we going to drive revenue, increase margins, and improve productivity? Thinking about shareholder value is a way of focusing the mind.

There are a lot of people doing a lot of things under the banner of being customer-centric. If you were to ask them, "Why do you want to be customer-centric? What does that really mean?" the answer is like the Emperor's New Clothes—there's nothing there. People are just afraid to challenge an executive who says, "We want to be customer-centric."

Because nobody wants to ask, "What do you mean by that?" A thousand ships are launched under the banner of being customer-centric. The chief sales guy says, "We want to sell more to customers," and the CFO says, "Well, that's expensive to do, so let's have the call center guys start calling people." And they start calling people during dinner. Now you've gone from being customer-centric to calling people during dinner. We have a chapter in our book, *How to Eat the CRM Elephant,* on how man becomes ape—reverse Darwinism. You have to be careful.

Sales has always had a cowboy mentality where they are out in the Wild West and have become the heroes. "Against all odds, I closed the deal. I didn't have the right information and I had to do unnatural things to close it, but I landed the deal." I think sales is transitioning somewhat from that mentality to the corporate citizen model. The challenge is to get people to be good corporate citizens while still maintaining their creativity and entrepreneurial flavor. These characteristics make good sales people, so it is a delicate balancing act.

Sales people have to be willing to share data. They have to be willing to be visible and accountable and not just have the sales cowboy mentality of, "Well, I'll see you when I've got another one." In a business world where things aren't changing very quickly, the cowboy approach works because you can generally apply averages and pretty much know what's going to happen.

But when the economy experiences tremendous change as we've seen in the last few years, and will probably continue to see for a few more, you need to have more positive, accurate visibility into pipeline close rates, trends, who is buying, who is not buying, and on future sales.

You need this information not only from a financial projection standpoint, but also from an inventory standpoint. You need to know how many products and services to build. If you have an unknown pipeline, it's very easy to just keep building; and you'll keep building inventory into a downturn. Likewise, you won't see an upturn coming if you don't have accurate sales information. All this means that reporting discipline is essential in today's volatile economy—the cowboy is gone, off in the sunset.

Strangely enough, I think the CRM companies themselves are good examples of discipline. I think Siebel is an unbelievably disciplined company. The way they manage their sales force is incredibly disciplined. Right now, there are cultural implications of that discipline. You can go overboard in discipline and get to the point where the company is no longer a good place to work. And, as soon as the financial benefits run out, the people leave.

Software companies tend to need very, very disciplined sales forces to survive. However, sales forces in the financial services, retail, or communications industries have a long way to go to reach effective use of information and discipline around sales management.

We've gone through the hype cycle where CRM is the cure-all: install this software and your customer satisfaction will magically go up 15%, and your revenue will increase by 20%. That's a bunch of malarkey. But the fact remains that companies need to effectively manage customer information. Companies need to know what a customer has purchased and any service issues that customer is experiencing. When a customer calls for assistance, the person who gets the call has to be able to answer his questions.

Providing this information does not require a magic snake oil solution; it just needs common sense. I think CRM is at its best when it's had a heavy dose of common sense. CRM that's done in the name of intergalactic connectivity generally leads to a lot of wasted money. A lot of companies have wasted many, many years and a lot of money chasing this elusive "integration means 'all things CRM' across the entire enterprise" idea. Focus on a specific and narrow business result to be successful.

GLENN LELAND

Glenn Leland is National Vice President of Business Development for American Medical Response, the largest and premier emergency and non-emergency medical service provider in the U.S. Glenn started his Emergency Medical Services (EMS) career as an Emergency Medical Technician (EMT) in the 1970s and has served AMR and other firms as a paramedic, training officer, operations manager, marketing manager, director, consultant, president, and CEO. In 1994, he was awarded the American Ambulance Association's highest award for his work on strategic planning for the industry, as well as his leadership in development of a contracting guideline for community officials. That guideline is the principle text used in EMS undergraduate and graduate degree programs around the world.

BT

> **After seven years of acquisitions, AMR has spent the past three integrating all 265 pieces. As you can imagine, this created a monumental challenge in terms of creating an effective sales team in an organization, industry, and culture that has little sales history.**

AMR is in two distinctly different businesses that are operationally run together. Our first line of business is contracting with the government, local government, or entities of local government, to manage the 911 system. We are the community's paramedics and the largest responder to 911 calls in America. This represents about 65% of our business.

Our second line of business is contracting with health care. We provide inter-facility transport for health payers such as Kaiser Permanente and health providers such as hospital systems. We also provide transport for health care providers in a retail fashion. All of this represents approximately 35% of our revenues. We transport patients from one health care venue to another at a variety of sophistication levels. The high end includes critical care transport that, at a minimum, is nurse-staffed. It can also be a physician-staffed ambulance transporting patients from one intensive care unit to another. At the lower end, it may not even be an ambulance—it might simply be a mini-van or a wheelchair car.

AMR is the largest provider of emergency and non-emergency medical transportation services in the U.S. with operations in 36 states. We have about 19,000 employees and 4,000 ambulances that transport approximately five million patients on an annual basis.

In our business, we've recently gone through a period where we've been able to attract a significant number of new customers; but at the same time, we've had a higher than average churn rate. We haven't been retaining the same number of contracts, so the net effect is that we're not growing as we'd like. To be successful we want both: excellence in retaining a significant amount of our existing business while expanding and growing our client base.

When we have a contract or a written relationship with a client, our business has been pretty stable. The increase in defection has been in what I call our retail markets, or ambulance services. In ambulance services, an individual nurse or case manager—a user buyer—working in a hospital has to make minute-by-minute decisions as she picks up the phone: what number am I going to call? Which ambulance service am I going to use for this routine inter-facility transport? Ambulance service selection is closely related to the user buyer's most recent experience.

In some cases, smaller, more nimble organizations have been able to focus more narrowly on these user buyers. They have a more personal relationship with the customers or have recently performed well for them. Or, perhaps they have been given, or have asked to be given more retail calls. Adding everything up, we've seen that the David's have been able to whittle away at the Goliaths' market share by focusing more closely on the customer. Because AMR is large, our organization has been structured to focus on our large accounts, major contracts, or major customers. We retain and grow those quite well. It's the small ones that have presented the greatest challenge.

We recently completed the first phase of a comprehensive strategic planning process. We conducted primary market research to measure customer satisfaction and loyalty in our non-emergency retail markets. While we received world class customer satisfaction scores which any company would be happy to receive, we also realized lower scores in response to our loyalty questions. In fact, over 25% of our highly satisfied customers said they would switch providers for a 2% price reduction. But they rated price as a very low priority when selecting an inter-facility ambulance provider. And, they don't pay the bill; third party insurance companies do. Those findings lead us to conclude that we provide great patient care, but are undifferentiated in non-emergency situations.

Therefore, our new focus is on creating a higher level of service support for our inter-facility customers.

Organizing A Cohesive Company Structure

Organizationally, AMR is a company that grew to its current size by acquiring smaller companies. Our annual revenues are approaching $1 billion. We acquired 265 small- to medium-size, but highly fragmented ambulance businesses, over a seven year period. For the last three years of our 10 year history, we've been trying to bring some order to the chaos of 265 different companies. We've boiled it all down to four major cultures that reflect the four geographic regions. There is one corporate unit that coordinates strategy for all.

Each of the regional units has a CEO, a vice president of operations, a business development executive, and a number of other staff members. Each region has its own business development focus and business development executive, typically the vice president, who reports to the regional leadership. This person also has a dotted-line reporting relationship to me and the corporate office.

Our level of service varies from community to community. In many towns, we staff the 911 center. We interview the caller, determine the situation, and provide pre-arrival instructions, such as first-aid instructions, over the phone while the paramedic unit is responding. We also operate the paramedic crew. Most often the crews are in ambulances, but in some cases they operate on helicopters, boats, motorcycles, bicycles, horseback—you name it. We've tried every means imaginable to mobilize our crews.

We even staff fire trucks in rural areas; our paramedics ride on the fire engine with the fire department staff. We also have some public/private partnerships where it works the other way—we operate an ambulance and one of the members of the ambulance crew is a firefighter.

▶ Cultural Transformation

When we first started acquiring companies, the basic plan was to find great companies, buy them, and then leave them alone because they were already being well managed. As we accumulated a certain critical mass, we started leveraging our purchasing power, collaborating and cooperating on various initiatives, such as national purchasing and national uniform programs. Over time, additional issues have been identified that may benefit from standardization or centralization. This sometimes meets with opposition by the local operations and cooperation has varied from topic to topic.

Today we're embarking upon the next level of standardization. Let me clarify that standardization is not centralization. Standardization is defining best practices, sharing them across our national offices and encouraging their adoption throughout the organization. Centralization refers to functions. For example, we brought the accounts payable function to our Denver corporate headquarters and process it all here.

In our business culture, standardization is supported by the local units, while centralization is rarely supported. We are focused on determining when we should standardize, when we should not standardize, and when we should just leave well enough alone. I think that is a challenge for every organization and calls for a transformation in culture.

When it comes to sales and marketing, our history provides some interesting challenges. We grew rapidly through acquisitions our first eight and a half years. We never had any sort of corporate culture for growing the business through contract or sales activities.

The companies we acquired had grown through a variety of mechanisms. Generally, a small, local owner/operator went out and built relationships in his community, provided a good service and won the business, in some cases decades ago. It was the relationship between the owner and the various people in the community that really retained the business. Everybody knew and loved Fred, and called Fred's Ambulance Service. Most of those owner/operators have subsequently retired. They sold their businesses and moved on to other chapters of their lives, leaving behind a management team that, in many cases, didn't have those personal relationships.

For a long time, we didn't have a process that recognized that change in management. We had grown rapidly through acquisitions. We thought like an acquisitions company and lost a bunch of contracts. In the last couple of years, we've started to focus professionally on the issues of business retention and business growth. We're bringing that into the mainstream of the organization because we can't rely upon the previous owner/operators to do it.

▶ Monday Morning Quarterbacking

I can imagine people saying that we should have seen this coming. Certainly there were pockets that recognized it and took action, preserving or growing their businesses on their own without any national coordination or incentive. Accomplishments occurred because someone locally knew to take action. And they were usually rewarded in the marketplace.

At the same time, our industry and the organization was going through a fair amount of change. There's been tremendous pressure from health plans for reimbursement, so we saw an increase in costs but a decrease in revenues on a per-unit basis. Consequently, much of the management team's focus was on achieving efficiency.

Cost containment was the order of the day; the issue of retaining business became less of a priority. A little over a year ago, our CEO recognized this problem, created a national business development function, and asked me to head it up.

We identified a cultural issue: we thought of ourselves as an acquisition, cost containment, and efficiency management company, and did all those things very well. But to retain and grow the business, we needed to become an organization that was much more in tune with its chief markets. We created an infrastructure of business development, appointed regional business development executives, and started to create a sales force.

A variety of people in the organization had customer service or contract management duties, but they weren't actively going out and pursuing new business. We gained some structural control over that population and started training them to be a sales force. As the first professional sales training exercise, we put the sales force through Miller Heiman's *Strategic Selling* and *Conceptual Selling* programs. We saw significant results. The sales force became adept at identifying prospects, developing a strategy, and communicating with clients.

We now have lists of prospects to visit and have started closing business. In fact, we've seen the most significant growth in business since our days of acquisition. We're growing on an annualized rate of approximately $60 million over the course of the last year. This is mainly due to a significant change in our sales process.

Still, we had not addressed the business retention piece. The focus was on getting a fledgling sales organization moving forward and not so much on retaining business other than our major contracts. We lost some major contracts and remained essentially neutral in revenues. We began shifting our focus towards building a better business retention program.

We started off with a crude set of sales tracking and reporting tools, which essentially were spreadsheets we e-mailed out. We now employ a sales force automation toolset for use on an enterprise-wide basis. But the toolset hasn't been standardized; I asked each regional vice president to come up with his or her own reporting and managing process and they each have a different style.

▶ Measurements

Each week we measure a variety of things. For example, we measure each division's sales call plan. How many sales calls are they going to schedule? What priority will the calls be? With what types of customers? Each week, the divisions submit their reports for the coming week, and their actuals for the previous week. This allows us to track what are they actually doing, and how close to their plan are they able to stay.

We also measure visits to existing customers when an opportunity has been identified. Sales calls are follow up visits where the sales person has a single sales objective. Maintenance calls are visits without an active sales objective. These are tracked and reported separately.

Rather than having the managers or me arbitrarily assign call volumes, our business development people create their own targets. They look at their assigned accounts and plan their territory. Then we prescribe a call frequency for maintenance accounts—how frequently they should see an account based on a variety of factors. They combine maintenance calls, sales calls, and single sales opportunities into a sales call activity plan. Actual activities are reported against this plan.

Typically, they have more maintenance calls and fewer sales calls than they had forecasted. This seems to be the pattern today as we're shifting the culture. As you might imagine, we have frequent discussions about this issue.

We encourage our business development folks to work closely with our operations team to identify what's really going on. Why are we doing so much maintenance? Is it because we're not performing as well as we would like to operationally? Are we having a service issue? What is the dynamic that's creating higher maintenance than anticipated; or should we plan to maintain that much?

Putting Training To Work

For openers, we've allowed each region to decide whom they want to send to sales training. Since I became an instructor I've taught 23 classes to about 260 attendees. AMR pays for the training, so the regions can send anyone they want with no restriction.

One of our regions has sent all of their senior operating management. In one particular division, the vice president of operations really latched onto the process and saw that, for this to work, he had to drive it in his division. This person has created a monthly target meeting.

His management team and business development staff meets monthly to review each account from a strategic standpoint and brainstorm how they can improve service to that account. They also discuss every sales objective as a complete management team and come up with an action plan for the next month.

These monthly meetings have helped this division understand their market penetration. When they started this process in January 2002, they believed that they had about 90% market share with no room for growth. Since then, they've grown over 25%.

They've also created some service innovations that they say would never have surfaced without this process. This is happening predominantly because their business development people are out interacting with clients on a daily basis. And the people back at the office who manage the operation are communicating and treat each other as teammates.

Traditionally, the sales person says, "If only they'd get the product right, it would be easier to get my job done." The operational people think, "If only they sold the right product, it would be easier to do this." Our organization had that same natural tension between sales and operations, but by sitting down together and going through specifics, they've seen each other as problem solvers. Now they ask, "How can we better serve the client and how can we improve the relationship?" It's grown their business dramatically. For the eight months this group has been following this practice, they've had an even greater impact on profitability than they've had on growth.

We don't rank divisions by size or profit, but by their compliance with plan. They plan to produce a certain amount of business and we track actual versus plan. When we started measuring, this division was fourth from the bottom, or 21st of 25. Now they're in the top seven. With half the year gone they had to make up a lot of ground. Even though they were significantly off plan in January, they will end up ahead of plan by the end of the year.

We have highlighted this operation's approach for the other vice presidents of operations and have shared the data about its impact on performance. We've suggested this approach as a best practice and have encouraged other VPs to emulate it. In the last two months, eight of 25 vice presidents of operations have adopted it.

A lot of the training program's success is due to all of the students understanding its importance to the organization. Having the national vice president personally teach the class is also a factor. For every class, I asked the regional CEO or a vice president to join as a student. All of our

CEOs joined. One CEO attended three times. He wanted his team to understand that this was important, and backed up his belief with his presence. He also saw it as an opportunity to interact with his team and reinforce some points that he thought were particularly important.

Everybody talks about management commitment. It's very easy to measure. It's simply a matter of involvement and follow-through. When I go out into the field and am interacting with the sales reps, I'll stop the discussion and say, "Let's get out your blue sheet (a copyrighted form from *Strategic Selling)*." In many cases early on, I found they didn't have them. So I'd take one out and we'd complete it together right then. It reinforced the process and showed we were serious about following it.

Still, we continue to get passive resistance in some cases, particularly with the blue sheet. People don't feel they really have to fill out the blue sheet, so we've had to be a little more stern. I've found it effective to call their VP and point out, "I came and spent my time to teach your people how to do this, so they can at least follow through on using the process. If they don't, why am I leading the next class you've requested?"

Introducing Technology

I think CRM is going to be an innovation for us. It will help our natural evolution towards building a set of tools to help us manage the process, the data, and the various interactions. And while we've made a lot of advancements in this area, once we started looking at how to move to the next level and started evaluating vendors, we saw that we would be better served to buy a solution and continue to try to innovate. But we also created access databases and a variety of other tools to manage the process and the data.

We have specific objectives for this implementation. We currently use a series of weekly and monthly reports to manage the sales function, which will be turned off on October 1, 2002. In order to continue complying with their reporting requirements, the regions will have to seamlessly and flawlessly implement this project. I've requested this because I've seen so many CRM projects fail when it wasn't clear that the organizations really had to comply.

Because of our compliance requirement, we've resisted the temptation to use every single bit of functionality. We've limited it to the functionality we already had in our manual system. We're just shifting over to the new CRM system as the vehicle that we use to report, very much the same way we did manually.

We are also providing online training to better ensure the compliance and results we want. One part is provided by our CRM vendor, and an online AMR version will follow. In addition, each of our operations departments has scheduled a series of face-to-face training opportunities.

Partnering With The Competition

We have been talking about shifting our culture to partner with what has previously been viewed as a competitor: namely, the local fire departments. We've attempted this in the past, but are now reaching out more aggressively. Specifically, we sought out fire leaders and asked them what challenges they have. We then shared with them what we see as our unique strengths. Then we posed the question, "Wouldn't we better serve the community if we did these things together?"

The response we received was dramatic. Fire services said, "We've never looked at it quite that way. We always saw you guys as the evil empire, the 800-pound gorilla that had the potential to really harm us." We recognize that we can grow faster by working with the fire departments than by working against them. And if we can figure out how to do this in a win-win way, then it also better serves our customers.

As an example, we have a partnership program in San Mateo County, California. One of the most important things in emergency ambulance service is the response time: how quickly can we put a paramedic at the bedside of a sick or injured person? Those minutes can mean life or death for the injured party. However, cutting down those minutes costs a ton of money and the shorter the timeframe, the more expensive it is.

In San Mateo County, we were the paramedic ambulance provider. We met with the fire department and posed an idea: what if you had paramedics as well as firemen on the truck? In many cases, the fire engine can get to the patient's bedside faster than the ambulance. If we had paramedics on both, we'd stand a better chance of a rapid response. In order to pay for that change, let's elongate the ambulance response time, which will save money for us. And we'll pay you; we'll provide the funding, training and equipment necessary for you to upgrade your fire department to paramedic service.

At first they thought we were crazy. Then they realized we were serious—and that it could be done. We went to the local government, got approval, and implemented a program that has slower ambulance response times than it had before, but with an enhanced first response by the fire service. The result? Better quality to the constituent at no significant increase in cost.

The significance of this story is that we tapped into the resource of the existing fire engines, better integrated them into the EMS delivery system, and reduced our own cost in the process.

Today, fire departments' roles have dramatically expanded. EMS is now responsible for responding to bioterrorism, mass destruction, and a variety of new activities they have not previously been asked to manage. Now we live in a post-September 11th world. I think that has helped us deliver our message: we focus on one area of the overall emergency medical services mission, which we are very good at. We say to fire departments, "Why don't you let us manage that, and you can take on the bigger mission of helping people in times of need?"

GERHARD GSCHWANDTNER

Gerhard Gschwandtner is the founder and publisher of Selling Power, the leading sales management magazine with a circulation of 200,000 subscribers in 67 countries worldwide. Gerhard and I first met at a Customer Relationship Management (CRM) Summit in Boulder, Colorado, several years ago and I was immediately impressed by his passion for the sales profession. Gerhard started the magazine on a shoestring budget in 1981, without outside investors. Two years ago, Selling Power moved into its own office building on a four acre lot in Fredericksburg, Virginia. Together, Gerhard and his wife, Laura, are the sole owners of the business and have three daughters. Laura is the editor of the magazine and writes novels in her spare time. A native Austrian who speaks three languages fluently, Gerhard is the author of ten books on selling and motivation, and two books on photography. He loves to ski, sail, golf and kayak. His publication's website address is www.sellingpower.com.

JD

As publisher of Selling Power, I have the opportunity to talk to many CEOs and vice presidents of sales in many different industries. During these discussions, I get their thoughts on the state of the union, if you will, for selling and marketing. Two key challenges seem to be emerging that we are going to have to address if sales forces are going to meet their business goals.

The Marketing Challenge

The first challenge I see is central to the marketing organization. The key problem today is that we are not giving sales people the right messaging or information tools to satisfy customer needs. Until we deal with this issue, sales organizations will continue to perform below their potential.

To understand why this problem exists, we need to start by looking at how we have structured sales and marketing. In many companies, sales and marketing function as big separate silos that very rarely collaborate. Marketing is immersed in the theoretical world of data analysis and comprehension of the 'ideal' customer, while sales focuses its activities on the wide variety of customer types that exist in the real marketplace.

Sales and marketing departments often live in two different worlds, and unfortunately the messaging that is created in the world of marketing does not always have relevance to the world of sales. In talking with a number of companies, I understand that of all the marketing materials created, more than 50% are not utilized regularly by the sales team. The problem is that the content does not correspond with the sales process, the way sales people actually sell.

Too often, marketing material is designed for the abstract, theoretical, ideal customer. But in the real world, that prospect does not exist. What exist are lots of different types of customers, in different markets, in different industries; and these people have different responsibilities, expectations, and authorities within the prospect company. Given these conditions, boilerplate marketing materials will not help a sales person convert a fresh opportunity into a sale.

▶ The Marketing/Marketplace Disconnect

The main reason this problem exists is that marketing is often not in touch with the marketplace. I know of very few companies where marketing managers or product managers actually go out with sales people on calls. They rarely have the opportunity to question customers directly.

As a result, marketing does not get firsthand feedback on how customers are using the product, or how they value it compared to a competitor. Marketing is often in the dark as to what kind of financial matrix prospects are using to determine the value of the product or service, or how customers see their needs changing in the future.

There is an additional challenge in that sales teams have to be very flexible; they often sell into many different markets, to many different channels, and have different sales processes for each. Based on this situation, you need a variety of messages for any given product, not just one. Perhaps your 'A' sales person can keep up with the customization of messages, but your 'B' and 'C' players cannot. In this case, a major portion of the sales force is not very effective.

However, this is not just a sales effectiveness issue; it is a marketing effectiveness one as well. You begin to understand the magnitude of the problem when you start to follow the message trail. Statistics show that when an average company prints, let's say, 5,000 brochures, only about 3,000 actually reach the sales people. If out of that 3,000, the sales team uses only 1,500, then you have a gigantic waste of time, effort, and money that marketing could have better invested elsewhere.

▶ Customer Messaging Management

To deal with this disconnect, there is a new discipline I see emerging that is loosely referred to as Customer Messaging Management. This concept aims to put some structure and rigor around how we develop and produce the messages we want the sales team to convey in the marketplace.

Some companies are on the cutting edge of solving the disconnect problem, such as American Express, EDS, and Federal Express. These firms are experimenting right now with Customer Messaging Management software and tools, and are implementing systems to create what I would describe as a Sales Intelligence Center.

American Express is one of the innovators in this area. They have established a Sales Intelligence Center that is available to their account executives who call on businesses interested in setting up merchant accounts.

Before the center was enabled, account executives had to spend three, five, or sometimes ten hours to create an individualized presentation for a merchant or a chain of merchants. In it, they would adequately explain all of the benefits of accepting the American Express card and the impact it would have for the company. To prepare for these meetings, an account executive might have had to search as many as 100 different databases to get the information he or she needed for that specific customer.

Now with the implementation of the Sales Intelligence Center, account executives can go to a single source for all their messaging needs. The Sales Intelligence Center contains details on all the marketing collateral and programs that are in place: data sheets, customized PowerPoint presentations, even customized white papers. By utilizing it, account executives can now access much higher quality material in a fraction of the time that it took before.

▶ Delivering on the Customer-Centric Promise

I recently had a conversation with Mike Bosworth, who is writing a book on customer-centric selling entitled *The Customer-Driven Sales Process*. During our discussion, Mike pointed out that many companies are really only paying lip service to the concept of being customer-driven. He said that if sales people are really going to be customer-centric, they are going to have to be more adept at calling on the executives of prospect companies.

Sales people are challenged by the lack of company-provided material, or the right material, to satisfy individual market or executive needs. They need to be able to talk to the CEO in a different language as compared to talking to the VP of Sales, or the CFO, or the CIO.

That is why implementing centers like the one at American Express will be the wave of the future. The smart companies will produce marketing collateral not just by market segment but also by job title. They will make it easy for the sales person to sell at all the appropriate levels of any given enterprise.

The Gartner Group perhaps feels the same way, as they appear ready to create a technology category to cover this concept. Recently, I have also seen a number of the established CRM players toying with the idea of adding Customer Messaging Management to their offerings. Some smaller CRM players have already released tools in this area.

The Sales Challenge

▶ The Creative Sales Opportunity

Sales is facing another challenge all their own. Right now, we are in a business environment where I think creativity has a tremendous premium. The reality of sales today is that it is less of a science and much more of an art. When the economy is good, any kind of sales approach is going to be profitable. High sales can mask a lot of problems, deficiencies, and inefficiencies. But when the economy is tough and challenging, I think the creative sales person has a tremendous edge over the average sales person who just goes into the market with a boiler-plate sales approach.

In this tough economy, the decision-making level has migrated upward one or two notches. In this new world, focusing on leveraging old relationships no longer works, and continuing to use old messages no longer works. Now, the sales person needs to become the customer's trusted advisor, at not just the recommender level in the company, but the executive level as well. He needs to come in with solutions that can really have a measurable impact on a company's bottom line.

If that is not the case, if sales people cannot be competent enough to do a needs diagnostic, or if they are incapable of formulating creative solutions to discovered needs, then there is no sale and the company will not be successful.

In this economy, where everybody is greatly challenged, sales people need to recognize their prospect's issues, quickly prioritize them, and then zero in on one or two where they feel they can really make a difference.

Here, they need to not only demonstrate they can make a creative contribution to the company, but also document what the impact will be, and how they will achieve specific goals. You cannot sell in this market with promises; promises are nothing. You need to sell in this market with proof.

▶ Executive Support in the Sales Process

You need to approach this sales challenge from two perspectives. First, management has to be more involved in the sales process. The sales leader has to mobilize upper level management and get them involved in supporting the sales force. This is something I don't just preach; it is something I also practice. Here at *Selling Power*, our top sales executive regularly involves me personally in the sales calls our advertising sales people make.

A vice president of sales should call on at least 20 accounts a year or more. There should be an absolute minimum. And if the CEO doesn't make at least ten substantial calls a year on key clients, he is not worth his salt. CEOs can have a tremendous influence by sitting in a sales meeting, showing up at a regional meeting, or assisting a national account rep with a top client. This is a time when each person in the company should see him or herself as a sales person.

There is a significant side benefit for getting CEOs more actively involved in working with clients. I hear from several consultants that CEOs are increasingly dissatisfied with their vice president of sales and their vice president of marketing. That dissatisfaction often stems from the fact that CEOs do not have a common vocabulary to communicate with their chief sales executive. Many CEOs don't have a background in sales or marketing; instead, they came up through the ranks in engineering or finance.

Some CEOs are installed into their jobs by venture capitalists or the board of directors, who select someone who can watch their investment and maximize the value of the company. For these appointees, the sales and marketing functions are usually not as familiar.

With no firsthand experience, a CEO might feel challenged when it comes to evaluating the effectiveness of sales and marketing teams. So, becoming actively involved in the process can go a long way towards education. The CEO will be able to see the issues that sales and marketing executives struggle with on a daily basis, which in turn should help build better relationships among all parties.

▶ Creative Solution Selling

Second, we need to bring to bear all the necessary resources required to help the sales people design and deliver solutions, versus simply sell products. At *Selling Power*, we have made it clear to our sales team that we are not in the business of selling space. We are in the business of helping customers with creative solutions. In order to meet a customer's real business need, we are willing to make all of our media assets available to our sales people.

In some cases, this means that we may need to deal with complexities such as having print ads married to an e-mail blast or tied to an online web presence, in support of branding a client asset. Or, in implementing an online newsletter or advertisement campaign, we may have to get involved actively in some of the creative development work for a client.

On several occasions this year, we have had clients come to us after rejecting two or three campaign concepts from outside agencies. Because we already speak the sales manager's language, we offered those clients access to our creative people and have been able to develop some very effective marketing programs. By going beyond the idea of just selling ad space, we have created win-win relationships with our customers.

Recommendations To Sales

▶ Set Clear Expectations

What advice would I give to sales organizations? Trying to be universal in my perspective, the first thing I would think we all need to focus on is what the company and top sales executive expect from their sales people. The larger companies grow, the more amorphous their communications process becomes. The vice president communicates with the regional manager, the regional manager with the district manager, the district manager with the field sales manager, then with the account reps in the field, cascading down like molasses. What often happens is that the corporate vision, values, and style of execution tend to get diluted.

UPS is one company that does an exceptional job in this area. UPS is a very hands-on organization with an expectation of continuous improvement. They go the extra mile. They communicate this relentlessly to everybody, and everybody knows what their mission is, and what is expected of them. Because those expectations are so clearly communicated, everybody knows the score, and the sales organization is one of the most effective in America.

▶ Measure Performance—Good and Bad

The second thing that I would recommend to a vice president of sales is a matrix for measuring the sales force. Ideally, this would include not only an intelligent reward system for good performance, but also a warning mechanism for when expected performance levels are not met.

A lot of companies overdo it on the rewards side. They invest a lot of money and resources on incentive programs, sales clubs, etc. to reward top performers. However, when it comes to dealing with under-performers, sales people who need to be salvaged or rescued, they have no real recovery system for helping them.

Too often, under-performers are placed on a performance plan without being offered any help to improve, and then are summarily fired after 60 or 90 days. As a result, sales organizations can have horrendous turnover rates of 30%, 40%, even 50%. This is a huge cost to a company in terms of lost sales, as well as recruiting and training expenses.

Some companies are dealing very effectively with this issue. I remember talking to a division manager of AT&T. He shared with me the system they had developed for working with sales people when performance levels were not met. When this type of problem occurs, the sales person is placed on a 60-day 'intensive care' program whereby the manager aggressively attempts to help the sales person remedy the situation.

The manager works actively with the sales person to cover the territory more effectively, and to ensure that the sales rep has all the fundamental skills necessary to do the job. Performance expectations are well defined, support services are made available, and the consequences for failing to make changes are crystal clear.

If the sales person recovers, if his sales recover, then everything returns to normal. But, if after the pre-defined period of time sales do not improve, the account executive is given the choice of either finding a non-sales related job within the organization or seeking permanent employment elsewhere.

▶ Continually Challenge Your Sales Process

The third thing I would focus on is the sales process, because it is something that can make or break the sales force. Too often, the way we sell becomes a tradition. The problem is that in today's economy, tradition cannot always keep up with the demands of the marketplace. The traditions of any company, or any sales organization, can inadvertently inhibit performance because traditions can limit available options.

That's why you have to look at the sales process every single quarter and see how you can improve every part of that process. Everything you do should be up for review; nothing can be held as sacred. If you are selling direct, should you also look at selling through channels? If you are selling over the phone, should you also have a field sales force for big accounts? We cannot continue to rely on what has been successful in the past to help us be successful in the future.

We need to look deep into the process and understand all the details of what we do. For example, you should be able to gauge how effective you are with proposals. If you have a proposal library, you should be ranking those materials just like Amazon rates books.

If you have 29 proposals in your library, you want to know which one is used the most often and which one is used the least often. The ones used the least need to be revamped. The ones used the most need to be tested and measured for effectiveness. If they are overused, but not effective, then you need to remedy that situation.

We have to find a way to really measure and evaluate everything we do in sales. We cannot just rely on tradition to take us forward; we have to make decisions and take action based on the realities of how well we are performing in the current marketplace.

Recommendations To Marketing

Until recently, marketing has not been accountable for their efforts; that is their dark side. Marketing's focus has been on 'doing things.' They create messages. They develop and print brochures. They design and implement numerous campaigns. They create elegant websites. They conduct a large variety of activities that look very glamorous and creative, but they are hardly ever measured.

Too many companies implement direct marketing campaigns without finding out later how effective they were. Or they do advertising campaigns and never measure how many leads they generated, and how many of those leads actually translated into sales. They do extensive media campaigns and then never report the results.

The biggest problem that a vice president of marketing needs to address is this: "How can I make my marketing team more accountable, and what kind of a matrix should I use to measure the effectiveness of the department?" We have to get our hands around understanding what the real return is on our marketing investments. Just as we should be constantly assessing our sales process and looking to optimize the way we sell, we should also be evaluating our marketing process and assessing the effectiveness of those activities.

Staying The Course

The ironic thing in this economy is, at the same time that everybody is complaining about sales and profits, we are cutting back on the very investments we should be making to deal with those problems.

We are cutting back on sales, and on marketing, and everybody is cutting their advertising budgets. What comes to my mind is a little poem that is very corny, but I will share it with you anyway. It goes like this:

> 'He who has a thing to sell
>
> and goes and whispers in a well
>
> is not so apt to get the dollar
>
> as he who climbs a tree and hollers.'

We need to stay the course. If you believe in yourself, if you truly have the products or services people need, then you need to continue to make the right levels of investments in marketing and sales. You should know why you are making those investments and what the expected returns should be, but we have to spend the money if we expect to make money. That may be a hard thing to do today, but it is the right thing.

JACK LANE

Jack Lane is Senior Vice President of Administrative Services for Spherion Outsourcing, an organization that provides quick-response administrative and sales support personnel and systems to major corporations around the world. Jack's understanding of both the sales cycle and the sales executive has been honed during a 30-year career that has included a number of high-level positions in sales, marketing, and business development at such companies as IBM, Attachmate, and Accenture. His company's web site address is www.spherion.com.

JD

> ***Sales quotas can only be met if sales people are in the field, talking to customers, meeting them face-to-face. In an age of tight budgets and self-enablement, however, many sales people spend more time performing administrative tasks than they do selling. Hiring in-house administrative staff is no longer an option. Neither is increasing the size of the sales team. If projections are to be met, if sales people (and their managers) are to keep their jobs, if companies are to stay in business, another solution must be found.***

Your sales are flagging, and you're having trouble meeting your projections. Your sales people are working around the clock but still coming nowhere near making their numbers. You're wondering what the problem could be.

The answer may actually be pretty simple—a matter of basic arithmetic.

The solution, of course, is a little more complicated. There is one, but we'll get to that in a minute.

First, think about what it takes to make a sale. Recently, we figured out that for one of our clients to make 16 sales, they needed to start with 1,350 targets. These targets produced 450 leads, only 150 of which were qualified. Those qualified leads led to 48 assessments, which translated into 16 sales.

Factor into that the amount of time a sales person should be spending identifying the market, figuring out and researching the targets, understanding the issues these companies are facing, learning who's who at the target company, determining how your offerings match the potential client's needs, preparing for the calls, planning the meetings and the presentations, following up after each meeting, managing the relationships—and you've got a very busy sales person with a very full time job.

But then, with that job description in mind, take a look at some extremely sobering statistics recently released by the Insight Technology Group (ITG), a Boulder, Colorado-based think tank that's been charting how sales people, these days, actually spend their time (see below). On average, their research shows that a sales person today is spending as little as 17% of his or her time doing face-to-face selling and 21% of his or her time selling over the phone. That means that less than 40% of a sales person's attention is focused on doing the very thing that sales person was hired to do.

Sales Professional Time Allocation

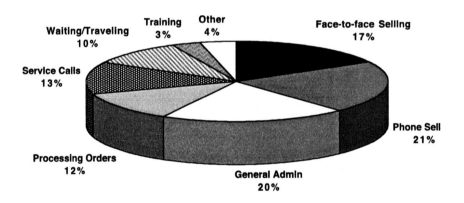

The Sales Person's Day

What's that sales person doing the rest of the day? Fully, 45% of his or her time, says ITG, is taken up by administrative tasks—preparing mailings, scheduling appointments, coordinating schedules, creating presentations, updating customer records, tracking orders, doing rudimentary client research. The remaining 17% is spent on such relatively unavoidable—if unfortunate—tasks as traveling, waiting for appointments to start, and training.

Given that all those administrative tasks have to be done—and that someone has to do them—it's understandable, at least when you do the math, that there's little time left for selling. And if you've any doubt that that's the case, listen to what the sales team will tell you when you ask why their quotas haven't been met: "I wish I could have made more sales calls," they'll say, "but I had to do the sales forecast…I spent all day doing research…I was preparing the PowerPoint for tomorrow's presentation…I have to get the proposal done for Monday."

All true. All familiar. But the question remains: How did things get this way? Why is the sales person consumed with administrative duties when his or her chief mandate has to be bringing in the sales—and meeting the projections?

You probably already know the answer. The combination of tighter, recessionary times and a movement toward self-enablement has stripped away the support layer from many sales operations. Today's sales person may well be heavily equipped with technology—hardware and software to help him or her perform many administrative tasks—but there are few human beings around to pitch in where the technology can't yet go.

And this cycle, stalled by a slow-moving recovery, has become somewhat self-perpetuating. The C-level decision makers are wary of providing support through increased headcount because the economics don't justify it. Stick-wielding managers can ask sales people to work longer, more productive hours, but, truth be told, the administrative work needs to get done, and countless studies have documented the loss in effectiveness that too many hours on the job can bring.

Moreover, few sales managers would advocate bringing in additional sales troops to bolster the effort; while that might boost overall sales, given the expense of paying sales professionals, this clearly would not be a cost-effective move.

So sales departments continue to miss their numbers. Sales managers continue to miss their bonuses. And talented sales people, drawn to organizations by the promise of both professional challenge and increased personal revenue, achieve neither. Instead, they often become burnt out and leave—creating additional problems, and expense, for your organization: the cost of replacement and the loss of knowledge capital.

Learning From The Call

Consider this scenario:

In an ideal sales world, a sales person would complete a visit to a client, pick up his or her cell phone, go into a mail box and dictate the following report: "I've just had a great meeting with Jane Doe at the Client Company. We talked about a new marketing campaign and a number of other new initiatives. I think we'll close this sale in about three months. Should be a $100,000 deal. A couple of next steps: Please send her an umbrella with our logo, an invitation to our next seminar, and a thank you from me saying I enjoyed the meeting, appreciate the time you took, and look forward to our next meeting."

After a week's worth of sales calls and a week's worth of such detailed sales reports, the sales person could easily provide a comprehensive record that could be analyzed and acted upon. Not to mention the fact that he or she has made sure that customer relationship management is at top form and the company has an increasing storehouse of client knowledge to draw on in the future.

But relying on himself or herself alone—and stretched in so many directions—a sales person is more likely to wait until Friday, when the sales report is suddenly due, and, working from memory and through fatigue, simply catalog the headlines, missing the details, dropping the analysis, and, possibly, losing the sale. That Friday message, in contrast to the one dictated immediately after the meeting, would sound more like this: "Met with Jane Doe. Think we can do something here."

Clearly, something is broken that desperately needs to be fixed. Sales need to be made; budgets need to be met; sales people cannot continue to collect sales-level salaries while performing administrative-level work. The dilemma is finding the tools that will fix the problem—efficiently, cost-effectively, and for the long run.

Fixing What's Broken

However, if internal fixes—hiring more support staff, bringing in more sales people, or asking the existing sales staff to work longer and harder—aren't available or appropriate, what other routes might be considered? Increasingly, we've found the answer to be outsourcing sales support services to an external organization whose core competency is in the provision of these administrative services.

That, of course, is our business; we are an organization that, as its core competency, provides administrative services on an outsourced basis to a host of companies. But ours is also a business that has mirrored changes in how companies operate; it's a business that has developed out of demand. Over the course of the last several decades, more and more corporate front offices have found themselves unable—and unwilling—to provide the level of administrative support to which executives had long been accustomed—and so, that level of support was gradually whittled away.

As you have found in the sales environment, advances in technology helped take some of the pressure off; in addition, there were numerous areas where self-enablement made sense. In time, however, the front offices came to realize that, in their efforts to save costs and streamline their operations, they'd sometimes thrown the proverbial baby out with the bathwater. Regrouping, they looked at redeveloping the support structure they'd eliminated, but realized that was both unviable and unnecessary.

The solution for many of these organizations was outsourcing. And as we've provided outsourced administrative services to the front offices of these organizations, we've come to see a number of parallels between the front office and the sales department—parallels that point the way to similar solutions, with similar results.

The standard solutions to the problems faced by sales departments today—hiring more support staff, hiring more sales people, just demanding better sales results from already harried and scattered sales people—are easy to envision. They might not work; they might not be feasible; they might not provide results. But they feel familiar. It's easy to imagine how the path might be followed and it's just as easy to see how it might fail.

Two Related Approaches

Moving toward an outsourced solution—especially if you haven't done it before—might be harder to fathom. For a sense of how it can work, let me share the experience of one of our clients, John H. Harland Company, an Atlanta-based firm that sells checks and business forms to financial institutions. When we started to work with them, Harland was providing its sales people with few consolidated administrative services.

To support Harland's sales force, most of whom work remotely from their home offices, we focused on three core services:

- a *sales resource center* to handle such everyday needs as word processing, presentation creation, and transcription services;

- a *sales supply group* to manage collateral distribution and inventory; and,

- *a branch fulfillment center* to handle the distribution of customized collateral for Harland's customers.

Though we were leveraging the knowledge we'd gained in our work with other companies—particularly in front-office applications—our real charge in this project was to develop workflow processes that met Harland's needs and fit into that company's way of doing things. The result, directly attributable to this project: an increase in face-to-face selling time of at least 25%.

At the other extreme, an existing, strong, centralized, administration support 'hub' at IBM was moved to a remote configuration designed to boost the level of support provided to professionals on the move. The program, called Principal Response Team (PRT), allows specialists to provide sales people with such services as calendaring, teleconferencing, meeting planning, mail management, travel planning, word processing, and presentation creation support.

Proof of PRT's success is that through a combination of selecting, training, and retaining well-qualified workers—as well as leveraging workflow management techniques—the ratio of the number of people supported by a single administrative person is three times higher than when we started and user satisfaction has gone up.

Getting Started

Faced with the seeming intractability of the problem they're facing— competent sales people not making their sales goals because their time is eaten up with administrative tasks—and the success that companies like Harland and IBM have found through the outsourcing of administrative tasks, the choice of an outsourced solution might seem both logical and inevitable. But there are often obstacles in the path of adopting it.

Sales people, accustomed to self-enablement, comfortable with the 'excuses' the current situation provides, and doubtful that outsiders can serve them the way they—or an onsite sales assistant—can, will often, somewhat understandably, resist this sort of change.

At the other end of the company, CFOs, burnt by extensive investments in CRM and Sales Force Automation programs that haven't performed, and not clear about the type of return on investment an outsourcing arrangement can provide, will often, and understandably, resist making yet another investment in an outside service.

To allay fears from both directions, it's useful to understand how an outside services provider, such as Spherion, would approach taking over tactical administrative services, thereby freeing up sales professionals not only for the strategic thinking that's behind effective selling, but for the actual sales calls themselves.

First, it's important to assess the current situation: Who does what? What do they do? How could that task be done better?

We find it very helpful to look at the entire sales process and determine how many steps have administrative components associated with them. If the sales person is involved in those tasks, we want to see if there's a better way to get the job done. Once we've done that assessment, we develop a gap analysis, showing the space between where the sales force is and where the sales executive (or the budget) thinks it ought to be.

With this baseline established, we can work with a client to build a system that supports the way people already work, rather than expecting them to drastically change their methods to support a seemingly inflexible system.

In developing the system—and the sales administrative infrastructure that is its foundation—our experience has taught us that there are six basic components to consider:

- **Work space:** The design of office space has a tremendous impact on workflow.

- **Work practices**: To ensure high quality, fast delivery, and optimal procedures, it's important to know how long it actually takes to perform certain tasks, whether it's typing a letter or creating a complex presentation with graphs, animation and sound. We have a wide range of tools that allow us to document, benchmark, and monitor these tasks.

- **Skills/competencies:** You need the right people with the right skills and competencies available at the right time to perform those tasks. We do extensive pre-hire occupational skills and behavioral assessment; we segment people into jobs that leverage specific skills sets; and we provide extensive coaching, training, and e-learning. The last thing a sales person needs to spend time doing is training his or her support staff to do the tasks that have been outsourced to them.

- **Connectivity:** The sharing of information needs to be facilitated by the connectivity tools—phone, fax, e-mail, instant messaging— that the sales reps actually use when they're working remotely.

- **Communications:** Sales reps and the administrative staff—the Vital Support Representatives—who support them need to build warm, trusting relationships that are geared toward helping the sales team achieve its goals. Without that confidence, it's likely that sales reps will simply bypass the administrative support staff and revert to doing the tasks themselves. In that case, everybody loses.

- **Measurement:** Baselines are important, but the timeliness and quality of work needs to be monitored continuously, with all issues addressed quickly and professionally.

Tailored Solutions

With an assessment of the current situation, an understanding of the sales process, and an analysis of these six components as they relate to a client's specific situation, we're able to tailor not only the work flow but also the work balance. So, for example, when we manage the resource base for one of our clients, we know we need to make more administrative staff available on Wednesdays because sales people need to be ready to present their sales opportunities at the management meeting on Thursday.

Similarly, through trend analysis, by tracking the available administrative time and anticipated work-turnaround times, and matching these with the required skill sets, we can optimize the resource management capability across a wide group of individuals, making sure that service is always available to fill the demand—well beyond the confines of an organization's staff, well beyond the confines of a typical eight-hour day.

That means, for example, that if, one day, one of your sales people lands at an airport, presentation in tow, only to discover that world events have made a key element of his presentation not only irrelevant but embarrassing, there is an administrative staff person a mere phone call away, ready and waiting to set things straight—reworking the presentation, getting it printed, and making sure it's sitting at the sales person's hotel's front desk as he heads off for his all-important meeting.

The alternative, of course, is not so pretty. It's scrap the presentation. Or paste over the offending words. Or try to explain it away, while looking less than cutting-edge—and jeopardizing the sale. But it's an alternative that, in a world where sales people double as administrative staff, is all too common. Unless, of course, the sales person isn't even in the field at all.

Win-Win

The benefits of freeing up the sales person's selling time are manifold— once the sales person has grown accustomed to this new freedom. Besides the obvious goal of meeting projections, there are likely to be:

- **Higher win rates**: With more time to concentrate on strategic selling, targeting will be tighter; sales people will be less likely to be blindsided during the sales process.

- **Higher margins**: With more time to concentrate on developing solid business cases for potential clients, discounting will be more of a last resort.

- **Better sales force morale**: And, better retention rates, which can clearly and easily be monetized, given the high cost of replacing an experienced sales person.

- **Speed of response**: When sales people are backed up around the clock by trained, qualified, and tuned-in administrative staff, they can respond more quickly to customer needs, increasing customer satisfaction and loyalty.

Many companies have found themselves in a dead-end, no-win situation. Where the economy once allowed sales people to achieve wild success while functioning as glorified order takers, just meeting sales projections is now demanding nearly unprecedented levels of creativity, energy, and initiative. But those levels are impossible to sustain in an environment where self-enabled sales people are not only spending a vast percentage of their days performing administrative tasks, but are finding their creativity, energy, and initiative sapped in the process.

The cost-effective and efficient solution to this problem appears to be finding an outside service provider who can function as an administrative partner to the sales force, providing economies of scale and round-the-clock, personalized service. The benefits are clear. The risks of either maintaining the status quo or taking routes that have proven ineffective are just as obvious—for the companies, for the sales people, and, of course, for the sales executives, whose jobs so often depend on the performance of the sales team they run.

JANET DOLAN

Born on a farm to a fourth generation of Minnesotans, Janet set out to be an attorney. After graduating from the William Mitchell College of Law in 1976, she worked for four years as a trial attorney with The Southern Minnesota Regional Legal Services, where she assisted low-income clients in dealing with such issues as immigration and housing. From there, she moved on to the Minnesota Lawyers Professional Responsibility Board, becoming its First Assistant Director in 1981. When I met Janet she had already served as Corporate Counsel for The Tennant Company and was then Vice President of Sales. In 1999, she replaced well-respected Roger Hale as President and CEO. Today, she is one of only 22 women CEOs of companies listed on the New York Stock Exchange (symbol: TNC). I enjoy every time I have a chance to connect with Janet and am impressed with her enthusiasm, upstanding character, and ability to handle the big jobs without taking them or herself too seriously.

BT

The Tennant Company has been in business for 132 years. We've twice been listed as one of Fortune's Best 100 Companies to Work For and are on the leading edge of the quality movement. All of this gives us a certain perspective; we attract and hire people with a certain mindset and value set. We used this foundation to build bench strength and pull away from competitors with short-term focus and challenges.

New Approach To An Old Challenge

▶ Communicating the Plan Early and Often

Clearly the past couple years have been challenging times. Often you don't have anything clever that helps you get through, but I'll tell you something that we did. Our business is dependent on capital spending, which gives us a cyclical view of things. We know there are certain leading indicators that, when they start appearing, barring the stars lining up differently, you know you're headed into a slump.

These indicators showed we were in for a rough ride about February 2001. When we knew that we were going into a recession, we pulled together the worldwide leadership group for our company, which is the top 30 or so people, and said, "We can batten down the hatches and do this the way we've always done it before and die of a thousand cuts, or we can choose to do it differently. We could say to ourselves, 'Let's not look at going into the recession; let's look at coming out of the recession, and how we want to position ourselves to really ride that recovery curve in as good a position as we can.'"

So we put together eight guiding principles that we have used throughout this recession. And then we put in place a huge communication plan throughout the organization. Of course, we didn't realize at that time how long it would last, whether it would be two quarters or two years. It turned out to be eight quarters and still counting.

▶ Surgery with a Scalpel, Not a Machete

For example, we invested in the major strategic get-ahead initiatives that we thought we had to keep going throughout the recession. Some of these initiatives included new product development, our SAP implementation, and our channel brand strategy because we were going to market with multiple brands. We decided to keep going forward in those areas.

This sent the message to our organization that we would be hiring people in those areas even though we were laying people off elsewhere. Because we were clear about this message, we didn't have people grumbling around the water fountain, saying, "How come they are spending money in that area and not in ours?" We identified the key areas so everyone would know where we'd be investing; all other areas we'd be scaling back.

We actually stepped up our engineering expense. We spent several million dollars on a new CAD CAM software system. We did a number of things through the recession while we laid off 10% of the workforce. And we've stayed pretty clear on it. We also said, whatever cuts anybody bears, they will be greater on the top than on the bottom. So, for instance, we took a salary cut across the organization except for the income-producing parts. I took a 10% cut and everybody else took a 3%, so it was staggered.

'I Feel Your Pain'

We said that whatever headcount reductions we had, we would make them disproportionately at the top. So, out of the 10%, we didn't allow it all to come from the bottom. I took out two executives on the senior team, and we took out five or six of the next layer. We didn't want people to feel, "Oh it's easy for those guys because they never suffer the pain."

And we did everything we could to cut smartly. For instance, we didn't take a headcount reduction in the plant. We took a reduction in hours and rearranged the plant schedules so everybody worked four ten-hour days. The plant went to four-day weeks rather than lay people off. In essence, they took a 10% reduction, but they did it in hours, not straight salary, because we didn't need the production and, more importantly, we wanted to hold on to the skilled labor. When the recovery comes, we won't be out looking for untrained workers.

Actions like that were important and consistent with the tone we set. And we stated that, if we take a salary reduction, we will continue it until we see two quarters that indicate that we are getting back on steady ground. We didn't want to say, "Hey look, we think it will be three quarters, so that's it." We said, "This could be two quarters or it could be two years. Whatever it is, we are going to weather it. So, we will be looking for signs of recovery before we replace people."

We cut back on travel and labor, all the discretionary areas. We said, "We'll try to reduce everything we can, like discretionary spending, but we still need to travel for business." We also believe that you should use this recession as a time to really build your bench strength. We urged managers to deal with low performers, and, more importantly, to hire good, strong performers. Slow times are an opportunity to recruit talent you cannot get in the good times.

If you've got high-potential people, get them trained. If you've got know-how that you should be spreading horizontally across the organization, do that. We have emphasized that it isn't just about hunkering down; this is a different phase of our development and we need to use it wisely.

Making Solutions Fit The Situation

We wanted to avoid blanket statements across the organization or around the world. It's too easy to say, "No travel or training," but that may not be appropriate for everyone. Instead, some people invested in training and developing their people further. Others decided to cut training, travel, everything before reducing any headcount. Some people will cut headcount willingly because they said they'd much rather have the remaining people be happy; others feel headcount reductions leave those remaining spread too thin. There was room for these differing approaches.

Another reason a blanket dictate wouldn't work is that 20% of our revenues come from Europe. These initiatives are harder to implement in Europe. We took some salary cuts where we could. A lot of labor in Europe was by contract because of the labor laws. In the plant, we tend to have what they call temporary labor so that you can flex more with volume. It's easier in the plant.

What we did in Europe was focus more on profit and proven efforts that would, over time, systemically reduce our fixed cost structure. We outsourced some of our manufacturing to the Czech Republic and we're moving to a central call center. We moved to a Pan European operating model. We reduced our infrastructure in five countries by centralizing finance, customer service, and logistics in one European center. 'One SAP' worldwide allowed us to move to this leaner, more transparent operation.

This is the kind of thing we are going to keep and not stop midstream. It all sounds good, just like listening to Jack Welch always sounds good. However, this did not all happen without a lot of pain. We have many employees who would say, "We didn't cut back near enough on the activity. We cut back people, but we still kept doing way too many things—too many initiatives. Everybody is stretched thin and they are layering on too many activities."

Widening The Gap

We came up with a name for this entire approach so that it would be easier to communicate. We call it 'widening the gap.' In other words, we're going to use this recession to widen the gap between us and our competitors. And that is actually the theme of our annual report. We tried to make it tangible, not just a flavor of the month. 'Widening the gap' was the theme of every conference call, quarterly earnings call, and company meeting. A beautiful picture of two sailing ships, one out ahead of the other, graces the cover of our annual report, and the report is titled *Widening the Gap.*

Most of our competitors are financially stressed. Our industry has seen tremendous consolidation where companies have bought out and/or are being bought out. For many of our competitors, the recession was going to be a lot tougher because they had as part of their cost structure a large debt due to acquisitions. By contrast, Tennant is a cash-generating company. We didn't generate as much free cash flow during the recession as in good times obviously, but we still managed to generate a fair amount of cash with zero debt. Being in this position can help you weather tough times and, in Tennant's 132-year history, we've seen both good times and bad.

We went through a substantial strategic review, asking the tough questions and challenging our core competencies. One strength we underestimated was our real core competency for taking the long view—making decisions that assure that the company survives. I mean, we've been here 132 years. We've always made money. Even in '82—our worst year—we never lost money. So, you hire people with a certain kind of mindset. You reward them in a certain way. But, there is a deep cultural appreciation for longevity and making things work—we don't zig zag a lot.

It's Now Hip To Be Boring

In a time when major companies are folding or seeking bankruptcy protection, some of the more conservative, dare I say 'old time values,' seem to be getting a whole new shine. It's the Warren Buffett philosophy: If I can't understand how you make money, I am not going to invest in you.

The horror stories from anyone who was knocking on fund managers' doors just a few years ago, between, say, 1996 and 2000, are just staggering. The arrogance, herd mentality, and ignorance were just unbelievable. This potential conflict of interest between analyst and investment bankers under the same roof was well known.

This practice that sell-side analysts generally would not provide coverage if there was not investment banking opportunities for their firm was well known. It was the height of cynicism. Because Tennant was trying to get sell-side analyst coverage, we had little debt (i.e., no need for investment banking), and we were also thinly traded which counted against us, so it was just taken as orthodoxy of the marketplace. No one was interested in us. Those analysts were no longer as independent as they once were at generating good, thoughtful analyses that the brokers in the firm could rely on to advise their retail clients. They had become shills for their investment banking business partners. And that was all well known. The current effort to change this practice just affirms it.

Also well known, especially in the mania years '98 and '99, was firm managers saying, "If you don't have multiples of high double-digit or triple-digit P/E ratios; if you don't have market caps in the stratosphere; and if you don't have 'dot-com' in your name, you're just boring. We're not interested in you."

When you get in the middle of a mess, nobody wants to look around and say, "You know, we all had a hand in it." Every one of us was deluding ourselves. 401(k) people thought they were going to get a 15% increase in their fund performance every quarter, and fund managers said, "I'll move that money in a nanosecond. I couldn't care less about your strategy or your long-term performance." Everybody had a hand in it, but you can't find them now.

Selling Smart – Deploying The Sales Assets

Back on the sales side, 2000 was fabulous. But the bottom dropped out in

2001. When you have a direct sales organization, you can more quickly change how you deploy the resources; but they are also largely a fixed cost. We were constantly trying to look at markets that had money. For us, last year during the recession, sectors with money were education, government, the drug industry, the healthcare industry and, post 9/11, the defense industry.

We constantly tried to say to our sales reps, "Don't visit 60% of your customers anymore. Put them on a planned-call list, because they don't have the money anyway." There's no use pushing something that doesn't work. So, you redeploy. We went to the top. Many of us were out going to the top customers. We focused on our commercial business because that's less cyclical compared to industrial.

For us, commercial would be 'walk behinds'—smaller equipment that the operator does not ride on—and below. These are lower priced products, driven less by capital and more by operating budget. These smaller units tend to be viewed as more of a necessity because they are used for day-to-day cleaning and facilities that are not impacted by the recession. So, hospitals, schools, office buildings, cafeterias—anything with carpet, tile, floor—fall in the commercial category. And these commercial products tend to be sold to contract cleaners who are going to purchase for their business anyway.

We also put a real focus on accounts receivable, working on the balance sheet. Our view was, if it's not going to come from the income statements this year, let's work on the balance sheet. Let's get the inventories down and stretch out delivery times wherever possible because then you can do more just-in-time manufacturing. And your sales force gets more involved in that. You just try to think smart and use your resources smartly.

When The Going Gets Tough, The Tough Prepare For The Future

We looked at all of our resources. Tennant has a reward system focused on shifting toward economic profit (EP). We're just into it two years and, unfortunately, they have been two pretty ugly years, so we haven't given it a fair test. Luckily, I have enough political capital left that they don't think I put it in just to rob them.

As an EP company, at least for the VPs of sales and for the regional managers of sales, a significant part of their at-risk pay is based on the economic profit of their business unit (North America). So they and the operations people and the functional people in North America are all getting rewarded on the same thing: How much do you generate in capital improvement year-over-year? To the extent we collect receivables or improve revenue or reduce inventory, they all get rewarded for the same thing. The EP for North America is contribution to the bottom line as a business unit.

We fundamentally have one corporate or enterprise metric. And all the people who have at-risk pay have some portion of it based on the enterprise. For the people who are more clearly aligned with one of the business units, they would have less of the enterprise and more of the business unit. Everybody has both an enterprise metric and a business unit metric as part of their number. Our new head of North America comes from the consumer marketplace. He's moving the sales organization more toward a focus on 'profitable sales,' not just sales. With SAP and better tools in the hands of the front line team, we can better drive EP through the organization.

All of this is really helping all of us—not only the sales executives but also other people on the team—to understand their part of the EP contribution and to be better business people which, in the end, is what I think tough times teach us. We made the decision to look ahead and work toward improving our position for improving times. With the efficiencies we have put in place during the slow times, we should see strong results in the good times. Meanwhile, we'll continue to develop our bench strength, tighten our processes, and invest in our strategic initiatives.

STEVE RAMSEY

Steve Ramsey is a Chicago-based Partner in Accenture's cross-industry Customer Relationship Management practice. He has global responsibility for leading the Marketing and Customer Strategy practice that houses Accenture's functional expertise in brand strategy, marketing effectiveness, customer strategy, and CRM-related business transformation. His primary areas of focus are related to helping companies with sales, marketing, and customer service related go-to-market issues, and helping drive higher return on marketing and CRM investments. Steve has an MBA from the University of Chicago and a BS in Mechanical Engineering from Lehigh University.

He and his wife, Sherri, are blessed with two sets of twin girls, currently 4-year-olds and newborns.

JD

> **This year, while marketing spending by Global 1000 companies continues to climb and exceed $1 trillion, marketing productivity and program effectiveness are declining. The issue is not necessarily the amount being spent, but rather how and where dollars are allocated. This is being solved by an interesting combination of process and technology.**

Marketing expenditures can be broken into two types: marketing spend and marketing management. Marketing spend represents the lion's share of this number, accounting for 75% to 80% of the total amount. These are the dollars invested in TV and radio advertising, print ads, direct marketing, web marketing, etc.

The remainder covers the cost of managing the marketing function. These are all the expenses associated with managing the process of program definition to the point where you have a final campaign that can be implemented through the appropriate medium. This would include expenses for people, creative, and so forth.

Clearly, when you are looking at investments of this magnitude, it is imperative that you are able to determine accurately your return on investment (ROI), but marketing organizations have historically been at a loss for how to do this. Today, this lack of information is no longer acceptable to the Chief Marketing Officer (CMO), not to mention the CFO and CEO.

The Marketing Effectiveness Challenge

In a survey of marketing executives in the United States and the United Kingdom, Accenture found that 68% had difficulty measuring the results generated from their marketing programs. The reason behind this was that these organizations lacked the appropriate metrics to make conclusive decisions on how effective were past programs.

This does not mean that they were not measuring anything. On the contrary, many of these firms did significant amounts of classic marketing performance measurements, such as conducting focus groups, user surveys, impressions tracking studies, etc. But these efforts only shed light on individual pieces of their marketing efforts, versus providing insights into the marketing mix as a whole.

Rarely was there any process in place to aggregate all those measurements into a single view of how each separate marketing element compared to the rest of the marketing mix spend. Without those insights, it was impossible to calculate a definitive ROI that could then be used as the basis for determining which marketing vehicles and market segments justified future investments.

Effective marketing management represented its own set of challenges. In the course of interviews with CMOs, Accenture's Institute for Strategic Change uncovered the following four obstacles to optimizing marketing efficiency and effectiveness:

- Formal marketing processes are for the most part non-existent, so individual marketing teams develop their own ways of working versus leveraging consistent, proven approaches.

- Collaboration techniques are rarely used, requiring marketers to invest excessive time in managing all the internal and external resources required to develop and implement programs.

- Marketers lack the ability to access, use, or repurpose existing marketing assets (photos, video, music, copy, etc.), therefore requiring the investment of significant time and money to recreate these items.

- Employee turnover means that a great deal of knowledge generated from past program successes and failures walks out the door when these people do.

These are the key issues that companies need to deal with if they expect to increase the effectiveness and productivity of their marketing efforts.

Marketing Resource Management Components

In response to this need, we are seeing the emergence of a fundamental new approach to marketing. The area is so new that it is a solution still in search of a name. Some people refer to it as Marketing Process Management. Others view it as part of Enterprise Resource Management. At Accenture, the term we have gravitated towards is Marketing Resource Management (MRM).

The focus of MRM is to leverage people, processes, and technology to successfully optimize the way we market. The components of MRM are integrated planning, proactive workflow management, continuous program financial management, portfolio asset management, and program performance impact analysis, all managed within a single framework.

Before we examine how MRM will redefine the function of marketing, let's first review the various innovations that are available today and are turning the concept of MRM into reality.

The first of these components is econometrics, which is a science that has been around for years. These methods are now being applied to analyzing multi-year data streams and are found to be very useful in determining which marketing mix drivers are really effective; and, just as important, which ones are not.

The ability to do this type of modeling is supported by the second component of MRM, which is a new class of Customer Relationship Management (CRM) software applications. Until recently, the focus of most CRM software for marketing was geared towards campaign management. This new generation of systems moves beyond that to provide the analytics necessary to support the analysis of all the elements of a company's marketing mix spend.

Two other classes of CRM software systems, which represent the third and fourth components of MRM, are emerging to help with the challenge of effectively managing marketing. The first of these systems are applications to support project management. These applications help improve the consistency of program management by reinforcing a structured approach around the process of marketing. They also support collaboration by facilitating communications and the sharing of information among all the various groups involved in creating and implementing marketing programs.

The other set of software applications are designed for knowledge capital management. They allow marketers anywhere in the enterprise to easily get access to work previously done by their peers. This includes project plans, content, visuals, creative, etc. By accessing and leveraging the work of others, teams working on new projects can complete their task in less time and at less expense than ever before.

MRM In Action

The MRM software marketplace is currently still in its embryonic stage, and probably will not reach its full potential for another five to seven years. That being said, significant advances in marketing productivity and effectiveness can still be achieved today using the technologies and processes that are currently available.

We are currently engaged with a variety of companies in various industries, such as consumer packaged goods, pharmaceuticals, automotive, financial services etc., and are applying these various MRM components to solve real world challenges.

▶ Analyzing the Marketing Spend

For example, we are working with a Global 1000 electronics equipment manufacturer who invests in excess of $900 million a year in marketing spend, and makes media buys on a worldwide basis. They support 43 operating subsidiaries and have 13 unique product categories. Their key challenge is how to best align their marketing spend to support the optimum profit opportunities for the company.

Every company we have dealt with has this issue if they are a global player, and in the past there has been no way to make an apples-to-apples comparison of the various opportunities at this level. Instead, companies have tended to rely on the current momentum of a business entity or a given brand. In most cases, this resulted in a simple extrapolation of high level financials rather than the bottom-up evaluation of the underlying business drivers. Many times, the business case to justify investments is made by a brand manager, and the more vocal individuals often are awarded the lion's share of the available funds. This type of decision-making process often sub-optimizes your marketing spend ROI because in many cases, you fail to put the proper level of investment behind the right growth element.

We tackled that problem with the equipment manufacturer in this example. To be honest, initially it was a considerable challenge to collect all the data elements from all the various parts of the enterprise. But once that was accomplished, we leveraged a variety of analytical techniques, including econometric models in order to really understand growth dynamics, by product category and by country.

For example, we were able to analyze the strengths and weaknesses of the various brand attributes relative to the competition. In doing so, for the first time we could assess the resulting impact on the firm's competitiveness if we were to put more or less money into programs for a given brand. We could also determine how the profit characteristics for each brand were trending and how much margin was being created, now and into the future.

Working with the management in each of the specific countries, we were able to develop certain sets of assumptions, which were now supported by quantitative data, to create a decision-making application that helped reallocate their available funds. The end result was not necessarily a black-or-white decision, but for the first time we were able to clearly identify significant issues of misalignment by countries or product lines that before might not have been evident. With these insights now surfaced, management could challenge their past allocation assumptions and make better investment decisions going forward.

Typically, in this type of exercise we are able to identify 15% to 20% profit improvement potential that can be driven through a more effective allocation of marketing funds. Of course, you then need to balance that against the implications these changes could have downstream. For example, if you make a decision to turn up the volume of TVs sold in a certain country, you may need to address an issue with your plant manufacturing capacity.

But clearly, if companies are going to achieve the type of structured, controlled growth that they all desire, they'll need this level of visibility into the impact of their marketing efforts.

This initial project was followed up with a second initiative to optimize decision-making down at a very detailed level. Assume that based on the first level analysis, you decided to allocate to a given brand—let's use the examples of TVs for now—N number of dollars. What is the best vehicle to spend that money on? Should you go with TV advertising, print ads, radio, or direct marketing? Here again, econometrics comes into play.

If we are able to get two or three years worth of data on the various marketing inputs, and we also have a clear understanding of the sales dynamics of the marketplace (i.e., how much revenue has been generated), we can then create a very reliable model for determining the return for individual marketing mix variables. That knowledge leads to a better allocation of funds within a specific brand plan.

We have done similar projects for clients, leveraging the knowledge that has been gained over the years, applying econometrics to the CPG market, and to other industries such as consumer electronics, pharmaceuticals, retail, utilities, automotive, high technology, etc. In all cases, these techniques show their value in really getting to the heart of the issue of determining which advertising programs are effective and which are not.

▶ Optimizing Marketing Management

In addition to increasing revenues by more selectively funding marketing spend activities, there is also a significant potential to reduce or optimize the costs associated with the management of marketing. To accomplish this, you need processes that turn marketing into more of a science, and technology that supports and reinforces those processes. At Accenture, we refer to this as Enterprise Marketing Management (EMM).

Transitioning to EMM is a huge shift for many marketing organizations. Traditionally, marketing has been all about creativity. If you look deep into marketing teams, you tend not to see a lot of process-oriented thinkers, even though much of marketing revolves around project management.

A common problem for many companies is that the real marketing and brand knowledge is stored in peoples' heads instead of saved in marketing systems. Since it is never captured, all of the knowledge is never translated into processes and a set of knowledge assets that can be leveraged across the enterprise, even when people have moved on.

So the challenge for EMM is to bring some level of automation to marketing that assists in brand management, marketing management, and asset management, so that we can continually leverage our best thinking and cease recreating the wheel over and over again. Done right, this is not only a great efficiency driver, but can also significantly increase the effectiveness of a marketing organization.

▶ Optimizing Brand Management

The concept of measuring brand strength has been around for quite a while. But the value resulting from these exercises has often been questionable, as they typically stop at simply measuring consumer awareness of the brand. The use of analytics and MRM technology is poised to take this analysis to a whole new level.

The components are in place today to allow companies to create what we are calling the 'marketing funnel.' Essentially, what this allows marketing to do is segment various groups of customers according to not just their awareness of your brand, but their commitment to it as well.

At the top of the funnel would be all consumers who at least have a minimal awareness of the brand. As business rules are further applied to these customers, the funnel narrows to the point where at the end, you have the customers who are extremely loyal and represent a highly concentrated value stream for the brand.

This type of analysis can give you key insights into your marketing effectiveness. For example, when looking at brand 'A,' you may find you have great awareness, but minimal loyalty. On the other hand, a review of brand 'B' might show that while many consumers lack awareness of your brand, those who do recognize it are fiercely loyal. With this knowledge in hand, it would become clear that for brand 'A' you need to focus on encouraging more consumers to try the product, while in the case of brand 'B' you have a super star offering that needs more promotion dollars backing it.

Currently, this type of analysis requires a significant amount of work to gather the information and data required to fuel the system. But the value that can be realized by being able to achieve this level of understanding of brand effectiveness can easily justify the investment. In addition, as the MRM systems mature over time, this new approach to brand management will become easier.

Marketing Performance Workbench

As I said before, the software tools in this space are just coming of age, but they still provide solid value and today allow you to deliver what we call a Marketing Performance Workbench. This workbench incorporates three major components. First, it provides a marketing process work space which allows you to develop and execute marketing projects. Second, it offers marketers a toolset that facilitates access to digital and knowledge assets. And lastly, it provides enterprise integration capabilities that support the sharing of information across multiple applications anywhere in the enterprise.

This workbench will allow marketing professionals to work much more effectively. Consider the following scenario: a marketing manager has been assigned a new project. This could be designing a new media campaign, conducting a focus group research effort, managing a customer satisfaction study, or whatever.

The first thing the manager would do would be to access the process workspace tool. Using this capability he or she can tap into all the collective experiences the enterprise has developed by doing those types of projects in the past.

The manager starts by selecting the correct project type from a pull-down menu. The system will then automatically generate a project management framework outlining all the steps involved in that type of initiative. Linked to each project step are suggested timeframes, resource requirements, templates for content creation, best practices examples, and a list of the required marketing digital assets. Marketing teams can then customize these items to fit their needs.

Next, the manager may want to find any existing digital assets owned by the company that could be leveraged. Using the digital asset management capability of the workbench, he or she can develop a detailed search request and the system will then inform him or her what video, audio, photos, copy, etc. are available for use or re-purposing.

The system provides administrative management capabilities to handle content check-in and check-out, version control, user access, etc. Managers can also find out who created the original material, so they can contact that person directly. Leveraging what already exists can significantly cut down the time required to complete a project, as well as greatly reduce the costs associated with reinventing creative materials.

Marketing teams often need sales or financial information that may reside in a variety of other sources, such as internal systems or scanned data; or information from retail customers, competitive intelligence information, and so forth. With some customization work by a system integrator, they can use the third component of the workbench, the enterprise integration management facility. With it, they can enter data from all these various data repositories in a fraction of the time it would take otherwise. This greatly enhances their decision-making ability.

Technology-Enabled Marketing Mandate

I sometimes get the reaction that applying this type of rigor or structure to marketing will stifle creativity. On the contrary, based on what we have seen when we have implemented these systems and processes for clients, we find that the changes actually accelerate creativity.

What we are really talking about is leveraging process and technology to automate many of the time-consuming and mundane tasks that marketing is forced to do today. This will free up marketing professionals to spend more of their workday on value-added tasks.

Other enterprise processes, like finance and supply chain, have undergone a technology-enabled redesign over the past ten years, and the outcome has been a significant increase in both efficiency and effectiveness. The demand on marketing today to improve performance and document the ROI from their efforts will mandate the types of changes we have been discussing.

Fortunately, all the components, in terms of both process and technology, are falling into place to allow marketing to make this transition, and these capabilities will only get more robust over the next few years. For companies looking to create competitive advantage with their marketing efforts, MRM will become the means to achieve that goal.

DICK LEE

*We've known Dick Lee for over ten years and enjoy his friendship and icono-
clastic, often caustic observations of sales, marketing and CRM. Dick currently heads the Customer-1 consulting practice of Minneapolis-based
Caribou Lake. The practice is dedicated to helping clients implement customer-centric business strategies and information systems. He is the author of The Sales Automation Survival Guide (1997), The Customer Relationship Management Survival Guide (1999) and Strategic CRM: The Complete CRM Implementation Manual (2002). He is also a regular columnist
for CRM Magazine. Dick has spent over 20 years in relationship marketing,
co-founding Gelbach Lee and Consulting as High Yield Marketing. He was
one of the earliest voices in the SFA/CRM movement to suggest that more
than technology was involved, and continues to advance this perspective
through his four-step methodology for implementing customer relationship
management.*

BT

> **Buyers are grasping the amount of leverage they have, but
> business execs and sellers are fighting it. The principal reason
> for the lack of sellers' understanding is that businesses have
> very poor listening skills. In business, we have been very lax
> about putting in systems and methods that enable us to capture
> as much customer input as possible.**

Alignment With Customers

In the marketing arena, I think excellence is defined as alignment with
customers. Alignment means the ability of the company to offer products
and services consistent with customer interest, and to offer them in a way
that is consistent with customer buying preferences. That sounds a lot
easier than it actually is to attain. If you look at marketing today what you
see is massive misalignment. Companies are trying to sell products that
are not geared to what customers are actually looking for This creates
products that are in the best interest of the seller's company but not the
buyer's. Companies are also offering these products in ways that are in
the best interest of the seller and not the buyer.

I encounter a classic example of this misalignment every time I read about a CEO couching his financial results for the quarter by saying, "We were below plan because of the failure of our sales force to close key deals." To me, that is code for, "We want the customers to buy when we need them to buy, not when they are ready to buy." They are trying to force the selling cycle into the revenue needs of the seller, not the buyer.

This orientation creates much distress and tension among buyers. It's an old method of selling, or really of marketing, because it's mainly about the approach to the customer, and it doesn't work anymore. It's a complex problem because you've got analysts who want more steady revenues per quarter and don't want to see sales yo-yoing up and down. However, more and more customers are saying, "Hey look, this is our ballgame. We're playing by our rules. We're going to do business when we are ready. And if you push us, you are going to push yourself right out the door."

Right now, senior execs reading this might be saying, "That's bulls—t! We're in the market but we have performance numbers we need to meet." I think this pushback is a reflection of old paradigm versus new paradigm. I think that what executives are really saying is, "I want things to go back to the way they used to be."

Crossover In Supply-Demand Lines

When I do presentations on environmental change, I use a very simple chart that shows the crossover in the supply-demand lines. During the early 1980s, we started bringing on-line new technologies to help us produce more, faster. At the time, I was consulting with clients like 3M, and we were seeing the window of opportunity getting narrower and narrower because people could copy designs faster. And product options and availability have been increasing ever since as we've continued to improve our product design, manufacturing, and service delivery methods.

What happened was all about productivity gains. Our potential to produce product and deliver services continued to elevate at a very sharp rate. But, and this is key, overall market demand was not rising as fast.

So in the '80s and '90s, we experienced a gradual crossover, industry by industry, of the supply-demand lines. After 40 some odd years, in most markets, buyers finally began to realize with greater certainty how much leverage they had. The recession helped them understand this, as did the advent of the Internet.

Buyers are grasping the amount of leverage they have, but business execs and sellers are fighting it. Executives say, "Yeah, but we're in business and we've got to do our business." To me, that sounds like a statement of denial; either, "I don't get it," or "I refuse to get it."

Business Has Very Poor Listening Skills

The principle reason for the lack of sellers' understanding is that *business has very poor listening skills*. In business, we have been very lax about putting in systems and methods that enable us to capture as much customer input as possible. And what's interesting is that when I work with a selling company on CRM, one of the principle points of resistance, or points that generates the least interest, is the ability of CRM to bring qualitative information back up the line into the corner office.

Basically, a lack of qualitative information doesn't touch anyone's hot button. You really have to sell the point that it is a big advantage of CRM; that it can, if implemented correctly, create a framework, a structure, and a culture for retrieving information from the customer. A CRM solution can then enable communication to executive management, product development, and engineering, or to wherever that feedback needs to go.

In my experience, I've found that if the right people want customer data, they'll get it—because they'll set up requirements for obtaining it. Granted, sometimes feedback comes into sales or marketing and stops there; it may never get to the 'C level' of the organization. But when the C level is really aggressive about getting the information, they get it. The challenge is getting them to be aggressive about it, getting them to want and care about it.

CRM Software Is Not A Silver Bullet

I think many companies thought they could substitute CRM technology for genuine customer care and communication of their needs across the organization. At some level, it seems companies were saying, "We have this whole collection of things that should happen, and if we buy Siebel, it will happen." But buying Siebel does absolutely nothing to increase executive level appetite for customer information.

In fact, buying CRM software does nothing in and of itself to bring that information within corporate walls. More than anything else, acquiring customer information is about *cultural change*. It's about creating the understanding that the information is needed and valued. Furthermore, this information can be gathered and disseminated across the organization even without CRM technology. The critical factors are the attitude and the value system of the organization, rather than any specific technology.

Attitude Change Is The Hard Part

For example, I have a client right now who I'd rate not an 'A,' but a solid 'B' in terms of wanting to get customer feedback. Currently, they have product development laboratories developing a constant stream of new products based on woefully inadequate customer feedback. As a result, the 'hit rate' for new products is disappointing. This particular client realizes the problem and is willing to take steps to build more customer information into the product design loop. Maybe not to the full extent we'd like to see them do it, but enough to make a significant improvement in customer receptivity to new products. The technology part of this? Easy. The attitude change is the hard part.

On the flip side of the coin, I met recently with a major player in the telecom industry, where customers are in a very sluggish buying mood. I was talking with them about the importance of being very perceptive in order to figure out a) what customers will buy and why they will buy it, and b) once you have figured that out, how to shift your product line accordingly. To this line of thought, their sales training person responded with an emphatic, "No! The role of the sales person is to sell, sell, sell." Wrong, buddy. Selling today is about listening and learning as much as it is about taking orders— or forcing them. With their current self-focused attitude, this company is going down.

There are a couple of key elements needed to effect change in the selling environment. One, you've got to have leadership who understands that in today's marketplace, you can no longer force the issue. You can't ram stuff down people's throats. Some CEOs intuitively realize this and are able to respond and work very, very hard at adapting to customer needs. But just having the CEO feel that way isn't enough; the CEO has got to take a very visible, proactive leadership position to sell those values throughout the organization. These two factors combined are really what's needed.

Changeover In The CRM Software Market

In 2001, I co-authored a customer satisfaction study on CRM vendors. This survey included people who had, in fact, purchased and had some interaction with the vendors they were rating. Grossly simplified, the results showed that all the major, multi-function CRM software vendors were failing to please customers. The vendors received mediocre ratings. Two of the biggest issues were the lack of adaptability to user needs and long, expensive implementations, which are largely due to the complexity of large footprint, multi-function systems.

In today's market, smart vendors are shifting away from mile-wide and inch-deep solutions and toward inch-wide and mile-deep solutions. Those that do maintain a multi-function profile are relying on a small footprint, component-based architecture like the ones developed by Optima Technologies and JD Edwards.

Optima has an excellent CRM product which primarily strengthens sales automation by developing knowledge management tools that attack very particular customer problems. And they are continuing to grow as a company right through the recession. I think JD Edwards has done the same thing in terms of understanding what the CRM software market is looking for. And there are a few other CRM software companies out there that are customer sensitive just by nature.

Product Management Versus Customer Groups

Wising up is a hard thing to do. There was a company I tried to work with last year, but we finally parted ways because we couldn't agree. As it turned out, their whole CRM initiative went right down the toilet. This company is driven by product management. Product managers are held accountable for selling the required amount of their product, and their compensation is linked to their performance. So of course, they will push marketing and sales to sell enough of their particular product.

Now, as a CEO you can make all the pronouncements in the world about being customer sensitive—listening to customer needs, and developing products and services to meet those needs. But if you don't disband that product management system, you will fail. Freud's definition of insanity comes to mind: doing the same thing over and over again but expecting a different outcome. This company cannot get closer to customers because of its product management-focused business model.

This dilemma was also something that Proctor & Gamble discovered a number of years ago. They disbanded their product management system, which was a very painful process. They reorganized around identified customer groups in a very significant way. They do have brand management, but the focus really shifted towards customer groups and customer markets, rather than product management. As an example, P&G was among the first companies to really establish the specialization of selling to older consumers.

Successes

Has my work resulted in major turnarounds? I'd have to say that outcomes have been mixed. I've had some wonderful successes in getting people to respond to their customer base. And I've had situations like the company with the product management issues and a 'technology-cures-all' IT department where I've felt like I was beating my head against the wall.

A very positive, current situation is H.B. Fuller, a global adhesives company. My client is the Chief Technology Officer, who stopped sales and marketing from going ahead with CRM because they hadn't developed a customer model yet. They really didn't have adequate customer input. He did the same thing with supply chain management. He knows that supply chain management changes the parameters of a relationship with customers. He talks in terms of customer permission and knowing how customers are going to react to changes in their shipping parameters. He also knows the danger of making changes arbitrarily because they may look good on paper and may drive costs down, but you could very readily drive business away if you don't know what customer attitudes are.

The net result of their efforts; those of the CTO, a CRM team with some customer-sensitive line people, and very forward-thinking senior management, is starting to emerge as an 'old line' company starts to turn a new face to the market. While these transitions are painful, they're also a beautiful thing to watch.

Not Just Listening – Educating and Cooperating, Too

At the same time, with H. B. Fuller, we may have to do some serious customer education to convey that just-in-time ordering has associated costs. In a market where margins are razor thin, if you don't cooperate with suppliers, you wind up paying for it. That was a whole learning experience that happened in the food industry in the early '90s, which is why the food industry really led the supply chain management initiative. Things were starting to spin out of control. Nobody was making any money, customers were getting more and more demanding, and finally, something had to give.

Supermarket chains started going under and there was really a profitability crisis. Nobody was making money in the industry and this is how activity-based costing really got off the ground. Activity-based costing is basically assigning costs to individual customers. Customers are made aware that their behavior is influencing the cost to serve them and that they are going to have to pay extra if they engage in behavior that makes it more expensive to serve them.

As an example, there were supermarket chains that were notorious for keeping trucks idling outside for eight hours before they could unload. And what finally came back was that the distributors and producers said,

"If our truck is idling out there for eight hours, you are paying by the minute because we can't afford to do it and we're not going to pass the excess cost on to more cooperative customers." It's a really interesting overall case—things went from conflict to collaboration within a pretty short period of time.

Some of this conflict was also simply due to not sharing order information with suppliers. Now in the grocery industry there is tremendous information sharing that allows for predictability of who is going to need what, and when.

I see that same opportunity existing in, say, semiconductors, professional services, financial services, or manufacturing. Unfortunately, the word collaboration has become jargon. I went through a stack of back issues of *InformationWeek* and, after a time, I felt that if I saw the word 'collaboration' one more time I was going to throw up. But collaboration does work much better than the adversarial stance. When people get together cooperatively and say, "Here's how we can work together more effectively for our mutual benefit," then good things happen.

CRM is not a silver bullet delivered through technology. CRM is, except in very rare cases, a culture that is sustainable only in the presence of new technologies. So, which is the chicken and which is the egg? In today's market, I would say that there is enough technology. What must come first, then, is management taking a visible role in moving this thing forward. In fact, we're in the midst of strategic planning right now at Caribou Lake. I met last week with Mark Kale, our founder and CTO, and asked for his insights about the technology market during the next three to five years. He thought for a minute and said, "There will be a whole lot less doing, and a whole lot more re-doing."

Creating Value With What Clients Already Have

In our current economy, clients are saying, "I'm not bringing in another new mammoth system. I want to maximize the mileage out of what I've got." If Oracle doesn't hear that message, they will miss the market by a mile. If Siebel stays focused on selling new implementations, they will miss the market by a mile. If I were running Siebel or Oracle in this market condition, I would start shifting my business as fast as my little feet could move in the direction of helping clients create more value with what they have already purchased.

From a CRM perspective, what can we do for customers that will address their core needs? The answer is coming back that we can help rescue failed implementations where somebody went out and bought technology, didn't know how to configure it, and didn't know what it was supposed to do. The company wound up with a big mess and then called in a Big 5 consulting firm, or worse, a software company, to fix the problems. And their new solution? Throw it all out and start over again.

That's not going to happen in today's economy, as it did back in the year 2000. Now, people aren't going to throw out millions of dollars in licenses because they think they bought the wrong software. The main issue and challenge is to get the mess straightened out. Part of Caribou Lake's mission as a CRM practice will be to help clients who have purchased software, gotten into a mess, and still are not experiencing a positive ROI. We will come in and review the whole situation and help them unravel it.

We have defined four steps for completing a successful CRM implementation:

1. Develop customer-centered strategies.

2. Redesign roles and responsibilities to carry out the new strategies.

3. Re-engineer work processes to carry out the new work flow.

4. Support the technology.

Today, most consultants who are addressing CRM issues do not have strengths in the areas where the projects are failing. Their consulting strength is in steps 3 and 4; however, the problems with the implementations are in steps 1 and 2.

Innovative Relationships: Everyone Wins

Our work with a credit company represents a classic example. Our initial charge was to help them expand their outstanding credit balances in the credit line business. So, we went out and did about a year of very painstaking statistical analysis of the marketplace and their customers. We also conducted qualitative research and gathered more subjective opinions. Through our efforts, we learned that the customer wanted help getting out of debt, and did not want to take on any more.

We then studied the psychology of being in debt and why it is so hard for people to dig themselves out. One of the things we came to understand was that people have a tendency to try to get out of debt too quickly. They have very high expectations and set unrealistic goals for eliminating their debts. By doing so, they set themselves up for failure. The first disappointment comes quickly, and the whole idea of living debt-free seems impossible. So they fall off the wagon and often get themselves even deeper in debt.

Remember, our initial charge was to sell more credit lines, mainly through database marketing. The idea was to increase what are called 'outstandings,' the balances on which customers pay interest.

It really took some internal selling, but we persuaded our client to design an entirely new product that was actually a throw back to the old installment loan. We looked at the debt situation people were in and considered how they got there. We discovered that to some extent, it was because the industry abandoned the secured installment loan. People used to buy a refrigerator by making 36 payments over the course of three years. If the customer missed one payment, it was 'bye-bye refrigerator.' However, with the new borrowing model which gave the customer more freedom and choice, there was limited accountability for spending.

So we designed a product that provided more structure, with an automatic withdrawal from customer checking accounts. We packaged it as a product, and internally called it the 'Installment Line.' The positioning was, "We're going to give consumers a slow but sure way to climb out of debt."

The interest rate wasn't the best, and we weren't offering short-term teaser rates, but we would loan them substantial sums of money for five years so that they could pay down their debt, as long as they would agree that principal and interest payments would be withdrawn directly from their checking accounts every month. We couldn't enforce this idea of using the money to pay down debt, but we strongly suggested it. As a result, the product was a smashing success.

Obviously, our client's fear was, "Well, gee, we're being the good guys in the marketplace, and all that's going to happen is we're going to get our own debt paid off while everyone else is out selling more and more." And we persuaded them that people don't behave that way. If they are in that much pain over plastic, and we knew how much pain they were in because of the research we had done, they will pay off the people they are mad at. If you come in and do the right thing by them, they will reward you. And they really did.

After this success, many of the plastic companies came out with copycat products. But they didn't understand what really made us successful. We didn't sell a product; we sold an attitude. And the attitude was, "We're going to do the right thing by you, our customer."

When you tell people, "Hey, take another credit card. Oh, by the way, you can use it to pay off your other credit cards too," you don't have any credibility. Which brings us back to our original dilemma: doing what is good for the company versus what's in the customer's best interest.

The two guys who wrote the bible of Six Sigma, Mikel Harry and Richard Schroeder, right up front identify that the only way to create value for the company is to create value for the customer. And I actually use their definition of Six Sigma as my definition for CRM: CRM means creating value for customers in ways that create value for the company.

ROBERT J. KNEBEL

When I first had an opportunity to work with Bob, he was the Vice President of Domestic Sales for the Citation division of Cessna Aircraft Company, which he joined in 1994. Over an eight year period, Bob and his team grew revenues from $500 million to $1.4 billion, with no significant increase in sales staff. Bob has over 20 years of sales and marketing management experience. After obtaining his Bachelor of Science degree from the University of California at Berkeley, he started his career with Gates Learjet and then served in executive roles for Gemini Distributors/Securaplane and Beech (Raytheon) Aircraft Company. Bob is one of those individuals who is very comfortable under pressure. He is committed to continuous improvement in people and processes and is recognized by his peers as a superior change agent, capable of motivating sales teams and customers alike. Since Bob always views the Customer as starting with a capital C, we have done the same for his interview.

JD

> **In our industry we have come to realize that it is not nearly as important that our Customers understand our strategies as it is for us to understand theirs. Our Customers will be the ones that define what 'competitive advantage' really means, whether overtly or not, and will somehow indicate that to us. To succeed, we had better be ready to listen and respond.**

The Era Of Customer Advocacy

Let me preface my comments with an admission that my perspective reflects my experience which has been primarily in the business jet industry. While many would consider this a particularly unique marketplace, I would venture to guess that many of the challenges faced by the aviation industry are universal in nature.

With respect to Customer relationships, our emphasis today is changing. Rather than focusing in a tactical manner on the immediate sale, while clearly that is always a part of our thinking, we are emphasizing the development of *trust and true partnership* in our relationships, which we believe will lead to mutual *advocacy*. That has now become one of our key objectives.

We find that advocacy is more meaningful, and goes far above and beyond mere Customer satisfaction. We have benchmarked numerous companies in a variety of industries, including those who hold themselves up as customer relationship management (CRM) specialists. Through this effort we have learned that Customer satisfaction, in many cases, has been measured in pretty shallow terms.

We have also spent some time thinking about Customer loyalty. A Customer can be satisfied and not necessarily loyal. Or, they can be loyal, but is that enough to ensure a partnership? What happens if the Customer no longer needs our product or service, or has outgrown our capability to serve them?

Recently, we have been trying to understand the next step up on this Customer relationship scale, ...beyond satisfaction, ...beyond loyalty, ...and we think that is *advocacy*. If a Customer believes in us, trusts us enough to *recommend* us to others, and *encourages* people they know to do business with us, then as an advocate for us we already know that they are loyal. If we can achieve that, then we can be pretty certain that if they have the need themselves in the future, they will do business with us again.

So our goal is to understand advocacy, and with it the processes we need to utilize to generate a high level of trust and confidence in our Customers so that we can meet their true needs, not just their product requirements.

We really want a more intimate relationship with our Customers, and if we can achieve that we will create a climate of *mutual advocacy*. When that occurs, then we have laid the groundwork that will create genuine competitive advantage, something another vendor will be hard pressed to take away.

Alignment Of Business Processes

This may sound like a lot of 'touchy, feely' stuff, but in association with this we are designing business processes to assure consistency in our Customer management approach, an element of rigor if you will, to ensure that we genuinely understand each Customer. Through this understanding we will be able to develop strategies to create a higher level of trust and intimacy with our Customer.

With regard to the subject of Customer intimacy, our industry has historically segmented its markets based on the products themselves. Lately we have started to realize that even a relatively small market, such as business jets, can represent a variety of Customer sub-segments we might target with different products and services, offering more value to these clients and creating new revenue opportunities for the company.

For each of these additional sub-segments, we are also developing sub-processes that will help us define in practical terms the value we can provide each Customer. This is a concept some other industries have adopted before, but it is new to our industry. It represents a significant change for us because for decades, we have been highly focused on the product, on performance, and certain operating characteristics of the aircraft itself.

In a break with that mindset, Cessna took a pioneering step 30 years ago when the Citation business jet program was launched. At that time, the company recognized that ongoing customer support was as important as the product itself. That focus on service has been one of the key contributors to the Citation's ongoing success.

But now we are entering a new era. Customers have much higher expectations. A greater variety of opportunities exist that go well beyond the product and the ongoing level of service we provide. Today, it is about understanding the unique expectations of individual Customers and being able to respond to those needs.

This has become a genuine challenge for our industry. While my previous comments about quickly and accurately identifying or developing solutions may sound like 'motherhood and apple pie,' our business has never been structured to provide customized solutions to business opportunities.

Because of our emphasis on products, speed in our marketplace has always been considered in terms relative to certification of new products. New aircraft, or even significant improvements to current models, can require years to certify. Likewise, change in organization or business processes has come very slowly, not at a pace the Customer finds acceptable.

From the Customer's perspective, purchase decisions today are as much about the company that they are doing business with, as it is about the product itself. With this new and different relationship with the Customer, products may still take some time to develop, but developing solutions that meet the needs of individual Customers is something we can and must begin to do much more quickly.

Focus On The Customer

This shift in strategy is causing us to develop new, innovative business models to support it. For example, we have adopted a targeted account selling methodology. This provides sales people with a comprehensive set of steps designed to accurately assess an opportunity, understand the Customer's requirements and their decision process, determine how competitive we are at being able to meet this Customer's needs, and determine what the value of the opportunity really is.

We have found this approach to be very powerful in helping us discover what it is our Customers value most. We are then able to create a solid account communication and development strategy that provides us a competitive advantage.

Along with this, there are new skill sets required by everyone who touches the process. This is profoundly impacting the way we select, train, and develop all of our employees, but especially those in Customer facing roles.

In the past, our people were focused on technical aspects of the product itself, as an operator or a pilot. We have all been caught up in the romance of flying. Today, we spend more time trying to understand how we create success for our Customers, how we support their achievements, how we best serve them.

In our market there will always be plenty of money and plenty of opportunities. The question will be, "Who gets the deals?" Our objective in establishing a competitive advantage will be to have our Customer relationships characterized by a very high level of intimacy, supported by a set of robust processes so that we can understand and act upon opportunities quickly. This will then allow us to further build on those intimate relationships and essentially expand our sales successes through our Customers themselves. It is only when advocacy has been achieved that you know you have established a true partnership.

Bottom Line Results

We have already begun to see significant benefits from this new approach to relationship management. We recently had an opportunity to present to a Fortune 50 company with whom we had never done business. They were already the operator of a large cabin airplane, looking to update and upgrade their fleet.

They themselves were going through a challenging period. While business was good, they, like so many other firms today, had been directed by their senior management to double their sales over the next five years. Already being a $20 billion company, that was no small task.

Now typically in our industry, when an opportunity like this arises, suppliers would provide presentations on their airplane, focused on technical specifications. Certainly mission performance is a prerequisite; however, based on our process work we decided to take a different approach.

We already knew our airplane would perform the types of tasks they had under consideration. So we began by asking ourselves what was keeping their senior management team awake at night; what were their true business challenges?

As we looked through all the information we had gathered on our potential Customer, we realized it was unlikely they could achieve their revenue objectives exclusively through organic growth. They were in a mature industry and subject to worldwide economic conditions. It was clear that their success would be dependent on their ability to leverage the power of their brand by either developing new businesses themselves or supplementing their organic growth through acquisitions.

Who knew where they were going to go? But wherever it was, in the stretch to double sales over the next five years, they were undoubtedly going to employ either or both of these strategies.

Now you can't do that sitting in your office. You need to have key executives traveling to more places, more often, and you need to do it reliably. In thinking this through, we also realized that this would mean executives would likely travel to some places without access to a major airport.

That became the challenge on which we decided to focus our presentation. We reviewed our perceptions of what was critical to our Customer, what mattered to them, and we then discussed how we thought we could support that better than anyone else. We focused on a solution for their business needs, and they found our presentation startling. It fundamentally changed how they viewed an aircraft and the process they should use to evaluate alternatives. After our meeting, they saw how their aircraft purchase decision tied back directly to their revenue growth goals.

We differentiated ourselves in the eyes of the key decision makers and became a successful supplier to that firm. In fact, our Customer was so engaged by the process we used with them that today they have altered their own internal presentations to other company departments—their own internal customers, if you will—using that same protocol and format in ensuring they understand the real requirements of their own constituents.

The Customer-Focused Organization

Fundamentally, customer relationship management is a process about understanding our opportunities, listening to and responding to the Customer, and then building a quality relationship with the Customer. Those are simple concepts, but you need to make sure that every employee,

Customer-facing or not, understands them and the need to treat all Customers as true business partners.

We are evaluating our Customer-facing employees with an eye toward developing training to ensure they all have the appropriate skills for properly handling Customers. As we add new employees, we are developing a list of relevant core competencies to be utilized in candidate evaluations.

We also began to look at our field-based people differently, and discovered that we had an internal cultural impediment that needed to be addressed. Essentially, there were a number of deeply rooted perceptions about roles, responsibilities, and general 'orientation' of our sales organization.

One of the underlying attitudes we struggled with in the organization was the impression that the sales people were purely tactical and focused strictly on immediate personal gain. For parts of the company, including company leadership, this was their view of the sales force.

Today, the company is being asked to view the sales person's role as that of a *business development executive*. We expect each of these people to act as an innovator and look for fundamentally new ways to make the business grow.

As we begin to think differently about those in Customer-facing roles, we recognize the need to also address organizational structure, measurement, and reward systems. Through changes in each of these areas we hope to create strategic competitive advantage.

We are also spending a lot of time making sure we are listening to and *understanding* the voice of the Customer. In fact, when we find a Customer who has something truly meaningful or profound to say, especially if the message is process related, we video tape them so we can share their views across our company.

Looking Forward

As you can see by my comments, we have begun to focus seriously on optimizing our processes and our people. However, we also have a very clear understanding that the productivity goals we establish for our organization, and the speed at which we will be able to execute, will ultimately depend on providing our people with the right types of technological support.

We are working to put the right information into the hands of the right person at the right time, not only for our Customer-facing people, but for all the people across the company with whom our Customer might be in contact. Currently, we are in the early stages of evaluating technological solutions to support this requirement.

Advice To Peers

What advice would I give my peers? My response may seem pretty basic, but for all the emphasis on processes and supporting technology today, I believe success is still primarily dependent on the people you select. Only settle for the best; always seek to employ top people. The performance of these individuals is what the Customer sees, and is the basis for how they will judge your company.

If you are instituting process changes within your sales organization, be serious about it. Be serious about demonstrating to all the individuals involved the value of the process and then be serious about ensuring that they use those processes.

Develop and embrace the belief that all members of the team must continue to grow. Make sure that you continue to invest in developing your people so that they remain truly vital contributors to the success of the organization.

Finally, never assume you know what the Customer is thinking. Go out and ask them. As I said before, the Customer will show you the way. If you actively engage with them, they will make clear what you need to do to turn them into advocates. Achieve that, and you are assured of success going forward.

MICHAEL HEFLIN

Michael Heflin is CEO of WhisperWire, a company that provides interactive sales applications that increase sales effectiveness. WhisperWire is currently focused on the telecommunications and financial services industries among others. Prior to WhisperWire, Michael was chairman and CEO of Fracta Networks, which he led through a successful acquisition. Before that, he was COO for Xelus, where his efforts doubled annual revenues in the core businesses and established Xelus as the leader in service supply chain software. Michael also previously served as vice president of North American Sales for Vantive Corporation, which was acquired by PeopleSoft in 2000. His leadership at Vantive helped grow revenue over 100% annually for five years. Whisperwire's web site address is www.whisperwire.com.

BT

> **Think of yourself as a snow skier starting off the new season. If you have skied double black diamonds the year before, you normally don't start on double diamonds for your first run down the hill. You start on an easier slope. The reason isn't necessarily that you've lost your ability to handle the challenge—the issue is your confidence about your ability to handle the challenge. So it is with sales.**

Confident Competence

Sales people are like different driving personalities. There's the little old lady peering over the steering wheel, and there's the NASCAR wanna-be weaving from lane to lane. In the first case, the old eyes know what to do, but they've lost the confidence to handle the situation. The racer will get you there quickly, but it'll be a scary ride. And, like the driver with little confidence, the driver with misplaced confidence can ride through an account, but leave behind wrecked deals and lost opportunities.

Ideally, every vice president of sales has a vision of what a sales force should be. It is a group of individuals with complete knowledge about their products and how to sell them; it is able to provide customers with a consultative experience that delivers real solutions. However, the reality is far from that vision—sales forces today are routinely not equipped with the right sales process, knowledge, and skills to effectively sell their portfolio of products.

The challenge of sales leadership is to create out of an ever-changing talent pool a confident, competent sales force capable of producing and caring for the customer. There is a cornucopia of tactical fixes for common weaknesses in a team. For example, if the team can't sell the product, we drag them into training. If the customer picks the bad guys more often than us, we develop a new pitch to demonstrate our superiority.

Unfortunately, we've been addressing sales skill sets with the same reactive approach we use with product sets. We preach to our sales staff to work accounts as strategic opportunities. Why shouldn't we lead our sales teams in the same strategic way?

Today's selling environment requires the same fundamentals that have been taught for literally hundreds of years regarding sales process, methodology, and philosophy. However, the environment today also has a unique set of increased pressures: much shorter time frames, an ever-increasing amount of information, and greater complexity in our offerings. Many sales managers continue to approach these fundamental issues in the same ways, but what is truly needed is a transformation.

Some thoughtful sales leaders are taking a different approach; they're looking at what their sales organizations need, not in simple tactical terms but in strategic terms, to address both their confidence and competence. They are looking to provide a suite of tools and skills that enable increased confidence and competence among all players.

When confidence and competence remain unaddressed, they result in a sales force ill equipped to drive the revenues and margins we need.

The Six 'Unders'

The ill-equipped sales force suffers some typical symptoms: a few sales people drive a large portion of the revenue while a majority of sales people have average or below average performance. Worse than the '80/20' rule (i.e., Pareto's principle), in my experience is the '97/3' rule. The result is that the sales team routinely sells only what they know rather than the high margin products; new product rollouts end up being unsuccessful; low margin products continue to be the largest part of the revenue base; or, on average, only a few products in a large portfolio of products are sold to each customer. In these scenarios, only a very small percentage of the sales force is truly equipped with the right processes, knowledge, and skills to bring in the high-margin, high-dollar deals that we all want.

I believe that problems arise in one or more of six areas. Specifically, sales reps: 1) are under knowledged, or they 2) under qualify, 3) under present, 4) under motivate, 5) under position, or 6) under value.

Let me give some common examples. A sales rep makes a call. He asks questions, but the questions don't lead to an optimal outcome. The rep doesn't know the right questions to ask or doesn't know how to translate a prospect's answers into solutions.

Another problem is over-reliance on scarce technical resources—perhaps sales reps too frequently call in product managers, engineers, or sales specialists to answer questions. Because of this reliance, getting a proposal out to the customer can take too long. As a result, the prospect cools, and the last thing on your sales rep's mind is cross-selling or up-selling additional business.

Sales forces experiencing these problems are often unsuccessful in selling products in today's changing business environment. The result is a crisis of competency and confidence.

▶ Under Knowledge

The first cause of ineffective selling is sales reps' lack of knowledge about their products and processes. The emphasis here is on the products they don't know or the proper sales process they don't follow. Focusing on a limited and familiar subset of products, they miss or ignore opportunities for up-selling, cross-selling and bundling products. There's an old saying that knowledge is power. Today more than ever, product and sales process knowledge are the foundation for confidence and competence.

▶ Under Qualify

The second cause of ineffective selling is under qualification. Reps don't know how to ask the right questions and target the right products to the right customers. In the end, they don't understand the customer's needs. They're like college freshmen in their second term who keep asking, "Where are you from and what's your major?" Time and again, sales reps approach qualifying prospects and opportunities with worn out questions and techniques that are no longer applicable to their current selling environment.

▶ Under Present

Sales people often lack real-time information about their products, pricing, and promotions causing them to fail to provide customers with the appropriate information to make a decision. For example, there may be a relevant and timely promotion that would close the sale, but the sales reps don't know to access it.

▶ Under Motivate

Sales leadership can clear the first three hurdles only to find that their sales reps are under motivating. The reps are unable to create a compelling reason for the customer to buy because they lack the ability to tie the products to the customer's needs. There is a magical moment when a match exists between the customer's wants and what you offer. It's sales' job to motivate the customer to embrace that match.

▶ Under Position

The fifth problem area arises when sales people can't effectively describe their differences versus the competition and crystallize those differences in the prospect's mind. Marketing has spent an enormous amount of energy and dollars trying to ensure that sales reps understand how to best position a product in a certain market with a certain type of customer. But sales may never get to that last mile. A breakdown can occur somewhere between the information and training that marketing delivers to the sales rep and the sales rep's conversation with the customer.

▶ Under Value

The sixth reason sales people can be ineffective is that they under value. They sell at lower prices because they haven't established the value of the product and the company. They can't speak confidently about the solutions—about 'why us.' They lack the confidence in their product offering to convince the customer of the value of buying at their price.

A Strategic Solution Set

Sales leadership can address each of these areas of under-performance with two umbrella components: in-process automation and real-time knowledge.

Imagine a professional football quarterback with coaches and an offensive coordinator whispering tactics and strategies in his ear. In addition to these resources, the quarterback has an understanding of the weaknesses of his adversaries. He has a full understanding of the playbook and uses it in a step-by-step process to make sure that his team drives towards the win. In-process automation and real-time knowledge can deliver this scenario for sales teams.

Now, don't misunderstand what the solution to these challenges looks like. The solution set that you deliver to your sales force is not simply an administrative one that's going to track their deal steps, administer their territories or provide a view into their pipeline. All of these have value, but the solution to this problem is one that addresses confidence and competency, and does so in real-time.

▶ In-Process Automation

Every company spends a significant amount of time to determine how best to equip a sales rep to approach, engage, and close a customer. This includes product positioning, market positioning, and sales training. Even then, all of that work and training typically ends up in a manual or on an Intranet site, but is not used during interactions with the customer. If you're going to deploy something that changes confidence and competency, you have to deploy something that guides sales reps through best practices *during* the sales call.

I'm not talking about something like, "Step 1 is to qualify, Step 2 is to analyze, and Step 3 is to present." Rather, I'm talking about understanding in-depth the products that I'm selling and the audience that I'm selling to. Take the 'three percenters' that produce the most sales and extract from their rich experiences the best analysis processes, the best engagement steps, the best positioning and offerings. Then, put all of this into a dynamic environment so that other sales reps can use it in engaging with customers.

This dynamic knowledge can be captured within an interactive selling system or sales effectiveness system that your reps utilize throughout the sales process. While key steps in the sales process might be 'engage, analyze and present,' an in-process automation tool used during the sale should support what the sales rep actually has to do.

For example, in order to sell a data network solution in the telecommunication industry, you have to understand many things about the customer's needs and environment. At the same time, you need to understand a significant set of data about the different solutions that you could offer. An interactive selling tool helps the rep to understand the specific types of business questions that should be asked, and assists in translating the prospect's answers into the types of services and products that could be offered.

This type of system is especially useful if it challenges the sales person to do things he or she has never done before. Whenever possible, the system should produce multiple solutions. This gives the sales rep the opportunity to sit down with the customer and say, "Let's get on the same side of the table and look at different options. Let's you and I work together and determine which one makes the best sense for you."

▶ Real-Time Knowledge

The second primary component of a strategic solution set is real-time knowledge: bite-size contextual information that transforms relevant marketing information into effective selling information. It specifically speaks to the reasons why a solution makes sense for a customer based on what that customer needs. When we speak of needs, we're not just talking about technical specifications, but also the customer's qualitative needs. We must understand that price can be more important in one case, and customer wants more important in another.

When two competitors walk in the door with offerings, all things being equal, they're just two different solutions to the customer. Real-time knowledge during the sales call creates a consultative relationship by again allowing the sales person to provide alternative solutions to the customer. The majority of competitors will bring in one solution that they will offer as *the* answer. Sales people can differentiate themselves by bringing multiple offerings to the table. This helps them to build better relationships.

This is especially true in industries where the actual solution set can have a degree of variance defining 'best.' For example, two banks recently approached our company with possible solutions to our needs. One of them brought a single offering; the other brought three different offerings. I spent a lot more time with the banker who brought three offerings, having him explain each and using those as tools to discover my true needs as the company's CEO.

Banks don't want to put only one solution on the table. The stated goal of most banks is to average six to eight products per customer. Yet the average retail customer utilizes one or two products. Increasing the number of products per retail customer has been a goal of banks since the '80s. However, as an industry, they have not elevated beyond one to two products per customer.

Now you have to ask yourself a fundamental question: Is it impossible to move customers to multiple products, or is there a fundamental problem with how we deploy our sales resources to get those customers to buy additional products? By giving real-time knowledge in bite-sized contextual pieces, you can actually deploy automation to make customers aware of your portfolio of accounts and services. The key difference is using automation steps to do this during the sales call. With real-time knowledge you can say, "I have multiple offerings for you to review; you may want to explore more than one based upon the needs we've discussed."

A Case From Telecom

In our work, SBC Communications, one of the largest North American telecommunications service providers, has deployed an application to over 5,000 sales reps across North America. If ever there was a nuclear winter for any industry, telecom is now experiencing it. The constrictions on demand, the oversupply of pipes in the marketplace, the financial pressures for performance, the combination of business failures and over-investments are all causing the telecom industry to reexamine where they're spending money and focus on cost cutting. At the same time, they are trying to drive top line revenues.

SBC realized that they needed to immediately improve the performance of their sales organization. They deployed a system that addressed specific issues in order to provide their reps with real-time information about a myriad of options. As a result, they've seen both quantitative and qualitative improvements including:

- *Shortened sales cycles and improved close rates*. Reps are able to deliver targeted solutions customized to meet customer needs.

- *Reduced reliance on technical support*. Reps are able to deal with less complex solutions, freeing technical support to focus on larger, more complicated deals.

- *Reduced time to transition reps from order taking to consultative selling*. The system allows new reps to quickly ramp to selling the full range of services.

- *Increased confidence*. The system gives reps dealing with more complex products increased confidence to sell unfamiliar products.

Critical Considerations

A sales effectiveness system is different from a sales automation system in three ways. First, the system is architected from its base to focus on the interaction with the customer, not on sales administration. Second, you have to embed into the tool your company's offerings, products and industry knowledge. This does not mean sprinkling the tool with words and a few pieces of workflow to make it look strong enough to be demonstrated. It means embedding into the application a full understanding of how your sales reps conduct themselves in a best practices manner, how they sell products, and how they sell to different types of customers.

Third, you must actually embed product knowledge; that is, you understand and develop modules around the products that the sales reps are selling to the customer. If business rules or product requirements necessitate a configuration or human intuition engine, include it in the system. Or, if there's something very special about the way that you analyze and classify need sets that is different from every other product, include it in that product module.

These three points—focusing on the interactions, industry knowledge, and product knowledge—make sales effectiveness a very different offering from sales force automation. You aren't just buying an application. You need to deploy a tool that covers the products for which your sales force really needs help. This tool might not cover every product or service you offer— you could start with less than your full array of offerings—but it is important to get it out to your organization to address their challenges.

Another issue for which you must be prepared is maintenance. A major cause of failure of knowledge-based systems, knowledge-management systems, and the like is that the maintenance—keeping the knowledge current—simply becomes a nightmare. To actually do this and make it work, you have to deploy the system in a way that matches the business processes and the organizational preferences of existing environments in product marketing and sales.

Moving Forward

There was a time when people believed that they could replace the sales force with automation. I'm confident that this is nonsense. Any tool used appropriately can produce massive leverage, but it cannot replace the sales force. Sales leadership must focus on appropriately using technology in combination with other strategic initiatives to improve performance.

We'll never make every sales rep a 'three percenter,' but if the bottom 30% can move their performance up to where the 40% to 50% performers are, and the middle third can move up 10 to 15 points on the performance scale, the company's ROI will be very compelling. By taking a holistic approach to developing their sales organization's confidence and competence, sales leaders can realize strong results in today's selling environment.

CLAY SAYRE

When I interviewed Clay Sayre, he was Vice President of Planning and Regional Development for Unocal Indcnesia in Jakarta. I first met Clay while he was on Unocal's Front Office Team, a small corporate group tasked with applying web-based technology to its core oil and gas business processes. One of the team's focus areas was management of critical external relationships, especially with foreign national oil companies and their governments. Since 1981, Clay has worked in operational and strategic planning, project management, business development, and change management for firms engaged in international oil and gas exploration and production. He has lived and worked in Southeast Asia for 18 years.

JD

Sales and marketing people spend a great deal of time attempting to create a relationship-based service model that will give them a competitive advantage in the eyes of their customers. We all would like to do that. But unless we have identified a customer who is interested in a relationship with us, and have a very clear organizational focus on what the customer is trying to accomplish with our products, we are unlikely to achieve our goal.

Creating a relationship-based service model for extraction of oil, gas, or other natural resources starts with knowing the customer and his needs. That's easy to say and hard to disagree with. But it is of value only if the customer is willing to pay a premium for the additional services we are able to offer. Our problem is that in our value chain, the customer, as we usually identify him, doesn't seem to care much about our services.

Understanding The Value Chain

In a generic energy-product value chain, we end the chain and name the user as whoever converts the energy product into another product or form of energy. Gasoline is converted into transportation; natural gas is converted into electricity, fertilizer, or plastic products; and coal is converted into electricity or steam heat. In those conversions, one value chain ends and the created product enters a new value chain where it competes with a new set of substitutes.

We need to view the entire value chain or we'll miss the full extent of the options the end user actually has. Those options create independence. If we focus on intermediate customers, we see fewer options and may get a false sense of the value of relationships. When the ultimate customer makes purchasing decisions with little supplier loyalty, it will be hard to realize a relationship premium from intermediaries in the chain.

The complete value chain for gasoline ends with a consumer who chooses to experience something that requires personal transportation, and then chooses to use a gasoline-fuelled vehicle. Only when those choices have been made will gasoline be consumed. The next choice we would like to see is that this consumer buys our brand.

In hopes of attracting this customer, and ultimately coaxing a higher product margin from him, we examine what else he may be looking for beyond simply enabling his transportation option. Seems like not much. We notice that retail gasoline customers are willing to add 10 minutes to their daily commute or make an illegal U-turn just to find a gas station where prices are five cents a gallon cheaper, about 50 cents for a typical transaction. Some invest this savings in an extra shot of espresso in their very next purchase, a $3 cup of coffee.

When we see this behavior, we wonder if a sustainable, high-value service model is possible for a retail energy product. Our products are viewed as commodities and therefore can and should go for the lowest price. So how do we make money? Some retailers have redefined the value chain and sell high-margin food and beverage products alongside low-margin gasoline.

Another energy-product value chain is electric power. The power producer buys natural gas, coal, or fuel oil and uses high-capital-cost equipment to convert fuel into electricity. If the marketplace for his energy purchases allows, he will swap suppliers and products to save a penny per million BTUs (British Thermal Unit). He is hardnosed in choosing energy supplies to ensure that his electricity products compete in their value chains. Natural gas, coal, fuel oil, and the electricity he generates are regulated, standardized commodities. It is inevitable that these power companies will not have strong loyalty to their suppliers and therefore will not pay a premium for a relationship with us.

Can we do anything to create a unique relationship with power producers? Stability of supply, consistency of the product, willingness to accommodate predictable and unpredictable fluctuations in demand are all service characteristics that should be valuable to the power producer. So we sharpen our pencils and analyze the cost of providing these services versus the premium that we might one day be able to extract from the buyer. But should we ever expect to find big value here?

A law of human nature is at work that, as applied here, would read something like this: *If your customer does not care about you, over time, you will learn not to care about your customer.* Some observers of our industry say that we have reached that equilibrium. We fill pipelines with natural gas, ships with crude oil, and trucks with gasoline. They never come back with a 'thank you' note from the customer.

If our sales cycle is placing incremental volumes of standardized, fungible product into a marketplace that readily absorbs it, then it may not matter whether we launch those products with arrogance or with heartfelt concern for the end user's business. Which stance do we choose, and do we get a different answer if we let outsiders answer that question? Internally, our company cultures feel very secure, very independent.

When an organization loses its sense of interdependence with its business environment, it loses a priceless source of vitality. Every organization is both independent and interdependent, depending on what aspect of its business is being viewed. It can choose how it sees itself. When it chooses to put its attention on its independence, it starts paying less attention to the information the outside world is sending it. Most of that information is intended to help it. Leaving aside any high-minded judgment of right and wrong, it's simply bad business for management to fail to direct the organization's attention towards areas of its most significant interdependence.

The value-chain framework puts our attention on our relationships with the energy product consumer. In our industry, that's a tough place to keep the organization's attention directed. It's literally thankless, and it may not make much money either. Is it possible that we have too great a proportion of our finite energy and attention on the customer?

We are interdependent with our customers, of course, but because our products are commodities, we may never establish significant relationships with them. If we agree that we need deep, interdependent relationships to stay healthy, where do we turn?

Who Else Could We Provide Value To?

Let's stay with the same energy-value-chain paradigm, but look at the other end of the chain: the suppliers. Our premise is that we can increase product margin through a high-value relationship. Can we develop organizational competence that consistently creates relationships that give us long-term preferred access to low-cost, high-quality energy supplies? A structural advantage here creates bottom-line corporate value, just as a famous brand extracts a higher margin from brand-conscious consumers.

Exploration firms do not create the natural resource; we just extract it. Our role is finding it, bringing it to the surface, transporting it, cleaning it up, and getting it to someone for distribution, not creating it. We will always be dependent on access to resource.

If we cannot differentiate our products to our end users, then it is critical that we have access to the highest quality, lowest cost raw materials. In oil and gas extraction, a 10-fold variation is possible in total exploration and production (E&P) costs, based only on the characteristics of the natural resource. The net effect of that cost advantage is greater on product margin than teasing a few pennies out of the end user. Can we influence this cost through relationships? In some locations, yes.

The marketplace for mineral rights is still very different around the globe, and clearly relationships do not matter everywhere. Consider the United States, a mature E&P market in which securing access to natural resources means buying mineral rights. This might involve a federal auction of offshore acreage or a transaction as simple as buying land with mineral rights from a Texas owner.

In the U.S., pricing models for mineral rights are relatively consistent and predictable. If we have not impaired ourselves with regulatory or legal trouble, or established a bad reputation with the public, then our money is as good as the next guy's. As long as we are a credible, mainstream player, investing in a special relationship with Texas landholders or the federal government is unlikely to get us preferred access to supplies.

The U.S. and other big national economies do not live or die by variations in energy prices, nor are they threatened by year-to-year fluctuations in relative volumes of energy imports and exports. The free market rules with ruthless efficiency. That is less true for developing economies competing with other developing economies for world market share of energy-intensive products.

If Country X imports energy for electricity at world market prices, and Country Y produces its own natural gas at 30% less total cost, then Country Y has an unassailable advantage in the production of energy-intensive products. For developing economies in mutual competition, natural resource extraction is truly strategic to development. Getting it right is potentially critical to survival. For all the right reasons, these governments closely control access to natural resources. We find them fully engaged in managing complex, long-term energy development programs.

To heighten the pressure, for some countries, their proven supply of domestic energy may be comparable to the time horizon of their long-term economic planning. This stiffens the challenge: they have a one-time opportunity to convert precious natural resources, the birthright of the people, into a sustainable economic base.

Bangladesh has recently discovered significant amounts of natural gas. Farooq Sobhan, president of the Bangladesh Enterprise Institute, described his country's challenge in a recent interview in *The Economist.* About Bangladesh, Sobhan said, "It can either squander its natural resources like Nigeria, or it can emerge as an Asian tiger economy that will one day rival Malaysia or Thailand. If done properly, the entire economy will be transformed, benefiting everyone from the humblest rickshaw puller to the wealthiest industrialist."[1]

If we are looking for high-value relationships, this is the type of environment in which to find them. What do government officials who feel these pressures need that we have? More meaningfully, what else might they find valuable that we could offer, and is there a business proposition for us?

Let's leave that thought aside for a bit and consider a framework for identifying the creative drivers of service relationships.

A Customer's Goal Pyramid

Within any enterprise is a hierarchy of goals, big ones and small ones. Visualize this as a pyramid of intent, with a single goal at the top. This goal is very crisp, described in a few words. It probably does not change over time; if it changes, it changes once in decades. This goal attracted most employees to join the enterprise and keeps the best ones around. Breakthroughs towards the goal excite everyone.

The enterprise thinks of itself as being this goal. "We are X," they say. We design the fastest computer chips, find cures for incurable illnesses, explore space. These goals are so well understood that we do not see them engraved down corporate hallways.

Underneath that primary goal are sub-goals. Sub-goals represent the areas in which the enterprise must realize constant progress to advance towards the ultimate goal.

Beneath the sub-goals are all the layers of strategy, tactics, programs, and projects organized by the many layers of management. This is where the enterprise becomes visible. Here is the action: issuing service and equipment tenders, managing contracts, designing new products, building plants, writing press releases, etc. Let's call this the base of the goal pyramid.

Service and product providers are invited into the base of the pyramid where they become part of that action. However that invitation came to you, that's where you are. The initial strategy is always the same: understand how you fit in; perform; exceed expectations; build relationships.

Then you evolve, working to understand the rest of your customer's goal pyramid. Can you work your way up a layer? The closer you are to serving your customer's primary goal, the better chance you have to realize a higher margin for your products and services relative to competitors.

For example, NASA approaches you and asks to buy a pump you manufacture. Assume that NASA's highest-level goal is unmanned exploration of space, and this pump is part of a project that is part of a program that is part of a sub-goal to go to Mars. Your pump is a long way from Mars. Does that mean that all you do with the contract is sell your pump? Of course not. Once you've harnessed your firm's talents to produce the best pump you can, you then use your emerging relationship with NASA to investigate other ways your firm can assist any or all of their programs.

Perhaps your firm cannot provide NASA with direct assistance in exploration of Mars, but you can still start creeping up their goal pyramid if you bring other value to the table. Start small. Maybe you have expertise in how your type of pump performs in low-temperature systems. If you offer this competence when other suppliers do not, you may be able to create a value proposition beyond the one for which NASA tendered. Your relationship with NASA starts to change.

Moving Up The Goal Pyramid

Now back to oil and gas. In international exploration and production, a key player in our success is the individual or institution that gives us access to natural resources. For convenience, let's give this institution a name and call it the minister of energy. We may view him as a supplier, but chances are he thinks of himself as the customer and views us as a service provider he invited to serve the needs of his country. Task number one is finding his undiscovered hydrocarbons in the vast expanse of the exploration acreage he has offered us. That's the big value creation in this game.

Depending on the competencies of our firm, we may also have a role in managing the development of the discovered resources and transporting them to market. For these services, we either take all that we find and pay back a percentage as royalty plus corporate income taxes on profits, or we take a share of the discovered resources and sell them ourselves.

However the contract reads, in the eyes of the minister of energy they are his country's strategic resources. They are the birthright of his nation and critical to the success of economic development programs with huge long-term growth goals. These resources may be the only assets his county has to fund significant change. He did not give us access to them without fierce debate. Do not doubt that at least one person in his government passionately wished that better options existed than giving them to us, and still feels that way.

We can refer to the minister of energy as our supplier of raw materials, or as the customer for our E&P services. Calling him 'customer' changes our point of view, and with luck, just that name change will start our organization thinking a bit more about what he needs from us, and a bit less about what we need from him. Whatever we call him, he holds the keys to our success and we need a deep and broad relationship with him.

A relationship in which we serve the minister of energy requires that we understand the complex forces acting on him. Whatever else may be going on, at the core of those forces are national development goals. So, we need to evaluate and form suitable relationships with other government agencies standing alongside him. Governments represent the people, so we find ourselves building a relationship with the country itself. It is a relationship in service of the people, working through a single point of contact with the minister of energy.

If that sounds too grand, let's replace 'the people' with 'the constitution,' something we can get our hands on and work with. A country's constitution, or its equivalent set of documents, is the only explicit will of the people we can reasonably access. As E&P contractors, we are working for the government in a manner consistent with the constitution. As straightforward as that sounds, is it too 'political' a position for a for-profit corporation to take?

The distinction is hardly noticed as long as the government is operating in accord with its constitution. A keen test of living corporate values comes when the government's actions depart from the intent of the constitution in a manner that forces the E&P contractor to choose between them. Over the long haul, supporting the constitution should be the right course; in the short term, it may be costly.

A test of this principle occurs each time the E&P contractor designs tactics to lobby decision makers towards a government ruling needed by the E&P firm. Are tactics selected to be consistent with the intent of the constitution and the government structures the constitution dictates, or are lobbying tactics chosen to be maximally effective? Can we lobby effectively within constitutional decision channels?

Though challenging, it is still not enough just to understand the laws, regulations, constitution, and government structures of the host country. We also need working familiarity with the informal decision-making norms for the host country. This in turn means integrating host country national staff with corporate decision makers in management teams that are actually working as teams, and have power. These are high standards, rarely met.

Let's assume we have come to terms with the application of our corporate values for work in the target country, and we have the organizational skills and structures that would allow us to manage relationships there. Let's say our corporate goals are aligned well enough with the country's goals so that we have not disqualified ourselves as partners before we open negotiations. Let's agree to view the minister of energy, the gatekeeper of acreage, as the customer and ourselves as provider of the services of identifying and extracting natural resources for his country. How do we work our way up the country's goal pyramid?

Environmental protection is an easy example to use for illustration. This country goal may be held inside or outside the energy ministry; it may be a higher-level goal than resource extraction, or lower. The goal will always be present somewhere, in some form. Our industry has learned that, whether stated or not, the goal of environmental protection needs to be met along with all the goals of resource extraction. The same applies to worker and community health and safety. We no longer debate this, and our host countries expect us to excel in these areas.

At best, performing resource extraction while satisfying health, safety, and environment issues is still one of today's competitive differentiators. Or, it may be yesterday's competitive differentiator and today's table stakes. How much future value can we expect from a strategy to differentiate ourselves as 'green' resource extractors?

Where do we look for tomorrow's competitive differentiators? We start by granting our host countries 'customer' status in our internal thinking, and looking for the next level of service we can provide them.

As E&P service providers, we first accept our invitation as offered and set goals to find the undiscovered hydrocarbons and bring them to the surface.

That is the unfailing initial strategy: understand how you fit in; perform; exceed expectations; build relationships.

Next, we work up the pyramid. Where is our task in the base layer of the country goal pyramid? Clearly, it is the country goal pyramid we have to study. If we look at the only the goals of the energy ministry, we can be sure we are looking at a sub-goal for the country.

Above all the energy resource extraction goals, however many billions of dollars they encompass, are tough, country-level issues. A generic energy, industrial, and economic development strategy would deal with at least:

- cost of energy delivered to the domestic market
- security of supply
- longevity of domestic energy supplies
- matching energy policy to industrial policy
- competitiveness of domestic industry versus cost of energy
- total economic cost of variations in energy price
- availability and quality of non-energy natural resources
- characteristics of skilled and unskilled labor
- determining the level of energy subsidies or taxes
- effect of energy subsidies or taxes on social policies
- national security
- geography
- historical trading partners

The list is generic, the result unique to each country, and of course it's complicated. The interactions we have with the minister of energy are influenced by hundreds of years of decisions around these issues. Does our operating behavior reflect awareness of the huge and complex problems our customer is dealing with? Are we asking ourselves, all throughout our organizations, where in that enormous field of problems can we help?

We may never be invited to review government policy, but policy makers may be interested in our advice nevertheless. Even if they're not, to the extent that we can think with the decision drivers our customer is experiencing, we have the opportunity to structure our product and service offerings in forms that are a better fit with our customer's complex needs.

The first step towards expanding our usefulness will be creating honest, transparent energy options for the energy ministry to choose from. At first, we should not expect to be skilled at balancing country-level decision drivers and recognizing, from the country point of view, good options from average ones.

If our sole product offering is a single resource discovery that we are trying to market, then our advice will be nothing more than lobbying for what's best for us. The super-majors in our industry will have more energy supply alternatives to choose from, more flexibility to swap risk, more financial strength, and hence overall, greater opportunity to create custom energy products and services.

Our own oil-field service suppliers have worked a similar strategy with us for more than a decade, and the dominant players appear to be set up as prospective E&P companies themselves. They might actually have the skills to compete effectively with us, but they have not chosen that course, and are unlikely to do so. They have developed these skill sets so that they are better able to understand our value decisions and work with us. They do a great job, and, of course, they expect a premium for this.

Farooq Sobhan, in a position of influence in Bangladesh, wants to transform the entire economy, "benefiting everyone from the humblest rickshaw puller to the wealthiest industrialist." The challenge to us is to work with him and others like him in partnership. If we do this well, we create enough joint value that we can keep a portion of that value as our premium.

Creating True Partnerships

Developing partnerships with a country as they transform non-renewable resources into sustainable industries is one future playing field for the E&P industry. That mindset creates new business challenges that are no longer limited to mastering resource extraction. The nature of our customer's problem means that if we are successful in creating that partnership, then we will be a partner for a long, long time, and will never again be viewed as just another oil company.

We would become the complementary half of a relationship that each successive government will see as a national asset, a firm that helps create and grow industries and is a thought partner for whatever economic challenges emerge. All such complimentary thinking would be well hidden from public view, of course.

This may sound fancy and theoretical, and if so, a perfectly reasonable question is, "When does this create bottom-line corporate value? Is this practical?" As to practicality, there is an easy answer: no, it's not practical. As a thought framework, it is not practical until it is applied. The art, as well as all the value creation, is in the application. Theories don't create a thing. Management will determine how much of this is workable. Commercial talent will figure out how to convert country-level relationship goodwill into corporate value.

This is a framework for thinking about ideal relationships between a natural resource extraction firm and its host country and government. As it is applied and working strategies are created, compromises are inevitable. Compromises are least destructive and most constructive when they are made consciously and with choice. The practical utility of this relationship framework is in enhancing awareness of those choices.

[1] The Economist, February 9, 2002, page 29.

DAVID MORRIS

David Morris is President and CEO of ZuPreem, a producer and distributor of specially formulated diet food for exotic pets and zoo animals. David descends from two pioneering leaders in companion animal nutrition. His grandfather and father developed and commercialized what were to become Hill's Prescription Diets, Hill's Science Diets for companion animals, and ZuPreem products. The family's company, Mark Morris Associates, was a specialty research and development organization that worked under contract with Hill's Pet Products, Inc. for the development of these products prior to its acquisition by Hill's Pet Nutrition, Inc. in 1988. Following graduation in 1992 with a law degree and MBA, David capitalized on a decision by Hill's Pet Nutrition to discontinue the ZuPreem line of diets for zoo animals. He established a company to continue the line, and since 1992, ZuPreem has expanded aggressively into the avian pet food market in addition to its traditional zoological park business. I found David to be well versed in the sales and marketing challenges facing smaller businesses today.

BT

Because small companies, by definition, have a limited number of people, we have to make the most of human, financial and technical resources. This means I have to grow as a leader and increasingly release authority to others so they and the company can grow. Having a clear plan, participating in education/entrepreneurial programs, and having a trusted advisory board have been key for me.

In the past, our company has not been particularly effective with respect to sales force management or the sales and marketing process. We are currently doing a lot of work to change that, but it's only been within the last year that we have had very effective leadership. My wife, Darlia Morris, a Doctor of Veterinary Medicine, joined the company a year ago. She brought with her over seven years of sales and marketing experience in the private sector.

At the beginning of 2002, we also recruited a new national sales manager who came from a much larger company. This new sales leader brings to us a much more sophisticated approach. While he is young, he's been

©2003 Sales Mastery, Inc.

exposed to processes and what for a big company is everyday blocking and tackling. For a company our size in an industry which is more 'mom and pop,' some of those concepts are very new.

For example, we recently completed our budgeting process. It is not that innovative, but my guess is that most small companies don't establish rigorous budgets through annual planning and then periodically review their progress against those plans. They may have a general goal in mind, but they don't always manage the business toward that goal. If the forecast comes up short, they don't always make cuts to keep to plan.

Finding Value In Entrepreneurial Resources

A lot of my thinking has been guided by two different factors. The first has been my participation in an organization called YEO, which is the Young Entrepreneurs Organization. I was introduced to YEO while attending MIT. There I went through a program called *Birthing of Giants*, a program that is sponsored by *Inc.* magazine, YEO, and the MIT Enterprise Forum. In the program, we met for four days each year for three years. We met people who are all under age 40, own companies of a certain size, and the experience was unbelievable.

The program was great; it was hard not to be enthused. Through hearing people talk about the different stages of growth and what it takes to be successful in business, I now have a deeper understanding of the real issues. And, if we don't want to get the same results we've always gotten, we actually have to do something different.

The second factor is being in Kansas City, where there are great mentoring resources. We are very fortunate to have access to the Kaufman Center for Entrepreneur Leadership (listed at www.entreworld.org). Kauffman was the founder of Marion Laboratories and owner of the Kansas City Royals. He was a very successful entrepreneur; basically, he sold his company and endowed this foundation. One of his passions is supporting the development of entrepreneurship in this country.

Other visionaries are also involved in mentoring the community. For example, Jana Matthews talks about the stages of development and how the leadership role continues to change. Our challenge is to really think ahead to the next step for developing our businesses.

It has been important to me to listen to other people, and understand that my challenges are not necessarily unique. Everybody is challenged in similar ways. What can be unique is having the confidence to say, "I'm going to move outside my comfort zone." Most entrepreneurs trap themselves by thinking, "I must do it all, I must touch every project, I must control everything." As a result, they absolutely become the bottleneck of their company. I'm committed to not repeating this situation in our company.

Think Ahead, Tap Into Trusted Knowledge

There are probably entrepreneurs who know they are not great sales and marketing people, but they can't afford to bring on a sales and/or marketing manager. I think that this then becomes a matter of priorities and degree of pain; it's always challenging to do more with less.

To help direct our efforts, we appointed an advisory board about a year and a half ago. These individuals are an absolute godsend. Not only do they produce a sense of accountability for me, there were times when they gave me the will to do some things that otherwise might have remained unaddressed. I never want to walk back into an Advisory Board meeting and say, "Yeah, that manager who we all know is under-performing and is not a fit, is still here."

Basically, the advisors look at my situation and provide information and insights based on their experience. We most recently spent two to three hours talking about leadership. They gave very specific examples from their careers, including who their mentors were and their specific traits and actions they took that made them effective leaders. That was a very valuable discussion.

Communicate Clear Objectives And Feedback

When you fail to put in place visible performance measures and to provide regular, specific feedback, management tends to be overly fair. They give people multiple chances in the event they hadn't been clear enough in the beginning. We're trying to get out of that vicious trap because it's not fair to the rest of the company to continue to accept anyone's under-performance.

Also, our management team's at-risk pay is based on two components: 1) company profitability; and, 2) their individual components. So now, performance and profitability are impacting people other than just the owners. There are lots of initiatives that we would like to implement, but we have reined ourselves in because we probably would have spent more than we were really comfortable with. Any over-spending would impact people's take home bonus in December. We've found that structuring our business this way creates a sense of reality for everybody.

At ZuPreem, everyone has objectives on which they are evaluated every quarter. The results of these reviews determine a person's annual bonus, as well as his or her raise for the next year. I think one of the biggest problems for a small business is that no one wants to do reviews. Often, the process is handled so poorly and it seems easier to avoid them. But without a solid, repeatable process in place, most managers will not provide constant, clear communication and feedback to their direct reports.

Some people say that you should do ten-minute reviews once a month. If you're giving that kind of consistent feedback, everybody has an opportunity to correct any problems or maximize successes. From my perspective, if companies avoid the review process, they have lost a huge opportunity.

The whole idea of communication is to reflect or pare back the conversation and to make sure the other person understands. In meetings, it's amazing how people can get stuck due to some miscommunication. Sometimes 30 minutes or more is wasted; it's unbelievable.

Track With The Growth Of Your Business

I decided that the company needed to step up, even though we had grown 25% each year for the past six years. That growth is on a small base, so by itself it's not that big of a deal. We're still proud of that success, but I felt we had started to plateau. Our company was continuing to grow but we were starting to outgrow certain individuals on the management team. As a result, my job was becoming increasingly more difficult.

Specific individuals were not able to scale with our business growth and tackle new challenges, especially on the operations side. We had a beloved employee that was one of the early people who helped get us from point A to point C—or even point D. Many entrepreneurs have a person like this on their team. In our case, this was an important go-to person, who had functioned as my right hand. However, as the company grew, she could no longer be in that role because it meant she'd become an absolute bottleneck.

Generally, folks like this are super loyal but their talents may not have grown with the demands of the job. They are the kind of people you could afford to hire when the company was young. As the company expands and transactions become more complex, there may be a slot for them but even that may be overwhelming. They often do not delegate effectively and feel the need to touch everything. They are almost like an extension of an entrepreneur who can't grow with the company.

In our case, it was obvious that the person was not happy and couldn't handle the job because of the size of the transactions. This person's view was, "I take care of this business and show my worth. I'm providing valuable service just by making sure that no balls get dropped."

Well, if you are making sure no balls get dropped, you are still trying to touch everything. You've got to approve everything, and the job becomes impossible; at least that is what our experience was. By the time I finally addressed the issue it was a very traumatic situation. Absolutely, I should have made that decision six to nine months before.

Create Culture, Visibility, and Accountability

The other thing we are trying to do is all about creating alignment and focus—making sure all the departments are focused on the right things, and to a certain extent, on the same things. If you don't set up systems that reward the behaviors you want, such as tackling problems, continuing to grow, and maintaining accountability, you're not going to get them. We're also working to ensure that the operations department understands their role and the two or three main things that they have to do really well. Those objectives will drive the overall effectiveness of that department, which will then serve as an example for the rest of the company. With everyone focused on specific goals in one area, we can more easily replicate the process throughout the other departments.

We have one department that is a little harder to quantify, but we can still do it. Like a lot of small companies, we've combined accounting, HR, IT, and all the non-variable overhead functions into one department. The goals for this department are somewhat different. With an overhaul of our budgeting process, they'll understand the steps we'll be going through next year; how they do each one of those steps is what I want them to focus on.

Looking back, I realize that we've always had a lot of personality issues that were solved when certain management team members left. Our two newest managers understand that for the company to grow, the management team has to function as one unit. We're shifting away from an entrepreneurial model where, "David is the boss, David does everything."

We're looking for much more of a team approach, which I am actually very skeptical about because there's been so much about the wisdom of teams in the business press lately. Despite my skepticism, I have to delegate authority if we are going to move beyond where we are now. I have to spread the load around the management team.

And as mentioned earlier, we've tied compensation to *team performance* to create alignment. That's real. Everyone needs to come together as a group to fix whatever problems we encounter. And, there's got to be a healthy dependency on each other.

I'm doing my part by getting out of the daily operations; I'm going to let my management team make the vast majority of the decisions. The rate of my involvement goes down as our two new key managers in sales and operations come up the learning curve.

What I've learned in the last year and a half is all about the importance of graduating from a manager to a leader. At the end of the day, I am responsible for two things: 1) the strategic direction of the company; and, 2) ensuring that we execute every single day to the best of our ability. Both of those things are more than full time jobs. However, in order to be effective, I better have time to reflect on what we want to do strategically and what our opportunities are, and to coordinate the departments and make sure we are achieving our goals.

There's always a temptation to reach down, to stay with what's known and comfortable. But I have made a commitment that I plan to stick with, and that is to move beyond my comfort zone.

Sales And Distribution

We have a couple of different distribution channels, and though we sell product around the world, the vast majority of our business comes from domestic sales. Our two product lines are pet products and institutional products.

Pet product sales come through the traditional channel: wholesale distributors who then sell to independent pet shops and clinics. For example, people can buy our bird food through PetCo, PETsMART, or another retail outlet. We also sell through some specialty channels like the Internet or mail order, but they're a pretty small percentage.

Our institutional product sales mostly come from the zoological sector. These same products are almost another category of product when we sell them either directly or through another set of distributors who cater to specific customers. For example, owners of unusual or exotic pets (primates, reptiles, exotic carnivores) might buy our Zoo Diets.

Most of our sales efforts are applied against the majority of our business, which is the independent pet trade. We have two to four outside sales people who are spread out regionally to cover the whole country. Our national sales manager also has senior level responsibility with distributor customers.

The Sales and Marketing Excellence Challenge

The main challenge we have is related to the distribution model of the pet industry. Like many industries, ours is contracting, which means having a smaller number of wholesale distributors selling to fewer retailers.

There's huge pressure on the part of the distributors to rationalize SKUs and to limit the number of duplicate lines that they carry. We compete in a category that is a small percentage of the overall sales of that distributor—we're a niche within that category. So, we are always competing to gain more mindshare with that distributor. We're actually looking for our unfair mindshare because our sales don't really justify the level we want.

The other thing that we've always done is to try to trace back from the consumer, to the store, to the distributor. And that's one of the reasons we embraced CRM technology, so that we would have a way to easily coordinate and communicate information to the sales force. To further assist we typically create teams, matching an inside person with an outside person.

One of the things we do to gain and maintain mindshare is to simply have people working in the field. I think for a company our size, we've traditionally had more sales presence in the field than anybody else (as a percentage of sales). We want to make it as hard as possible for a distributor to say, "Well, I'm not going to carry that SKU. I don't want to carry your line in general."

Our sales people build relationships and typically it's done face-to-face. Some transactions can be completed over the phone, but that method of communication is much more effective when maintaining an established relationship. Since we have access to capital, we're in a situation where we're able to front load our expenses as it relates to the sales effort.

Most small companies spend half their time just keeping up, then harvest some revenue, then reinvest it back into the business and stair-step it up. We've jumped ahead a little bit because we've been able to justify putting those people in the field; as a result, we capture the investment on the backside. It's always a little bit scary when you're front loading like that because the gross has got to be there. It gets ugly really quickly if things go the other way.

The risk is that things don't always work exactly the way we plan, which can lead to a higher cost of sales. But we've been fairly successful at holding our operating costs very steady. We've actually been able to drop some, and are significantly increasing our operating profit as a result. So, it's working out all right. That's been our approach to add more value for distributors.

I'm speaking on a relative basis; again, as a percentage of the distributor's overall business we're not going to add that much value. We just have to work harder as far as getting bigger mindshare. For us, working harder includes more frequent account coverage and better levels of promotion. It also means having a relationship where we can actually work with the distributor to get sales data on our accounts that they typically do not give. This information allows our inside sales group to be more effective in identifying opportunities for new product placement.

Sometimes, we will be proactive and call on resellers ourselves because we know we're not going to get much face time with a particular distributor. That distributor's sales rep has 4,000 SKUs to offer retailers. They can't talk about all 4,000; they can talk about maybe three lines.

A couple years ago we brought in CRM software to increase the coordination between the field and the inside sales person. We want our sales people to be as knowledgeable as possible when calling on the distributors. We also use the system for follow up activities. Our field people's territories are so huge that they may not revisit a local market for four or five months. If they go into an account and there's an issue, it's very easy for them to record the information and schedule a next action for the inside sales person to follow up on.

Initially, we built ZuPreem with an inside sales force. But to take the company to the next level we believe we need this high level of effectiveness in the field—without giving up that inside sales force. This is very critical: despite what I said earlier, you *can* build relationships over the phone. Let's take this example: we trace a sale back to Joe's Pet Shop, where Mary Jones buys bird food. If ever there is an issue with Mary and her bird food from Joe's, we can facilitate resolution. Because we trace the sales, we can deal with the issue and prevent it from happening with all of Joe's customers.

Or, if Joe's pet store goes out of business we can contact these people or send a post card offering a mail order option or referring them to another stock retailer in their area. Oftentimes, we can save that business or help transition that business simply because we know who our customers are.

Now, the retailers are not going to give us their account list. A lot of the information we have is based on calls into our center. But our people are also focused on getting this information. The distributors don't usually give us complete data, though sometimes they will. Granted, it's hit and miss but we do it to the extent that's possible. In many cases it's just a matter of asking the right questions; we're able to piece together the picture somewhat.

Applying Technology

As I mentioned, we brought in a commercial CRM package in October 2000; before that we had a proprietary program that was written for us that worked okay. However, since it was a customized program, every time we needed a new report our developer had to go back and write it. It was just a big pain. We also couldn't sync the information with the field. There was no way for us to communicate with people if they were not on the network, and that really forced our hand. We knew we had to get something else.

In general the new CRM program has worked pretty well. The extent to which it hasn't been successful has been a failure on our part to clearly define each piece of information and what the answer to each user-defined field would mean. The second difficulty has been keeping the database current so that we can actually leverage it and use it more effectively. That's changed very quickly over the past year. With the new sales manager's arrival and now the new marketing professional, I think we're really going to start executing against the data, not just warehousing it. Data becomes information only when somebody bothers to look at it— and use it.

For example, we have a distributor going out of business and dropping all their food lines, including ours. Since we know which zoos are buying from them, we are able to go in one at a time and say "Okay, we need to move you to a new distributor, or maybe we can take you direct." Whatever they want to do, we're going to move a significant portion of our zoo sales to either go direct with us or move to new distribution. Without supporting technology and customer information, we would have a tough time staying close to customers and successfully executing this transition.

We also want to use technology to create competitive advantage. We have a major web initiative right now to tailor our customers' experience based upon the animals that they are interested in. If we can provide information for a parrot owner versus a ferret owner, or a zookeeper or veterinarian versus a regular pet owner, we can add more value to their experience.

Our big challenge right now is to focus on getting new products into the channel and expanding our share of ultimate customers. We compete for a significant portion of what a typical bird owner will feed her parrot, for example, but I think currently we supply less than 50%.

So I think our challenge is to gain a larger share of customers on the consumer level, but the only way we are going to do that is if we can get new products into the pipeline and into the field. We will accomplish this by aligning behind a handful of key initiatives and executing on them exceedingly well.

ALAN ROSS

I first met Alan Ross in 1998 after he contacted me about an article I'd written on sales process. A Cal Poly (San Luis Obispo, California) graduate, Alan's education gave him a process orientation and he was interested in how this could be applied to his company's sales efforts. Alan is the third generation of the Ross family involved in Ross Printing and, with a son also trained and working in the industry, is committed to seeing the company grow into the future. Alan became President of Ross Printing in 1991. The company received the Gold Award for Management Excellence from the National Association of Printers and Lithographers in 1996. Located in Spokane, Washington, Alan has served on several local boards and community organizations.

BT

> **Today, it is all about making sales; that is the compelling, urgent need. To do that we need to create value-add relationships with our customers, and we have to better leverage technology.**

Ross Printing was founded 86 years ago by my grandfather, who was later succeeded by my father. I am also committed to keeping the family enterprise going; my son has earned a degree in printing management and is now employed in the industry.

Understand The Current Marketplace

That said, our company and our industry are facing extremely challenging times, unlike any in the history of our primary process, which is offset lithography. As a result, our daily efforts are very focused. We have a high sense of urgency to understand what is happening in the marketplace and how we are going to address the issues.

During the go-go years of the late '80s and '90s, our industry ran at full capacity. Press manufacturers in the U.S. and around the world typically shipped their goals and more. Eventually, new cylinders (drums on printing presses to which aluminum plates are attached) were introduced faster than old cylinders were being retired. Today, we have an imbalance in the supply and demand equation. We see a tremendous amount of competition, coupled with reduced demand.

Survival Tactics

In trying to sort out how to survive this particular time, and hopefully prosper as an economic recovery gains traction, we've had to revisit our whole business model and in some ways reinvent ourselves. We've taken a new approach to the market, which is oriented more around gaining market share than servicing and maintaining the top 40% of the market—our direction during more bountiful times.

▶ Focus on Market Share and Operational Efficiency

In a market share environment the focus is on cost per impression (CPI). How much does it cost us to put ink on a piece of paper and get it out the door? We measure CPI very aggressively and are attacking the cost side of the equation with enthusiasm and vigor; our assumption is that the only way we are going to create margins is to produce it faster, better, cheaper than the other guy. That's different from how we have done business for the past 80 years.

Print has been under attack from other messaging media as well. The bulk of our business comes from advertisers who have had reduced budgets and more choices, which in turn dampened the demand for print. For example, the Internet was a source of tremendous dislocation and billions of dollars of lost revenue in our industry, because of the infrastructure costs related to assembling, staffing and maintaining company websites.

Predominantly, funds for the above were taken out of print budgets. As the Internet evolved, and we still don't think it's reached its real second-generation water level, it was a very negative event in print buying patterns. Broadcast fax, e-mails, Internet storefronts, and cable television were all cheaper than direct mail. All of these, plus funding for Y2K upgrades, came out of print budgets.

We've seen our total market shrink over the last three years, and expect the trend to continue through this decade. So, it became incumbent upon us to identify what was happening and how we could counter that. We have embraced a couple fundamental points that we think resonate with our customers. And we're putting all our chips on the table and going for it.

▶ Maintain Solid Customer Relationships

I have two fundamental themes that I constantly reinforce throughout our organization. The first is the compelling and urgent need to increase sales. I act as the sales manager or Chief Sales Officer in our company, along with being the CEO and General Manager. Especially now, it's very important to maintain direct relationships with our strategic customers.

Simply stated, that means making as many face-to-face or telephone contacts as I can reasonably sustain to let customers know what we are doing about our cost containment. It also means addressing what we can and should do to increase our sales with each customer. What's changing about their business, and how can we better suit their needs? Now, that seems rather simplistic, but typically when we drill down into their needs, we get into the other key area I'm constantly monitoring.

▶ Utilize Available Technology to Create Value-Add

The second fundamental area of focus is the technology choices that we make on a regular basis to produce our product better, faster, and cheaper. Technology involves three aspects from our perspective: the Internet, internal networks, and computer assist devices for specific equipment.

The Internet, despite all the dislocation that it has caused with print buying patterns, has become a very potent tool to supplement the manufacturing process. We have customers that we've never met face-to-face and yet we produce high-end premium printing for them. For example, we converse frequently via the telephone and e-mail with a customer in central Montana that we never see in person. Given their location, it is difficult and expensive to visit. So, whether it's an important local account or one that is remote, in today's environment it is one of my top line responsibilities to convey appreciation and concern for our customer's issues—and to provide reassurance that we are doing things, like investing in technology, in order to provide a very competitive price point.

The Internet has been a tremendous vehicle for things like file transfer. In other words, a customer can create PDFs (Portable Document Format) and move them across the net to us. The Internet is a wonderful device for what we call remote soft proofing. We have calibrated monitors by which we can show a customer's work on a dedicated website, automatically trigger an e-mail notifying the customer to go in and edit it, invite other associates to review it, and gain final approval. The site then automatically triggers an e-mail back to us, and in many cases becomes the contract proof that goes to press. We utilize this process frequently in the label portion of our business.

Another very potent Internet tool for our work is content management. One example involves a customer that is out of state for us, but is a national player in the neutraceutical business (i.e., nutrition-based products, such

316

as supplements). This account was pretty much a transaction account for us (i.e., not strategic). They had fractured their label print buying among several suppliers and would routinely wash out printers. This drove the price point to a ridiculously low level.

When we saw what they were doing, we proposed that if they would dedicate all of their brand names and all of their label requirements to us, we would create and maintain a website displaying color PDFs of every single label in their inventory, which amounts to hundreds. They could download, print, and collaborate among the various branches around the country on the ingredients in a particular product. This is very important now, as the FDA tries to scrutinize the neutraceutical business, and as the space becomes increasingly competitive.

Our solution has worked out wonderfully. The customer just loves it. We can say, "We think you're saving probably one full person with the efficiencies gained through this dedicated website." You can debate whether it's a half or a full headcount, but when we translate that into savings for the company, our price per thousand on a particular label becomes less of an issue. We are adding value in another way; without the Internet we wouldn't be able to do it.

Another benefit of the Internet is speed. Say you are *Sports Illustrated* and have a very strict deadline. At the same time there is a need for distributed printing, because the postal service is now charging by zone. That is, if you ship across country mailing costs are higher than if you ship 200 miles away. So, today we have distributed printing plants that can download files and actually print closer to the point of distribution.

In order to create commonality of image, so we're not creating five or six hybrids of the cover of *Sports Illustrated*, they upload the file on the Internet where everybody has a color calibrated monitor that is managed with the same baselines. There they can go in and annotate with comments on color balance or skin tones or product match, and the master file is then edited; the download at the various sites will be common and look the same at all locations. That's called remote soft proofing. But, given cycle time issues, it often becomes the contract proof.

This occurrence is amazing, given the specificity that art directors would bring to the pre-press provider just ten years ago. They've made enormous concessions for the sake of speed.

While this process is saving headcount for the customer, it is also saving a person at our end, which translates into a lower cost per impression, and is where this discussion started. I don't have to be the lowest price provider, but I've got to be competitive.

It's the same everywhere; we're all chasing business. Unfortunately, we are trying to take market share away from each other because the market isn't growing. And it gets pretty vigorous. So we look at all of our tools and constantly reassess what we can do differently to make our offering better, faster, cheaper. It always goes back to technology. Despite the hammering the tech sector has received, I am still convinced that the United States is going to lead the world in productivity and our ability to integrate technology into the manufacturing process is going to be the way out of this mess that we are in.

Make New Technology Investments

Aside from a very powerful internal digital network, one of the most recent technology advances that made significant meaningful reductions in cost is the adoption of a totally digital work flow. I'll explain what that means to us.

As you know, files are created digitally. Whether a file is saved as a PDF, PageMaker, or an Illustrator file really doesn't matter to us. We take the file and manipulate it so the customer is happy with the press sheet. In commercial lithography, the file was then exposed by laser or, in the old days, a camera, to create film. The film was then mated with an aluminum plate and sent off to press.

Recently, the industry has greatly minimized the use of film; we are now exposing the image directly onto a metal plate via what we call a plate setter. This is called CTP—computer to plate—or direct to plate. This process has been an amazing evolution in our industry because it enables us to dramatically reduce costs. However, it is still a matter of controversy in our industry, since in some situations people feel that film produces a better result. As CTP has become more adopted, the price of film has dropped dramatically, therefore skewing the cost benefit equation to a certain extent.

While Ross Printing brings to the table a long history in the marketplace and a great brand name, it's still a price driven market, so we need to further distinguish ourselves. Quality is almost a given; it is assumed that if a printer has survived to this point, they are going to put out a quality sheet.

Turnaround time, however, is something we can talk about. Direct to plate is an enormous boost to reducing cycle time. That's very important in an environment where manufacturers want to minimize printed material inventories. They want to keep the window of editing opportunity open as long as possible, and once everyone has signed off, they want product in hand quickly.

Once the product is available, the vendor immediately wants to get it in front of the sales reps, the dealers, brokers, and customers. Things move so fast that a week can mean all the difference. One sale can more than amortize the cost of the project. If a competitor goes to market first with some new innovation, then it's a day late and a dollar short—and the market does move that fast.

The first generation of CTP required that the plates, after exposure on the plate setter be pre-baked; the hardened emulsion was then scrubbed and developed, and then post baked. This is a real energy-intensive and chemically dependent process.

In July, we hosted Kodak Polychrome Graphics; we are the first commercial printing plant in the country to test what is called a processor-less plate. It's a CTP plate but it's a water-washed plate. The byproduct after the plate is washed is completely water soluble and nontoxic. By utilizing this technology, we would eliminate all of those expensive chemicals, as well as the associated disposal process and costs. We would also be shutting down a line that generates a tremendous amount of heat that requires air conditioning. So, we are striving to get this new processor-less plate on line as soon as possible. The next step will be imaging right onto the press cylinder; a process which we think will have some commercial viability by the end of the decade.

Know Your Customers—and Adapt to Meet their Needs

As I said earlier, it all begins with the question, "What are my customer's issues?" We've discovered that he doesn't want to deal with a lot of vendors. So, we are providing other peripheral services such as inventory warehousing, fulfillment, and direct mail.

Publishers want to turn over the files and then limit their involvement from there on out. They'll look at a proof and might even look at a press sheet, but they want the entire transaction to be just as transparent and easy as it can get.

Even 'billing as shipped' can be a real value in the customer's eyes. For example, in contracting for a book printing, a publisher can say, "Alan, I'm going to give you this print contract. I think I have an overall demand over two years for 20,000 books. I'll pay you for all 20,000 books but I can't afford to pay you for all 20,000 up front. Our sales projections are such that we expect to ship 2,500 books each quarter, so I want you to print, warehouse, and drop ship to my retail sources starting with the initial 2,500 copies. And I want you to send me a bill for what you ship, and continue to warehouse the rest."

A scenario such as this creates some fun negotiations and very delicate cost accounting. One of the most difficult things that we have to face in our business right now is predicting sales. Several years ago, I learned about the importance of creating a growth-oriented, predictable, measurable, and sustainable sales model. However, it's *very* difficult now to predict sales levels for even a quarter out. If I can get a customer commitment to buy 20,000 books over the course of eight quarters, I have a hard number to plug into my forecast.

Even if I have to eat the cost of a second or third set up, it is not a deal breaker given today's technology. I'll print 10,000 books and send shipments and corresponding invoices. When I get to a certain inventory point, calculated by my inventory management system, another order is triggered. Then I'll buy the paper and ink, schedule the press time at my discretion, and print another quantity. It's just great to have the long-term commitment; it's very meaningful in an environment where predicting sales is one of our biggest challenges.

▶ Communicate and Educate

In differentiating ourselves from the competition, our history and reputation as a reliable provider are very important. A huge part of our customer base is comprised of advertising agencies that use us to print for their clients. As a result, reliability and predictability, as well as quality, are vitally important. The printing company's CEO preferably, or certainly the CSO, has to spend time with the customer. The agency is probably enduring tough times, too, so if nothing else, you convey how much the relationship means to you and what technological investments you are making that will help make them a star in their customer's eyes.

To keep a steady work stream and create a combined organization that can meet multiple needs, it is important to educate customers at the owner/ manager level. Although their print technology knowledge tends to be low, I won't allow them to assume that printing is printing.

At the same time, I feel it is very important that my sales people understand color management issues, remote proofing, PDF workflow, the actual cost savings of direct to plate, and so forth, even if the customer is not currently using them. I want each sales person to understand why a particular option is different, and its benefits—because you have to be believable.

Implement a Winning Sales Model

We also have invested in administrative technology. We use CRM software to monitor the effectiveness of our sales process. Our seven-step sales process allows me to manage, support and review sales performance very quickly—even from a remote location. If my activities draw me away from the office, and they should, I can still help my sales people orchestrate the next step of a big deal through utilization of the Internet or our own intranet.

The seven-step process is very simple and it's just terrific because if we can identify where the deal fell apart, we can coach sales people more effectively. In fact, we're almost at a point where our sales people don't even need to seek help from me. They can figure out what went wrong through going back to our pre-defined buyer and vendor responsibilities and identifying where/how we failed to comply with our own process—and as a result, why we lost the deal. It's worked out very well.

Stay Awake And Thrive

My CFO and my manufacturing manager are my key constituents. We get together at least once a month to review the manufacturing statement. And it's all broken out by ratios. Of course we track year-to-date, previous year, etc., to track down anomalies in any part of the manufacturing statement.

We have established new compensation packages for sales people that are very heavily weighted toward performance rather than base compensation. So, they have a high sense of urgency to create new sales—and they've done just that. I'm attracting good people in that area because our investments in technology are unique to this market. So the best craft operators and the best sales people, we think, will migrate to us. And that has now begun to happen.

The prognosticators in our industry said, probably four or five years ago, that by 2008, there will probably be half as many printers in existence as there are now (estimates vary between 25,000 to 40,000). That trend is unfortunately right on target. All of a sudden, we've just had so many bad things happen from 9/11, the crisis of confidence in the stock market, reduced demand for our product, predatory pricing practices from printers that are just trying to get oxygen until it might get better.

A lot of the adverse conditions we see in the industry today were predictable. In the late '90s, the handwriting was on the wall and unfortunately, all of our dire predictions have more or less become reality. But, it's a healthy process. It's basic economics. And I'm convinced that the survivors are going to be lean and agile, and driven by technology.

BOB THOMPSON

Bob Thompson is President of Front Line Solutions, which specializes in CRM strategic planning and research. Since 1998, Bob's groundbreaking research in Partner Relationship Management (PRM) requirements, best practices, and technology solutions, has earned him a reputation as the industry's leading PRM consultant and industry analyst. In January 2000, Bob launched CRMGuru.com, which has become the world's largest and fastest-growing CRM industry portal with over 175,000 members. CRMGuru.com publishes e-mail newsletters, provides a forum for thoughtful discussion, and allows community members to get support directly from an international panel of CRM experts. Bob is often quoted in publications such as BusinessWeek, Computerworld, and InformationWeek. He also speaks at conferences and seminars internationally. A prolific writer, Bob is also the editor and publisher of CustomerThink, an award-winning e-mail newsletter.

BT

As I've often said, "You ought to be smarter at the front end." A lot of business is actually about learning by doing. When you have the data and the systems to translate that data into real information, but you don't use it to determine how to build better relationships, that's a shame. Neglecting to do this costs us money and customers and I think this happens a lot more often than we'd like to see.

Today, I'm running a publishing and consulting company but I've spent much of my career working with large customers in manufacturing, airlines, and wholesale distribution. I am very relationship oriented and have won big opportunities over the years with major accounts such as Delta Air Lines, where I established a new 'application marketing' team that sold over $100 million of hardware, software, and services.

Marketing excellence means working with the right customers, being smart about who you decide to work with, and delivering messages that outline your capabilities in an effective way. When you get somebody's attention, you have a chance to do some profitable business. I'm not a marketing analysis expert, but it seems to me the most important role for marketing is to make sure that when a relationship starts, it's with decent prospects—those with the potential for long-term profitability.

I've written an article for a *BusinessWeek* supplement about marketing analytics technology. The article primarily focuses on how to optimize your current customer base. In this type of endeavor, marketing plays a huge role in ensuring that the sales force is working on the right opportunities.

Digging Through The Data

As for identifying which customers are profitable, not very many companies have figured out how to do it. The tools are somewhat complicated. The data is there, but the accounting systems and legacy databases are not organized to make profitability analysis easy.

The companies that have the most to gain from profitability analysis are typically financial services providers. Companies with lots of consumers or a large number of business-to-business technology customers would also enjoy a big payoff from a profitability analysis.

We've built all these automation systems that collect tons of sales, marketing, and customer services data over time. There are also transaction systems, point of sale, and retail data repositories. If you have collected these mounds of data, perhaps now is the time to dig through and figure out whether or not your current marketing and sales activities are focused optimally.

Respect The Relationship

Sales should be about serving your customer. The best sales people that I've ever run across create awesome relationships. These sales people do not manipulate, coerce or do anything untoward. They provide a solution, and they provide value to their clients. In my estimation, if you look at it from a customer point of view, it's not that they don't appreciate an aggressive sales person, but rather they want to get their problem solved. Effective sales should be about delivering the value that the customer wants and doing it in a professional, effective, efficient, and aggressive way.

I was always aggressive when I was in sales. I made my numbers, and the relationships were always intact when I was done. Occasionally, I got into situations at IBM when they wanted to push product X, Y, or Z. They'd say, "How come you're not selling that stuff?" or, "How come this deal didn't close?" My response would be, "We sold $100 million last year, but this project wasn't a good fit."

I had a bigger objective in mind, which was to maintain and nurture a long-term relationship. I was concerned about the next year's business, not just this year's business. I was not interested in any programs to go sell a particular product because it was a hot deal. Back then, you had to have some backbone to take that stand. And in my case, I can say that I've performed—I made my philosophy work. Whether or not others share my philosophy, I don't know.

Today, I'm sure there are folks who want to do the right thing, but at the same time, there's a dearth of leads. People are sitting on their checkbooks and are asking a lot of questions about ROI and financial viability, as well as productivity or revenue enhancement.

I'll give you an example of how a good relationship works. I buy technology for CRMGuru.com and am extremely cost conscious. One of my objectives is to keep expenses less than revenue, which is mostly made up of advertising support for the site. We're not trying to sell every square inch of the site in terms of ad space, but we need revenue to support our projects. When we do buy technology, we squeeze every nickel until it screams and then we squeeze it some more. That practice is probably more common now than it was a couple years ago.

For the last two years, I'd looked at e-mail distribution software. I wanted to find something more sophisticated than our existing system, something that would allow us to have a database of our readers. I consider the readers our customers, and I wanted to have a more sophisticated report on who's doing what. I wanted to know the e-mail newsletter open and click-through rates. There's a lot of intelligence to be gained through gathering statistics and managing this communication process—but it is expensive.

Until a few months ago, I couldn't find a technology that I could afford. This time, when I investigated the market I found a different selling environment. Pricing strategies were more aggressive and the vendors were much more willing to negotiate.

Based on our needs, we quickly narrowed our search to three companies. I discarded one because the company was launching a new product and I did not feel comfortable taking a risk on a brand-new piece of software. The vendor has a good reputation, and we're using their previous technology now. But for the new product, they threw everything away and started over. We would have been customer #1, and I couldn't take the risk even though they seemed to be price competitive.

The second company we considered was the Cadillac of the industry, who was willing to price the product like a really high-end Chevy. They really wanted the business and had a great solution. But I just couldn't afford it. I ended up having to tell them no.

We chose the third company, but that decision does not come without risks. It's a young company, and they have a few customers; some are big names that I recognize, such as Meta Group and Business 2.0. The company was willing to give references and be flexible in terms of working the package in a way that I could manage.

The value was there and the functionality looked very good; even so, there were some holes. I said, "You don't have X, Y, and Z." They said, "Fine, we'll build it for you. We know that we'll be able to prove our product and bring on other clients." They were willing to put that on the table, no problem. As it turns out, they've come through on all of our requests very admirably.

I drove this company's sales rep nuts. We were at the end of June, and had seen demos, developed specs, etc. I also met with their CEO. I wanted to look him in the eye and make sure I knew what his plans were. I was trying to assess the risk of working with a young firm. I was a customer betting my operation on their product, and enough money was at stake that I put all my energy into it.

By June 30th, their rep had been working with me for two months and had been just great. He asked, "Bob, can we get this contract signed today?" Those were not his exact words, but it was clear that he was getting a lot of pressure from his management, such as, "When are you going to get this deal done?"

So he asked me the questions he should have been asking. What kind of shape are we in? Are you planning to sign up and can we get it done today? I told him no. I said, "I'm not comfortable signing it today and I don't want to. We're going to be working together a long time and as far as I'm concerned, it doesn't make any difference whether we sign today or next month. I don't want to be rushed into it." To his credit, he backed off.

We ended up signing the contract about a month later. As it turns out, in the process of doing some testing we uncovered some critical issues before we signed, and I got these addressed in the contract. These were almost showstopper quality issues. Certain functions just didn't work the way we needed them to work.

In retrospect, maybe the company would have dealt with those functions anyway. We've since uncovered other issues and they have been very willing to work through them. But I didn't know that at the beginning. I wanted to make sure I didn't sign a contract and then end up regretting a hasty decision.

This process was very tough on the sales guy. He could have done a lot of damage to our relationship by pushing too hard. He could have said, for example, "Well, what if I give you a big discount?" Or, any of the tactics that are sometimes used to get a contract signed within a particular timeframe. He didn't do any of those things.

Whether he was considered a hero or a failure by his management, I don't know. But from my point of view, he kept working through the issues along with his technical people. We eventually signed a contract, and I'm a happy camper. And in return, they have a good, probably long-term customer, assuming they continue to perform well.

The relationship I've described reflects our current business environment. Sales reps have to adapt and manage a different type of sales process, one that truly supports what their potential customers want, and addresses their real issues. It's not wham, bam, close the deal and move on. Customers won't stand for that anymore.

My experience is that most sales reps don't have enough good opportunities to work on, so they expend a lot of energy either trying to make marginal deals fit or putting too much pressure on deals that do fit. I think an interesting question is, why don't they have more quality opportunities to work on as a normal course of business?

Finding Quality Leads

One possible reason is that their company has over-expanded beyond real market demand. There is always a lot of hype around whatever is the current hot product. During the dot-com era, there was a lot of business growth for all kinds of reasons, some not so good, and that growth created a false sense of opportunity. These companies and their sales forces scaled up beyond the real market demand, and then became frustrated by the cutbacks that followed. That's certainly one possibility.

There are other factors at work that could be equally culpable. Perhaps companies' marketing processes are not very effective, and are not producing enough of the right quality leads. From our vantage point at CRMGuru.com, it's interesting to watch our advertisers' strategies over time. Two years ago, we saw more branding campaigns. Right now, advertising objectives are purely about lead volume and response rates. Advertisers are running ads primarily to generate leads—a very tactical approach to marketing.

We ask our advertiser customers about the success of these tactical approaches. I've asked a number of customers if they've ever measured how many of their leads actually close. How well did their campaigns perform overall? And how did they experience working with us from an advertising point of view?

We don't do any screening on our web site and ask very few questions of our readers, so we cannot be 100% sure of who comes to the site. However, because our content is management oriented, we know we get people who are interested in management issues. Readers sign up and discover whether or not they like what we have to offer. They read our content and the ads; and if they click on an ad, then the advertiser is happy.

This arrangement has worked well so far. I've always felt that if it didn't work, the whole business model would fall apart. At any rate, what I've heard back from our advertisers is: a) it's currently about response rate and lead conversion—can they get somebody to click-through, and how many clicks do they get for the dollar? And b) how many of those clicks turn into a lead?

The questions remain: how many of those leads actually turn into sales? Do you have any statistics? Only one out of 30 advertisers has ever come back with answers. One such firm replied, "We figured out that we get one sale from about 300 unqualified leads." This firm is very savvy in terms of e-mail marketing and tracks things very carefully.

But with everyone else, the focus seems to be just volume. I've always wondered whatever happens to those leads. Are they ending up on some sales rep's desk and are being ignored, because the sales rep thinks the sales potential is low?

Marketing And PR Programs Work

I definitely think drip-marketing works. Back in 1998, I originally started my newsletter as a low-key marketing effort. The newsletter didn't include much marketing, but I wanted to have something that got our name out there. I had no idea what I was doing, but I figured, "What the hell," and I actually got some business. It took a while, though. A few times, I took the time to trace the origin of new business. I asked people where they first heard about me, and they'd say, "A few months ago, I started reading your newsletter," or "I met you at a conference," or some other contact point.

Gaining visibility in the industry didn't happen quickly. For a period of time I was very proactive, and even hired a PR agency. I never tracked that carefully—but I'm convinced that the combination of being proactive in marketing and PR, plus picking a niche such as Partner Relationship Management (PRM) helped me launch my business.

By getting published, putting out press releases, and writing my newsletter, I went from a 'nobody' to a 'somebody.' I wouldn't say a 'big somebody' by any means, but people knew who I was and became clients; I was off to the races after about a year and a half to two years. This strategy has worked out very well so far. Now, I don't have to spend anytime at all drumming up new business.

Bigger companies are also trying to find some nuggets out there. They have to implement mass e-mail or direct marketing programs or other activities to find good prospects. These marketing activities are exactly what led me to my e-mail distribution provider. They had a small ad on a surf engine someplace. I was searching online, the ad popped up, I clicked a link, thought the product looked kind of interesting, and then one thing led to another. The company was actually very responsive when I requested a demo or more information. They were right on top of everything. When somebody showed a spark of interest, they had a good process in place for working the opportunity.

If you try to intellectually work your way through it, you will always feel there's a better time than right now to start these marketing programs. For me, I started at a time when I didn't have a lot of extra money, but I took a stand and said, "Here's what I'm going to invest in," recognizing that it may not have been an immediate need, but it was important.

Making that decision is tough. In the general market, even after all of the upset, all of the character erosion, market cap collapse and people going out of business left and right, it's hard to find people who are saying, "We're starting a new program now. It may take a year and a half to bear fruit, but that's the way it goes."

Instead, I hear companies saying that times are tough and the sales guys just need to get out and work harder, do the right thing, and/or get with the program. It seems to me that you need a collective alignment towards marketing that says, "It's not going to happen overnight, but we all believe this is the thing to do. The sooner we get started, the sooner we'll get where we want to be."

Still, bigger companies get much more ingrained in how they do things; we've all seen that. Even I have a bigger operation now. I have other people to think about, more revenue, and all the things that come with a growing business. It's not as easy for me to turn on a dime as it was two years ago. That bothers me sometimes, but on the other hand, I've got more to turn. I'm still a little speck of a business compared to these big corporations, but the dynamic is the same. Someone in a leadership position—the VP of Sales, CSO, or CMO—needs to say, "We've got to do something different."

If a company is simply chasing a revenue number, they often don't take the time to acknowledge the lead time associated with a new program. Most times, it's going to hurt for a while until the new program starts netting some real results. It's like changing your golf swing. Tiger Woods didn't win immediately after changing his swing; however, he was willing to make the investment necessary to succeed in the long term.

How many companies do this? Given the pressures, I would think that they would work to overcome their inertia and make the changes and investments necessary to make their numbers. However, this often is not the case; they just flog the sales people harder. They say, "Let's send out even more e-mails or do more campaigns," but it's just more of the same tactics that didn't work before. As a result, companies still don't make their numbers.

It's easy to be a critic and I'm glad that I'm not in the situation I've just described. My vision has always been to build a substantial business, plank by plank, over the next 10, 15, or 20 years. I couldn't care less about growing revenue 300% a year or any arbitrary number. It has absolutely no meaning to me. I got over that in my last job where we went from zero to $30 million in two years, but we made no money.

I want to make some money. I want to have a sustainable business that is profitable and is a good place to work, for myself and anybody who works here in any capacity. As it turns out, we've been growing by 30% to 50% a year—and the profits have been growing faster than that.

Have Passion For Your Customers

It sounds kind of mushy, but as I've watched the business environment and the whole CRM boom unfold, I have a profound respect for the role of the CEO. Not the CSO, not the CMO, but the CEO. This is the person who really develops and sets the culture, who fundamentally communicates in verbal and nonverbal ways what is important, what are the principles, and what is the culture. A good CEO has a vision about the business that's bigger than the stock price projection.

My heroes in business are companies like Southwest Airlines, whose culture really stands out. They don't serve everybody and some people don't like flying Southwest, but Southwest is fanatical about serving its target market at the right cost. They take care of their customers and execute every minute. And they also make money. There is a spark or passion within that company that you can almost feel. How many companies have passion that is so palpable?

The Sales and Marketing Excellence Challenge

To position yourself amidst your competitors, having passion for the customer segment you've chosen is incredibly important. It's not just about sales effectiveness; it's a corporate strategy. Senior management not only has to create the vision and positioning; they must also go about executing it every day. That's what the real leaders in Customer Relationship Management do.

STEPHANIE WOLFSWINKEL AND PHILIP HALLSTEIN

Stephanie Wolfswinkel and Phil Hallstein are two of the more dynamic people I know at helping people realize their full human potential. Trust, commitment, and straight talk are all part of their vernacular. So are becoming centered and aware. Headquartered in Mill Valley, California, SportsMind has been working with teams and business leaders for two decades making pragmatic application of philosophical principles. Integrating various aspects of Eastern and Western disciplines into daily reality and producing powerful results is what these people do. Far from the 'woo woo' psychobabble of some programs, Stephanie is as direct a company president as you'll meet, grounded in principle and full of energy. Similarly, Phil comes from a strong consulting background of organizational process re-design and has consulted with the likes of Capital One, Microsoft, and American Express. These folks stretch your mind and challenge you to do something about it. Their web site is www.sportsmind.com.

BT

Responding to the pressures of the marketplace, many companies are investing in technology, sales skills, product training, etc. to increase the effectiveness of their sales teams. Those are all valuable, but to have a balanced approach to performance improvement, we should also be looking at what we can do for team members at a more personal level.

What Is Performance?

We each operate in a world where we are asked to perform, yet we seldom ask the question. For a sales person, does performance mean meeting your numbers this quarter? For a leader, does it mean mobilizing dozens, hundreds, or thousands to fulfill your vision?

The question of business performance is central to us at SportsMind, where we focus on improving the performance of managers, leaders, and teams. In addition to improving their performance (whatever that turns out to be for each of our clients), we also help them build *generative practices* for continually expanding their capability for performance.

The 'common sense' understanding of performance is how well one accomplishes something. And while this definition has some validity, we believe that effective performance is based on both personal and social competences. Our personal competences include the capacity to be self-aware and to self-manage. Our social competences include social awareness and the ability to create and manage our relationships. Optimal personal, team, or business performance can come about only through relationships with others. It is through relationships that we build personal effectiveness and produce results that are of value to others, whether they be mundane or marvelous. These skills are also reflected in the field of emotional intelligence (EQ).

The way we take EQ to the next level of effectiveness is by helping develop greater self-awareness by focusing on distinguishing between body and mind—and then integrating the two. We have found this integrated approach to be a basic foundation for improving performance for individuals, teams, and business.

Self-Awareness

Developing high performance begins with cultivating personal self-awareness. Self-awareness means having a deep understanding of our emotions, strengths, limitations, and values. Self-aware individuals or teams are realistic about their capabilities and are attuned to what 'feels right' to them. They do not abandon analytical reasoning, but balance it with self-reflection, thoughtfulness, and intuition.

Self-awareness in turn produces the capacity for self-management, because without knowing what we are feeling and thinking, we are at a loss to manage those impulses. Instead, our impulses manage us. Emotions, sensations, or internal conversations that operate below the level of consciousness often overwhelm our brain's thinking capacity to focus on the task at hand or cloud our thinking, resulting in poor judgment or ineffective action. This can seriously impact a sales person's performance.

Developing self-awareness, then, is necessary for improving our ability to self-manage, which includes:

- Emotional self-control—managing our impulses
- Authenticity—displaying integrity and trustworthiness
- Adaptability—exhibiting flexibility in changing circumstances
- Performance—driving to produce and improve based on inner standards

- Initiative—scanning for opportunities with a willingness to act upon them

In addition to self-awareness and emotional self-management, effective leadership or team behavior requires social awareness or empathy. We are always listening, but if we learn to attune ourselves to others, this attitude allows us to actually begin to see, hear and feel the world from that person's point of view. This in turn produces a mood of engagement, cooperation, and trust, out of which can come new possibilities, new actions, and new relationships.

Being attuned to others in the moment also allows us to express ourselves and our emotions, aspirations, and intentions in an authentic, grounded, and passionate manner. This attunement allows us to do what is most useful in the moment: calm fears, encourage openness, defuse anger, or mobilize action. We can see that much good can come out of learning to be self-aware, but how do we do it? Let's take a look at this crucial skill in conjunction with sales people.

Sales People As Effective Leaders

We typically think of leaders as being in a certain hierarchy in an organization, but in our view, anyone in sales is acting as a leader. Effective sales people co-develop a future with their customers; they listen—both cognitively and emotionally—to the needs and concerns of their clients. They evoke commitment from a number of players: their customers, their customer's organization, and people within their own organization. In short, they co-create a vision of the future with others and then work to mobilize the people around them to fulfill that future.

Ultimately, performance is an assessment that someone makes about your actions and their value to him or her. The assessment of good, medium, or poor performance rests on a certain standard of observation. Your actions stay consistent, but the standard used changes. Standards can change when your customer changes. While your behavior remains the same the assessment about it can change as the standards change. Your short, to-the-point e-mails become depersonalized communications; making the effort to get buy-in from all members of the sales team becomes a waste of time because 'you can just tell them what to do;' being direct and straightforward in sales conversations becomes confronting, challenging behavior.

As our business interactions include more and more people from different backgrounds, we can anticipate that the expectations of others, often unconsciously experienced and felt, will be more and more varied. Therefore, we need to become more attuned to the standards, expectations, and concerns of others. At the same time, we must be more aware of our own automatic tendencies, prejudices, and thought patterns.

Unfortunately, we are often unable to maintain the balance between the expectations or standards of others with our own expectations and standards. This is where self-awareness comes in. Some questions that arise include:

- What is it I need to become self-aware of?

- What should I be paying attention to?

- What happens when I forget?

- How do I know I am not still deceiving myself?

- How do I know if I am getting better?

- What will change if I do this?

- How do I wake myself up when I am unaware?

Unity Of Mind And Body

At SportsMind we offer a simple, but not simplistic, framework for building self-awareness of our body and our mind together—in an integrated way. Historically, these human dimensions have been perceived as separate and distinct. In our opinion, this traditional separation of body and mind has increased the likelihood of self-alienation among individuals, teams, and communities.

Business and sales success has always been based on the ability to optimize resources effectively and efficiently, to make powerful offers in the marketplace, and then to mobilize others to fulfill those offers profitably and quickly. By enhancing the integration of mind and body we are able to improve business efficiencies and create more powerful business relationships by addressing three of the greatest scarcities that exist in business today: *lack of time, lack of trust,* and *lack of attention*.

Lack of trust has become a tremendous cost to doing business, both in terms of time and dollars. People have lost trust in their institutions and in each other personally. Institutionally, we see a widespread hesitancy to invest because the institutions we have trusted (accounting/audit firms, SEC, Congress) to locate and punish unethical business practices have not held these businesses to historical standards of behavior; and we see the increased likelihood of lawsuits for wrongful dismissal or age discrimination. Lack of trust is expensive, especially in sales.

We have seen an increase in distrust manifested in the following ways: Customers are more skeptical and cynical about their vendors. People have greater difficulty committing quickly to new changes within a business. We need to overcome these trust concerns if we are going to develop meaningful relationships inside and outside our companies.

All day long the world demands our attention, pulling our focus this way and that. Our ability to concentrate, to bring ourselves back to what we were thinking, to manage a conversation with many people contributing, has become a muscle that has become essential in business today. By building our physical and mental 'attention muscles,' we can become more authentic, while moving in the spontaneous ways that our changing world requires. It is here, then, that we start with our practice for bringing mind and body into alignment in order to increase our power and ease in our lives.

Think about how often you meet people and are interested in getting them to trust you, and in learning quickly whether you can trust them. By building our self-awareness of our physical behavior and mental patterns, we can dramatically improve our capacity to create greater trust immediately. By building our awareness of others, we can also improve our ability to authentically move trust to a level where coordination and commitment become more likely, and we can do it more rapidly.

When there is self-awareness of our physical and mental states, we create a unity and integrity that lets us move with greater spontaneity, power, and effectiveness with others. The question is how do we build this practice in an authentic and responsible way? The first step is to notice two basic rules of self-organization: 1) control follows awareness; and 2) energy follows attention.

When we are aware of something, we increase our choices in the way we interact with it. What we are unaware of physically and mentally will act on us. By becoming aware of the internal conversations we have, we increase the possibility of shifting them to produce the kind of future we want, the relationships that have value to us, and the contribution we want to make to others. We refer to this ability to cultivate self-awareness as building a new kind of 'observer' of ourselves, and developing this skill can have a profound impact on how effectively we relate to our clients, our co-workers, and our managers.

As we learn to observe our own patterns of behavior, our own tendencies of mental thought and internal conversation, we also begin to notice where we are focusing our attention and how energy is following that attention. This connection is also demonstrated in the aphorism, "We move toward that which we think about." Our self-awareness or attention provides choice; this choice allows us to direct our physical and mental energies coherently and consciously.

Attention is the glue that holds the mind-body unity together. The authentic power that is produced by this unity provides vitality for living in the world. Connecting to the body in this way opens the possibility of shifting from a rigid, always-thinking-about way of being in the world, to one of more feeling and skillful action. When this unified way of being emerges, we become *present, open,* and *connected* in our bodies and our minds, and between our bodies and minds.

Center And Centering

We call this unity *center* and the process and practice of developing and sustaining it *centering.* In the course of our work with managers, sales professionals, and executives, we have universally found that those who have developed a capacity for centering are the consistent winners, have more satisfaction and fulfillment in life, and have a stronger sense of connection with friends, family, and the world.

The practice of centering comes from the Asian martial and meditative traditions. As a starting point, we typically introduce people to the unity of centering by learning to align the physical body. This alignment is oriented at the 'Hara' which is located approximately three inches below the navel. Although a centering practice begins with the alignment of the physical body, its implications go far beyond posture or a particular way of behaving. The deeper and more expansive possibility is that centering itself is a way of life. This means that every aspect of one's life is developed and experienced through center.

Center is not a thing, a physical place, or a particular way of being. Center is a living, evolving process of self-organization that increases our capacity for awareness, choice, accountability, action, integrity, and learning. Center is a state of wholeness in which effective action, emotional maturity, mental alertness, and spiritual connection are in harmonious balance. By building practices for centering the mind and body, we can create the authentic presence of someone who is present, open, and connected. To a sales person, this represents the foundation for creating meaningful relationships with clients.

▶ Centering the Body

The simplest way to begin to understand and experience center is through the body. To generate being present, open, and connected in the body, we begin by bringing our awareness to the somatic dimensions of length, width, and depth. All living things have these three proportions of top to bottom, left to right, and front to back. Centering the body begins by centering along the dimension of length. To do this, we align the head, shoulders, hips, knees, and feet directly on top of each other.

Once we've established an alignment along this vertical axis, we relax downward into the flow of gravity by releasing the tension in the eyes, forehead, jaw and chin, shoulder, abdomen, hips, pelvis, and legs. This lowers our center of gravity and our weight is transferred from the muscles to the bones. When we cease struggling to hold ourselves upright and allow our bones to support us, we enter into a dynamic state of relaxation. This increases our possibility for powerful and effortless actions.

As beginners, a simple way to bring ourselves to center is to drop our attention to our Hara. In our Western view, this point is the physiological center of gravity in the body. Shifting our attention from our thoughts to our center of gravity makes us present in the body and produces a stability and strength in action—anyone who is or has been an athlete whether a running back, dancer, cyclist, or martial artist instinctively knows this. By getting present in the body, that is, by bringing attention to center, we increase our capacity to meet the world with an alert, calm, and skillful action.

Once we are present in the body, we can move to the second distinction of center, which is being open. In this case, *open* refers to the opening of the nervous system and senses that occurs when we bring our attention fully to the body. Openness enables us to more fully experience the stream of life and provides a depth and texture to our range of experience. When I am present and open, life becomes fuller and every moment has a richness that is beyond my usual range.

Open physically is not a state we find ourselves in often. Managing stress is really about managing our degree of openness to the world and people around us. Our reaction to stress is often one of contraction. To remain open under pressure requires training, the capacity to be self-aware, and practice over time. But it is worth it in terms of the personal relationship, the ability to sense and move with the world, maintaining health and balance, and building relationships with others.

Being present and open leads me to being connected. This distinction of connection is at the same time simple and elusive. The connection we are speaking of takes form in three relationships. There is the internal connection of mind and body. This is the fundamental element of connection, the connection of the self. Without this connection, there is no capacity to maintain center or expand my level of connection.

The second level of connection is the connection of self to others. When present and open, I can experience the richness of connecting to others without generating either overly defensive or excessively porous relationships. By being centered, I find a natural ease with others. There is little need to actively set boundaries, as my centered presence provides them.

From this foundation of connection, I again branch out and deepen the quality of my connection with the non-human aspects of the world in which I live. I am connected to my environment. It may be that my environment is Manhattan and I am more fully aware of the chaotic nature of urban living, or my environment may be the open spaces of Colorado. In either case, being present and open enables me to be connected to my environment in a manner that enables me to experience and move with peace and purpose.

Centering at this initial stage introduces us to the power and flexibility of our attention and awareness. By scanning our body and locating our center of gravity, we begin to see how our attention can be willfully organized and directed to bring a greater vividness and control to our life. By expanding our awareness and focusing and organizing our attention, we're able to shift our moods, listen with greater depth to the concerns of others, increase our choices, and move in accord with the natural world.

▶ Centering the Mind

There is to date no universally accepted definition of what is, or is not, the Mind. In some traditions, the Mind is everything and all physical reality is merely the manifestation of the power of the Mind. In other traditions, there is no such thing as the Mind. It is seen as merely an invention of the Greeks to serve as a catchall for things they could not otherwise explain. For our work on centering, we will hold the Mind to be the hub of our thinking and feeling processes, and we will speak about feelings and emotions as an aspect of Mind.

To begin our practice of centering in the mind, we look for the opening move, which is to bring ourselves Present. In the realm of the mind, being present simply means to bring our attention fully to the body in the moment. That means that I am not sitting in a meeting thinking about the next one, or talking to a customer while I'm thinking about what's for dinner. To be present means to be fully in the moment. My mind is not off in either time or space.

To achieve this presence requires training of the awareness and the wholehearted engagement in the essential process of developing center. We have discussed centering in the body; we introduced the basic axioms of control and energy. Now we want to introduce the essential 'game' of center, the fundamental guideline for developing your practice. It is this: *Notice when you are off and come back to center quickly.* No one is ever centered all of the time. That is neither the point nor the culmination of the practice. The point of the practice and the purpose for training the awareness is to simply develop a keen capacity to notice when you are off center and come back quickly.

It is as easy to take my self off-center with my thoughts as it is to lose my center physically. Every time I move, there is the possibility of losing center. The same is true every time I think, and as a human being, I am always thinking. The mind is like Grand Central Station. Like the trains at Grand Central, the thoughts in the mind are always coming and going, a great noisy chaos of this and that.

To be centered in the mind is to develop the capacity to sit on the platform in the station and not get on any of the trains. That is to say, I develop my capacity to stay present to the task, conversation, or reflection in which I am engaged. As I am a human being, I will always find myself off on some unintended 'train of thought.' This is not bad. It is another chance to play the game of noticing when I am off and coming back quickly. An important point to note is that even time spent in judging myself to be wrong for being off-center only serves to keep me off-center. The challenge is to learn to notice when I am off and bring myself back without taking time out for assessments about being off.

As we look at the ability to stay 'open' in our mind, let's revisit the idea of being an observer of ourselves. To notice we are off-center, there is someone who is noticing this state. Who is doing the noticing? We call this 'other' our observer—this is, the mental part of us that is aware of self. This often shows up as the little voice asking, "What is he talking about?" or, "I know what he means." This observer also shows up as a constant voice narrating our inner lives.

Rather than let this automatic conversation rattle on, we suggest that we create an ally and begin to notice what this chatter is saying to us. Again, if we don't have awareness of this automatic commentator, it controls and shapes us. By learning to 'observe our observer,' we can shape our historical and often unconscious thinking and begin to manifest the life, relationships, and future we want. By noticing where this voice shuts down possibilities, where its prejudices keep us from experimenting, and where its reactive fear stops us from even considering making a move, we can stop extrapolating our past through the present into the future. In this way we can be open to new relationships, new possibilities, and new horizons. As we develop this openness, others around us will also. As we embrace or originate new possibilities, we foster the same in others.

Self-Awareness Is The Foundation

In summary, we have found that the key to improving the performance of managers, leaders, and teams is to provide them with tools and distinctions that will help them build self-awareness. With the foundation of self-awareness in place, they are able to move in a more powerful, efficient way, listening and taking action with a centered, unified mind and body.

JIM DICKIE

When I started to talk to Jim Dickie to do his interview for this book, the energy level in the room jumped about five levels. He has a passion for the professions of sales and marketing and it shows right away. Jim is the Managing Partner for Insight Technology Group, a research firm that specializes in benchmarking how companies are reinventing the way they market to, sell to, and service customers. He has over 25 years of sales and marketing management experience. Jim began his career with IBM and Sterling Software and then went on to launch two successful software companies. He is a contributing editor for CRM Magazine; author of The Chief Sales Officers Guide to CRM, Insights into High Tech Sales and Marketing, and co-author of The Information Technology Challenge. Jim is a board member for Baylor University's Center for Professional Selling and is an often-requested keynote speaker at sales excellence, CRM, and eBusiness conferences. Jim received his BS and MA degrees in behavioral psychology and personnel management from Western Michigan University.

Trisha Liu (TL)

> **In the course of benchmarking more than 2,900 sales and marketing effectiveness initiatives over the past ten years, six trends emerged that all companies are going to have to successfully deal with if they are going to survive, let alone remain competitive.**

#1 Understanding The Changing 'Buy Cycle'

As I was interviewing executives for this book, we talked about what they felt should be done to optimize the way they engage with their customers. I then asked how they liked to buy when they were on the purchasing side of the table. Every vendor is someone else's customer. Over the years, I have found that the insights that surface during discussions regarding what we value from our suppliers can be useful when looking at how we should in turn sell to our customers.

From these discussions, it is evident that companies are fundamentally changing the way that they buy. The first shift I have noticed is that customers are often starting 'buy cycles' without directly involving vendors.

Via the Internet, customers have access to a wealth of information on products. When I spoke at an eBusiness conference at 3M, one of the other presenters asked the audience how many of them had bought a car in the last three years. About half of the attendees raised their hands. He then asked how many of them went to the Internet for information before they went to a dealership the first time, and nearly everyone who had previously raised their hand raised it again.

A second change in buying habits is that when companies buy, they are focusing more on what products represent the best value, not just the lowest price. Unless they are making commodity decisions, cheap prices alone are not enough. Customers are considering the total cost of ownership of a product, the quality of one offering compared to another, and the risks associated with the vendor failing in the marketplace. They are also evaluating what additional value a vendor can bring to the table.

The third change we need to be aware of is that customers are demanding that vendors work together. In order to meet their ultimate need, many times products from multiple vendors need to be brought together. Customers are now placing the responsibility on the manufacturers to make sure that all the pieces of the puzzle work together, as opposed to taking on the burden themselves.

We are also seeing a move towards customers looking to establish long-term partnerships with vendors. If an existing supplier continually focuses on understanding their operations and can perform a new task at a reasonable price, why should customers spend the time and money to go out and do a new, multi-vendor procurement exercise? Product functionality and pricing advantages between vendors today are short-lived. It is the business partnership advantages that will influence purchase decisions in the future.

Lastly, customers are changing their procurement processes. They are centralizing their contracts to take advantage of the buying power of their company as a whole. Their ultimate objective is to have every order they place with a vendor be treated exactly the same, no matter where in the world it might come from. They expect vendors to know what the product, pricing, and service terms of the master agreements are, versus having to chase down that information on their own.

#2 Bring More Science To The Art Of Marketing

We will have to respond to the changes our customers are making in how they want to do business with us with a whole series of our own changes.

Our initial focus needs to be at the top of the funnel. We need to optimize the effectiveness of our marketing organizations.

One of the initial tasks marketing is going to have to tackle is doing a more effective job of defining exactly who is our 'perfect prospect.' As customer expectations rise, the ability of any single vendor to be all things to all people disappears. We therefore need to focus on being all things to all 'important' people, and it is up to marketing to tell the rest of the enterprise who those people are.

This will require us to do a much more effective job of market analysis and segmentation than has been achieved to date. We are going to have to apply the rigor of science to marketing. Analytics may not give us the perfect answer for quite a while, but they can provide us with the data points we need to triangulate in on what the realities are in the markets we are attempting to penetrate.

Once marketing has decided whom to focus on, they will need to figure out what the specific value propositions are that will motivate a given prospect to start a buy cycle. Awareness and favorable impressions are not enough; marketing needs to create buying action. Marketing will also have to wade through all the various vehicles they have at their disposal and pick the most effective methods for getting their messages out to the target users in the marketplace.

These targeted value propositions then need to be carried through all the materials that marketing develops for sales to use throughout the sell cycle. We cannot just provide sales with generic collateral; they need datasheets, presentations, proposals, etc. designed for specific audiences.

Marketing and sales will have to start working much more closely together to follow the disposition of leads through the sell cycle if we are going to accurately measure our real return on investment from marketing. We need to know what strategies and tactics are working, and which are not. Once these best practices are discovered we need to quickly share them across the entire sales enterprise. And we need to do all this dynamically so that we can anticipate market shifts in buying habits as they are starting, not after the fact.

#3 Changing The Way We Sell

Sales is also going to have to make a series of wholesale changes in the way that we sell. I see at least five key things that vendors will need to do much more effectively for customers in the future, if they are going to win or keep accounts.

The Sales and Marketing Excellence Challenge

First, we must formalize the way that we work with our customers. We need to instill a single sales methodology across the entire sales force. To reinforce and, in fact, enforce that methodology, we are going to need to develop detailed processes for how a sales person guides a customer through the sell cycle. Once the processes are in place, we will need to constantly monitor their effectiveness and fine-tune them based on shifting market conditions.

Second, we have to do a much better job of truly understanding our customers. In many cases, we are going to have go so far as to know who our customer's customer is, what challenges our customer faces in meeting the needs of their customer, and what value we provide in meeting those challenges.

It won't be enough to just keep track of where your customers have been. We will also need to know where they are, and where they are going. To accomplish this, vendors are going to have to have regular, meaningful dialogues with their customers about their goals, their objectives, and their challenges. To make sure we are all on board with those customer needs, we will have to collect and share information about our customer's business throughout our company.

Third, we will have to take on the responsibility of selling solutions versus products. We will have to become experts at what our products can and *cannot* do. We will have to propose solutions that best fit our customer's needs, and explain why our solutions are necessary, instead of waiting for customers to determine what they think our products do. That process can result in customers buying solutions for problems they don't have.

We will need to bring to the sale the knowledge we have gained from working with hundreds or thousands of other accounts, as well as selectively involve the experts within our own company who can best help the customer solve their problems.

The fourth change that needs to occur is that we need to make it much easier for customers to buy. A lot of this will involve getting customers the information they need to make a decision, when they need it. Early in the sell cycle, we will need to give them collateral customized to their needs. We will have to deliver customized demonstrations and comprehensive proposals that clearly show how we solve their problem, and what is the expected ROI. We will need to accurately configure the products they order so that they get exactly what they expect. We will need to make sure the terms and conditions under which they acquire our products are consistent with master contracts.

Finally, we will need to be much more proactive and thorough in the way we service accounts if we expect to get repeat orders. As soon as the sale is made, we will have to ensure that the information about the customer's expectations is shared with the people responsible for delivering and implementing that solution. We need to take responsibility for seeing that our products actually get used, and that they deliver the value we promised.

We will have to keep our customers apprised of new advances in our product lines, as they relate to helping them meet their future business needs. We also will need to evolve to more of a 'universal rep' concept, so that if a customer is talking to their account manager, they can get answers to questions about product shipments, new product announcements, billing discrepancies, customer support issues, etc.

As all other things become equal, service and account management will become the primary criteria for making purchase decisions. Ultimately, our people and our processes will become the only sustainable, long-term competitive edge we have.

#4 A New Class Of Sales Professionals And Managers

All this means that the days of getting by with sales people who *'demo, quote, and hope'* are over. The task of selling is becoming much more consultative in nature, and with this shift we will see major changes in the hiring profiles we use to select sales reps and sales managers.

The type of person who will be successful selling going forward will be someone who can gain the respect and partner with the one or more of the big C's in an account: the CEO, COO, CSO, CMO, CFO, CIO, etc. This will require that he or she has specific industry or process knowledge in order to understand his or her customer's business requirements and propose specific solutions to address them.

As opposed to the sales strategies of the '80s and '90s that focused on having product sales specialists, I see us moving towards having customer specialists. We will take our product expertise and integrate it into customer relationship management (CRM) systems. That, in turn, will enable and empower sales people to focus first on the customer. As opposed to having a bias for product A or product B, these new sales reps will focus on selecting the right solution, after determining what is the best approach for meeting the customer's needs.

These sales reps are going to have to be sharper between the ears. They will have to be good thinkers and great listeners, and they will need to be able to translate abstract customer concerns into solution requirements.

Because of this, the killer sales people of the future may well be the former middle managers of today. It is not likely that sales people will get enough classroom-based training to prepare them for the 'knowledge selling' that they will have to do to meet customer expectations. This may well require us to hire more experienced people.

The role of sales manager will also evolve. Any of us who have ever been in sales has a story or two about the old guard sales managers, the ones whose constant focus was to beat on the numbers: number of cold calls, number of presentations, number of demos, etc. They managed by activity and quota performance. There was a list of the top ten performing reps and if your name was not on that list, you were in trouble. This type of management has no place in selling today.

The successful sales manager of today needs to focus on shifting to a position of empowering self-managed individuals. The old guard management styles are already close to extinction anyway because CRM systems automate a number of the record keeping tasks that have occupied management's time in the past. A lot of those tasks will be accomplished by the 'sales-manager-on-a-chip' that reps carry around with them in their laptops.

Especially when you consider the high-level people who will become the sales professionals of tomorrow, the primary role of sales managers will become one of finding ways to help these sales people be more creative and innovative on their own. This objective will require sales managers to be more strategic coaches versus tactical ones.

They will need to continually analyze their own sales processes so they can keep fine-tuning their operations to be more and more effective. These are the people we will expect to determine what is necessary to create a learning and changeable sales organization.

This is going to be a shock for a lot of people presently in these sales and management positions. The kinds of people that will survive and prosper in these jobs will be those who can deal with all this change and have the ability to adapt their skills appropriately. Those who fail to do so will soon find the industry has passed them by.

#5 Supporting The Extended Sales Force

These changes in the way we sell will also need to extend beyond the walls of our own companies, to include our partners as well. Today, it is not just a question of what channel—it's every channel. We need to find better and more effective ways to move our products other than just relying on our own sales force. With that in mind, we need to take responsibility for helping our channel partners optimize their sales processes.

To accomplish this we need to understand what it takes for them to make 'sales out.' By sales out, I mean the sales our distributors make to the thousands of resellers and end users who need our products, but order them from the channel. We must dedicate a larger part of our resources towards creating demand pull for our resellers. This will require a much higher level of communications between all the players involved in the food chain to ensure we are all marching in sync.

A related step that we will need to take to support our sales out strategies is to evaluate every marketing program based on its ability to generate demand in key market segments. This process will require us to be able to track a lead through the complete sell cycle, so that we can determine what programs work—so we can do more of them—and what programs are failing—so we can quit flushing money down the drain.

#6 Successfully Leveraging Technology

We are not going to be able to deal with all these issues on our own. We are going to need to find our own solution vendors, our own business partners, to help us. This will cause major changes in the sales support industry (training providers, CRM vendors, consulting firms, etc.) itself.

The first trend you will see is the formation of more and more consortiums. Sales and marketing excellence requires the combination of process optimization, application software, infrastructure software, hardware, and communications expertise, which exceeds the ability of any one vendor to supply. Just as we will be expected to deliver solutions to our customers, we will demand that our sales support partners deliver complete solutions to us. We will expect them to invest in integrating their products and services with those of other firms to provide us with the comprehensive systems we need to deal with our sales and marketing challenges.

Another trend that will result from CRM suppliers having to focus on delivering solutions will be an acceleration of the rate that technology advances are integrated into products. As vendors are required to deliver systems that address not just sales rep efficiency, but sales rep, sales team, enterprise, and inter-enterprise effectiveness as well, they will turn to new technologies to develop the answers to our sales challenges.

Out of these changes in the sales support industry will come a group of companies that we can partner with to optimize our sales and marketing operations. It will be different than most markets where you end up with one dominant vendor, three or four followers, and everyone else disappearing.

In the sales support industry marketplace, I don't see us going from 500 vendors to five. I think it will be more like 50, with several sub-markets emerging along industry lines (consumer package goods, finance, manufacturing, etc.), functional departments (sales, marketing, and support), and go-to-market strategy approaches (direct sales, telesales, route sales, catalogue sales, ebusiness, etc.). Each of these segments will have its top five players. It will be critical that we partner up with the firms that best support our sales and marketing optimization objectives.

The Sales & Marketing Excellence Challenge Summary

So what are the challenges that face us? We must constantly review how our customers are changing the way they buy. Based on those changes, we must continually optimize the way we market and sell. We must hire the right sales people and managers to implement our well-defined sales processes. We must transfer the knowledge of the sales process to our channel partners. And finally, we must put together a process and technology support team to help us successfully leverage technology to enable and empower everyone to do their job.

In a nutshell, that is the challenge. Defining it is pretty easy. Achieving it will be more difficult. We will continue to see a number of programs fail because companies focus on the wrong issues; inadequately redesigning their processes, picking the wrong solution partners, and so on. But we will also see the emergence of more firms who really crack the code for sales and marketing excellence, which will result in them achieving dramatic gains in revenues, market share, and margins, all while reducing their costs.

We will see these firms highlighted on the front pages of the *Wall Street Journal, Business Week, Fortune,* and *Forbes*. We will see stock market analysts determining valuations for these companies based not just on *what* they sell, but *how* they sell, as well.

Life will be wonderful for these marketing and selling superstars, and it will be hell on earth for those who get left behind. Hopefully, you will find the concepts and ideas presented in this book, and in the additional interviews we will be e-mailing to you, to be useful in charting your course towards sales and marketing excellence. Once again, I wish you good luck and good selling.

BARRY TRAILER

My interview with Barry Trailer started, naturally enough to me, with why he and Jim undertook this book project. Yet as we continued it became clear that, in his eyes, this book is not about his views or even his experiences, but those of the people he interviewed. He talked about each of the interviews as though he was that executive's biggest fan. However, I suspect part of his admiration for their accomplishments is also a reflection of his own experience. Over the past 20 years, Barry has presented to and consulted with literally hundreds of companies with complex business to business sales. Many of these organizations are standouts and some of the executives he met along the way are included in this book. I got the distinct feeling that he and Jim enjoyed this project so much that they will likely be in touch with many more of these past acquaintances for a sequel. In the same way, I look forward to the opportunity of working with Barry on a future project to share more insights on sales and marketing excellence.

TL

What kept coming up in doing the interviews for this book is how much these folks 'think' about their business. They don't just show up every day and go through the motions; they're figuring out, or trying to figure out, what's really going on, what are the trends, and what they need to do to advantageously position themselves. They also demonstrated a surprising openness to sharing what they're doing, without fearing that they're somehow giving something up, in hopes that their peers might gain insights from their experiences in the trenches.

When Jim approached me about working on this project, it immediately struck me as a good thing to do. First, the playbook by which people had been operating over the past couple years had just been tossed out the window. Second, most books you read today were written at least a year ago, usually longer. Producing something really current just felt right.

Also, Jim had done a similar project ten years ago, interviewing executives about their view of what was happening and what was coming next, and I was keen to see what had changed over that time. This project provided the opportunity to connect with dozens of business leaders and hear their stories firsthand. Also, writing the interviews in the person's voice appealed to me; these executives' observations come through unfiltered. We're not providing 'our view' of what we heard from all these folks. We're presenting what the executives actually said so our readers can hear for themselves.

As soon as we started the interviews, it came as a surprise that it would be a lot of fun and that I'd learn a lot. Another big surprise was how accessible and open all the participants were. Sometimes when we reviewed edits with them, they'd say, "I can't be *that* specific!" Sometimes I think the interviewees were surprised by their own candor. But they changed very little; some of the common edits were to remove specific revenue or expense numbers, or to decide not to include the names of alliance partners.

Lessons Learned

There were a handful of lessons or themes that came up time and again. The first was the shift from product sales to solutions—total solutions. I might even say *real* solutions. During the 'bubble' years, a solution was, "OK, you have a problem, here's the solution (read: product/service offering)." Now, a solution includes a greater understanding of what is the buyer's business situation, who is the buyer's customer, and what pressures and problems are coming to bear on them. Within this fuller and more complete context, sellers are better positioning their offers.

Quality people were mentioned in several interviews and in several different ways. The definition of quality included those reps who would take the time and who had the intellectual capacity to present solutions. Beyond this, however, the best reps were those who developed and maintained quality relationships, both with customers and with associates. A willingness to share information and to be held accountable came up time and again.

Measurement was another common theme. The majority of interviewees talked about their companies once being 'fat, dumb, and happy,' and now having to become much more focused on margins, profits, and other metrics. Forecasting accuracy remains an elusive and important quarry.

Another concept that kept coming up was 'visibility into the pipeline.' I heard this a dozen times in different forms. Getting a grasp on lead flow, avoiding big surprises, and becoming increasingly proactive earlier when it was clear revenues would fall short were just a few of the forms these comments took.

One might have expected a reliance on technology to be a common theme, but it wasn't. Given my background the past dozen years, I was impressed with how little these sales and marketing leaders were looking to technology as the magic answer to their situation. Yes, CRM, marketing automation, and the rest were seen as useful *tools* but not *the answer* to the current challenges.

Solutions, Not Products

Two organizations with the largest sales channels, Microsoft and Check Point, are both looking to shift their focus to solutions and the 'customer's conversation.' With thousands of partners each, a major challenge in each case is educating the channel. With broad product lines and global reach, the direction is now to explore the buyer's situation, needs, and pain points, then speak directly to them.

Years ago, during my time at Miller Heiman, their *Conceptual Selling* program called this 'identifying the buyer's concept.' What struck me about this new-found adoption of old-time religion is that sales is returning back to the basics. Like the investment managers who questioned the relevance of Warren Buffet during the late '90s, I was wondering if the philosophies and practices I'd grown up with were obviated by the 'new reality.' In a sense, the answer was yes and no.

During the bubble times there was little time or need to delve into such prosaic details as business issues and personal wins. During that late 20th century gold rush, the order of the day was to grab business and market share. As noted in so many of the interviews, those days and attitudes are clearly behind us. In addition to the 'dot-com hangover,' sellers are suffering from the demise of the 'drive-by sale.' Today, you have to cover all the bases: uncover all the buying influences, demonstrate the economic viability of your firm, have a compelling business case, a competitive price, *and* have innovative solutions. And still, your prospect is as likely to sit on his or her checkbook as not. What's a seller to do?

The answer for many is to just shut up and do it. That is, do all those things and continue to develop as many leads as possible. For older dogs, this is simply a replay of tougher times, the most recent period being the early '90s. For new sales reps, closer scrutiny and demands for greater activity and accountability may not be fun but, hey, it's part of the job. Today's leaner, meaner streets mean a return to the basics in so many ways.

This is not limited to big companies. The smallest companies said many of the same things, though a few said they were increasingly focusing on *fewer* markets and opportunities, even as they expected *more* be done on each of those.

Entitlement Has Gone Out The Window

After the focus on solutions, quality people was the next most frequently mentioned component of sales and marketing excellence. During the heyday, a recruiter that specialized in sales personnel told me he had five offers for every candidate that was looking. Two years later, he had 250 candidates for each position he had to fill. Talk about a nasty turnaround.

The upside of this situation, as reported by numerous execs, was not having to offer huge base salaries, signing bonuses, and aggressive commission plans to people with sketchy and/or unproven track records. Young reps who'd made $250,000 or more in a year suddenly were expendable and gray hair was no longer automatically a bad thing. But maturity and tenure weren't automatic pluses either. The thing CSOs are looking for today are people who can orchestrate opportunities or channel partners and bring deals across the line to contract.

Jumping ship every year is once again a demerit, a change from the prior five years where there was a stigma if you didn't change jobs every 18 months.

However you define quality in people, one characteristic that sales managers and leaders are looking for today is the ability to develop relationships. The importance of meaningful and deep relationships between buying and selling organizations was, and continues to be seen as one way to continue to shepherd deals to closure. Even if a deal is not on the table, the importance of staying in touch, of letting people know you appreciate their business, and of understanding their business and situation (i.e., the focus on selling solutions, described above) features prominently in defining quality and excellence.

One of the standouts in this discussion was Savage & Associates, a financial services company in Toledo, Ohio. Over the past 25 years they have consistently brought on account executive recruits straight out of college. Growing their business by growing their ranks and the individuals themselves is built into this company's DNA and processes. Unlike some companies that made headlines by lopping off the bottom 10% each year regardless of performance, Savage & Associates mentors people to success. The insurance industry is rife with turnover, but the Savage & Associates sales reps average 17 years tenure.

Another way to characterize this theme is that the slapdash, run-and-gun orientation of the bubble times is over. Sales reps are taking a longer view and see they're in it for the long ride. But it's a long ride on a hard saddle;

you may not be able to drag deals across the line before their time, but you sure as hell better be actively working leads or deals everyday.

What Gets Measured Gets Managed

Measurement is back like never before. Years ago, Peter Drucker made the observation that the problem with management is that it's measuring the wrong things. Whether or not this is true, today's companies are measuring *everything*: number of calls, number of deals in the pipe, percent of plan, ranking by revenue, etc. But meaningful metrics continue to elude sales organizations.

In several cases, companies have a defined sales process but are not necessarily using it as a roadmap to sales success. More the norm, the 'sales process' has defined milestones—interest development, qualification, demonstration, etc.—and has arbitrarily affixed probability of close to each milestone. The problem is, if best practices are not identified and defined along with each milestone, little guidance is provided on how to actually improve. Having a systematic way to identify what's working and/or where to look in the entire identify-qualify-propose-close cycle is rarely seen.

There are notable exceptions, including American Medical Response (AMR) and Wells Fargo. Glenn Leland, National Vice President of Business Development at AMR, concentrates on process and identifying and publicizing best practices. Gary Lutz, Senior Vice President and National Sales Manager for Wells Fargo Commercial Banking, also focuses on process as an ongoing operating philosophy. Maybe it's a Denver thing since they're both located there, but their business development people cover several regions—all of the U.S., and west of the Mississippi, respectively.

Again, small companies can also use process to good advantage. Alan Ross of Ross Printing says that integrating his sales process with both seller and buyer actions has significantly streamlined sales discussions. It has also provided a basis for improving results over time.

Failing To Plan

The old axiom says, "Failing to plan is planning to fail." Across all the interviews I conducted, I was impressed with how organized these individuals were. They had clear plans and were working toward their execution with specific intermediate term objectives. Their plans were operating plans—living documents—as contrasted with annual business plans or strategic account plans that sit on the shelf with rare reference.

These people talked about exceeding or falling short of interim targets and adjusting accordingly. Specifically, if revenue targets were not being met, expenses were now being carefully controlled and could be throttled down very quickly.

David Morris at ZuPreem commented on the value of his business plan, as well as the value of a personal Board of Advisors. The word that kept coming up directly and by inference from the interviewees' comments was *accountability*. If the good times and double-digit revenue growth hid a multitude of sins, today's environment has stripped away any restrictions on inquiry. All areas of operations, including and maybe especially sales, are fair game.

Revenue is not the only thing being scrutinized. Staffing and headcount decisions are also on the table. Where enough good reps could not be had 18 months ago, companies have now seen one or two layoffs—including sales personnel. Things have gotten very tight and senior management has moved to reduce revenue-generating and customer-facing positions. As an interesting side note, these same companies have continued to invest in their own R&D functions, the thought being that new products will be needed to remain competitive when the economy finally does turn around.

Changing The Game

Many of the interviews suggested to me that the most significant changes in how the game is being played have to do with focus and discipline. That is, companies are no longer playing fast and loose, but are becoming both serious and organized during tough times. Applying both Eastern and Western approaches to focus and discipline are Phil Hallstein and Stephanie Wolfswinkel of SportsMind. This company started 20 years ago working with athletes and military units. Today, their client list includes top U.S. corporations employing their techniques for personal awareness and accountability, teambuilding, and leadership.

Michael Fields is playing years ahead of the power curve, working to establish an Internet research park in St. Croix, U.S. Virgin Islands. Included in this effort is working with local government and educators on the U.S. Virgin Islands, as well as members of Congress and businesses in the U.S. The reason? St. Croix, in Mike's opinion, won't continue to compete as favorably with post-Castro Cuba and other Caribbean nations for tourism dollars in the future.

The 9Ps of Profitability

As opposed to the famous 4Ps of Marketing—Price, Product, Place, Promotion—my colleague, Jim Dickie, talks about the 9Ps.

Are you solving the right **problem**? One of the biggest shifts from my point of view is the change in orientation of this essential question. In the past, companies would focus on solving their most pressing problem. In today's environment, the emphasis is on understanding and solving your customer's major problem. Two keen observers of the current scene, Bob Thompson and Dick Lee, talk about this shift.

Selling time remains a precious commodity. There can be a tendency during tough times to pursue anything that moves—any lead is a good lead. But companies risk spreading themselves too thin in a time of scant resources. Rick Cobb talks about reducing the number of verticals they pursue and carefully focusing on identifying the right **prospect** representing a reasonable potential.

Janet Dolan is leading her 132-year-old manufacturing company with an eye on the **position** they want to be in coming out of these challenging times. As opposed to battening down the hatches and riding out the storm, The Tennant Company is maneuvering with an eye on being in place to better serve the market when it recovers.

Jerry Ungerman talks about the benefits of having a great **partner** program and attitude. The leverage and success that Check Point gets from this approach to the market has paid huge dividends. Microsoft is no stranger to this concept and Ralph Young talks about what they're doing to educate their channel in enterprise solutions.

These two executives also note that, to attract partners—and customers—you must have a competitive **product.** Yet, as mentioned above, the orientation is to present this in the context of a complete solution.

Steve Pratt at Deloitte Consulting talks about how important it is to **perform**. He introduced the notion of the '100-Day Win' to tightly manage projects in achieving interim milestones and avoiding runaway costs.

When actual performance is below plan, Glenn Leland, Alan Ross, and Gary Lutz suggest looking at your **process(es)**. Are your processes clearly articulated, integrated into day-to-day business development efforts, and constantly reinforced and reviewed for ways to improve? My mental image of processes that are effectively implemented likens them to gravity. You don't get up in the morning and think, "Darn gravity—I'm still heavy." You don't think about gravity at all; you simply have learned to operate within its framework. Gravity isn't something you take time out from; in the same way, effective processes are *what* you do, not something you take time away from something else—say, selling—to do.

Ben Shapiro talks about **pricing** as a strategic initiative and suggests areas of investigation and consideration that do not normally come up in sales and marketing discussions. Mostly, I guess people are just too busy.

It reminds me of Stephen Covey's *Seven Habits of Highly Effective People.* The seventh habit is titled 'sharpening the saw' and derives from a story of a guy sawing wood all morning. By mid-morning, his production has dropped from earlier and by noon, his production is off considerably, though his activity remains high. When it's suggested he might want to sharpen his saw, the reply is, "Don't have time, I'm too busy."

Which leads me to the question, "What am I too busy doing?" Too often, I believe the answer is, "Working to make the number." Yet the conversations I've had over the past few months suggest to me that being too busy to plan is a poor trade off. Designing a detailed plan but failing to compare plan with actual performance on a regular basis is equally foolhardy.

And as mentioned in some detail above, surrounding all of these is the quality of your **people**. Michael Heflin talks about developing and supporting confident competence: investing in tools and training, then reinforcing these on an ongoing basis. Phil Hallstein and Stephanie Wolfswinkel work with companies every day in the powerful stuff of corporate culture, teamwork, employee and leadership development.

Leaders Lead

Retired Army General 'Stormin' Norman Schwarzkopf in reflecting on the most important lessons he'd learned over his career recalled being told, "When given command—lead." In the end, that's what each of these executives are doing and what their interviews are sharing. They have a vision of where they need to go, what needs to get done, and see their #1 job as making progress in that direction everyday.

In describing how they organize themselves, rally their teams, allocate resources, and address whichever of the 9Ps, each of them shared their own best thoughts in the hopes of making a further contribution. Many specifics were discussed, and this willingness to be open about how they view the world today and what will be required to still be here tomorrow impressed me. These are busy folks with full plates and real responsibilities, yet they proved accessible, introspective, and sincere in wanting to help others. It was my good pleasure to have the opportunity to interview them.

Not everything presented was brand-new, never-heard-of-before stuff. But even revisited ideas (e.g., selling solutions, not just products) reminded me of the notion of peeling an onion. Each new layer looks essentially like the one you just saw, yet each is seen at a different level. In many cases, what is different here is not the concept but the implementation of it. The stick-with-it-ness of these companies' stories, combined with the urgency of 'trouble times' following the 'bubble times' truly showed innovation.

The thoughts and actions presented were all terribly familiar and yet refreshingly new. In preparing the final interview, my own, I reflected on Mike Fields' comment that we are 'back to the future' and was reminded of poet TS Eliot's *The Road Less Traveled*: "And in the end, we come back to where we began, and recognize the place for the first time."

Special Bonus Offer

Turn this book into an ongoing educational process, versus a one-time learning event.

Your exposure to the top experts we interviewed does not have to end here at the end of this book. To provide you with further insights into strategies and tactics you can use in dealing with the specific challenges your organization is facing, we are offering to send you up to ten additional perspectives over the next year free of charge.

To register to receive these additional interviews, all you need to do is visit our website, **www.CSOInsights.com**, and fill out a brief profile to help us better understand the topics that specifically interest you. As we continue our research efforts and develop additional perspectives that fit your areas of interest, we will e-mail them to you with our compliments. Through this continuing exchange of insights, we hope to make this book an ongoing educational process instead of a one-time learning event.